CHICKEN SOUP FOR THE LATTER-DAY SAINT SOUL

CHICKEN SOUP FOR THE LATTER-DAY SAINT SOUL

Stories Celebrating the Faith and Family of Latter-day Saints

Jack Canfield
Mark Victor Hansen
with
Sherm and Peg Fugal

Health Communications, Inc.
Deerfield Beach, Florida

www.hcibooks.com
www.chickensoup.com

We would like to acknowledge the following publishers and individuals for permission to reprint the following material. (Note: The stories that were written by Jack Canfield, Mark Victor Hansen with Sherm and Peg Fugal, are not included in this listing.)

The Iron Rod. Reprinted by permission of Laura Craner. ©2005 Laura Craner.

My Heart Is Telling Me. Reprinted by permission of Annaliese H. Enderle. ©2005 Annaliese H. Enderle.

From Wings to the Temple. Reprinted by permission of Kirsten Rebecca Fitzgerald. ©2004 Kirsten Rebecca Fitzgerald.

The Faith of a Child. Reprinted by permission of Joyce Ann Pierce. ©2004 Joyce Ann Pierce.

(Continued on page 374)

Library of Congress Cataloging-in-Publication Data

Chicken soup for the Latter-day Saint soul : 101 stories celebrating the faith and family of Latter-day Saints / Jack Canfield ... [et al.].
    p. cm.
   Includes bibliographical references.
   ISBN 0-7573-0315-3
    1. Mormons—Anecdotes. 2. Christian life—Mormon authors. I. Canfield, Jack, 1944-

   BX8638.C45 2005
   28.3—dc22

2005051181

Publisher: Health Communications, Inc.
          3201 S.W. 15th Street
          Deerfield Beach, FL 33442-8190

Cover design by Lawna Patterson Oldfield
Inside formatting by Dawn Von Strolley Grove

To Halle, Maddie and Ayden

Contents

3. GRATITUDE

4. HOLIDAYS

5. MIRACLES

6. MISSIONARY WORK

9. SERVING OTHERS

Acknowledgments

We wish to express our heartfelt gratitude to the following people who helped make this book possible.

Our families, who have been chicken soup for our souls!

Jack's family: Inga, Travis, Riley, Christopher, Oran and Kyle, for all their love and support.

Mark's family: Patty, Elisabeth and Melanie Hansen, for once again sharing and lovingly supporting us in creating yet another book.

Sherm and Peg's family: Jayson, Cori, Ayden, Josh, Stef, Halle, Maddie, Jake and Jer, who are our greatest gifts and our best sources of inspiration.

Our publisher Peter Vegso, for his vision and commitment to bringing *Chicken Soup for the Soul* to the world.

Patty Aubery and Russ Kalmaski, for being there every step of the journey, with love, laughter and endless creativity.

Barbara Lomonaco, for nourishing us with truly wonderful stories and cartoons.

D'ette Corona and Kathy Frandsen, who helped get the job done.

Patty Hansen, for her thorough and competent handling of the legal and licensing aspects of the *Chicken Soup for the Soul* books. You are magnificent at the challenge!

Laurie Hartman, for being a precious guardian of the *Chicken Soup* brand.

Veronica Romero, Teresa Esparza, Robin Yerian, Jesse Ianniello, Lauren Edelstein, Jody Emme, Debbie Lefever, Michelle Adams, Dee Dee Romanello, Shanna Vieyra, Lisa Williams, Gina Romanello, Brittany Shaw, Dena Jacobson, Tanya Jones and Mary McKay, who support Jack's and Mark's businesses with skill and love.

Bret Witter, Elisabeth Rinaldi, Allison Janse and Kathy Grant, our editors at Health Communications, Inc., for their devotion to excellence.

Terry Burke, Lori Golden, Kelly Maragni, Sean Geary, Patricia McConnell, Ariana Daner, Kim Weiss, Paola Fernandez-Rana, and the sales, marketing and PR departments at Health Communications, Inc., for doing such an incredible job supporting our books.

Tom Sand, Claude Choquette and Luc Jutras, who manage year after year to get our books translated into thirty-six languages around the world.

The art department at Health Communications, Inc.: Larissa Hise Henoch, Lawna Patterson Oldfield, Andrea Perrine Brower, Anthony Clausi, Kevin Stawieray and Dawn Von Strolley Grove, for their talent, creativity and unrelenting patience in producing book covers and inside designs that capture the essence of Chicken Soup.

Thanks to Stan and Sharon Miller, who originated "Especially for Mormons"; Robert G. Allen and Tom Painter, who introduced the Fugals to Mark Victor Hansen; Matt Kennedy and Leonard Surprise of *LDS Living* magazine, who connected us with all the contributors, and who helped us market to the LDS market.

All the *Chicken Soup for the Soul* coauthors, who make it such a joy to be part of this *Chicken Soup* family.

Our glorious panel of readers who helped us make the

final selections and made invaluable suggestions on how to improve the book.

And, most of all, everyone who submitted their heartfelt stories for possible inclusion in this book. While we were not able to use everything you sent in, we know that each word came from a magical place flourishing within your soul.

Because of the size of this project, we may have left out the names of some people who contributed along the way. If so, we are sorry, but please know that we really do appreciate you very much.

We are truly grateful and love you all!

Introduction

Whether you're an investigator, a new member, a lifetime member, a less active member, a church leader or a missionary, we hope you'll thoroughly enjoy this brand new, never-before-published collection of personal stories written by fellow Latter-day Saints from every corner of the world.

You'll find delightful, inspirational stories about faith, family, gratitude, holidays, miracles, missionary work, overcoming obstacles, prayer and serving others. Stories that will make you laugh and cry, lift your spirits and inspire and motivate you. Stories you can use in sacrament talks and Sunday school, Primary, Young Men, Young Women, Relief Society and Priesthood lessons. Stories you'll want to share with your family during family prayer or family home evening. Stories you'll want to share while visiting or home teaching. Stories you'll want to include in letters to missionaries. Stories you'll want to give as gifts to family, friends, associates and investigators. Stories that will help others better understand and appreciate who we are and what we believe.

It is not coincidental that this volume is being published on the 200th anniversary of Joseph Smith's birthday, as well as the 175th anniversary of the Church. It is also not

coincidental that we were chosen to edit the book. If anything, our involvement in the project was providential.

Robert G. Allen, the bestselling wealth author and
trainer, has been a client of ours for thirty years. A couple
of years ago, he invited us to brainstorm with him and
Mark Victor Hansen, with whom he was writing a new
book.

In the course of conversation, we told Mark about our
success with *Especially for Mormons.* Mark was sufficiently
impressed enough to ask us to edit an LDS edition of
Chicken Soup. We could not have been more honored or
thrilled—or overwhelmed by the incredible responsibility.

Having collected, written and edited stories for five of
the eight volumes of *Especially for Mormons,* we were
tapped out and in need of all new contributors with all
new stories. Enter Matt Kennedy, the founder and publisher of *LDS Living* magazine, who generously offered to
place a call for submissions on his Web site and to e-mail
his subscribers. Hundreds of submissions poured in from
all around the world.

We began reading. We loved every story. Unfortunately,
we could use only about a hundred. We set aside the
others for potential use in future editions. Our long-time
editor and friend Kathy Frandsen came on board to read,
edit and proofread.

Though we have written and edited eleven books, we
have never worked harder than we have on this book. We
wanted to bring you the best collection of inspirational,
uniquely LDS stories ever published. Stories that would
give us a glimpse into the everyday lives of our fellow
Saints from all around the world. Stories that would
remind us of the marvelous work and wonder Joseph
wrought 175 years ago—and the great blessing it is to be
part of it. We think we have succeeded. We hope you agree.

Share with Us

We invite you to send us stories you would like to see published in future editions of *Chicken Soup for the Soul.*

We would also love to hear your reactions to the stories in this book. Please let us know what your favorite stories are and how they affected you.

Please send submissions to our Web site:

www.chickensoup.com

or mail to:

Chicken Soup for the Soul
P.O. Box 30880
Santa Barbara, CA 93130
Fax: 805-563-2945

We hope you enjoy reading this book as much as we enjoyed compiling, writing and editing it.

"You Mormons are so bizarre!"

$\overline{1}$

FAITH

. . . According to your faith be it unto you.

Matt. 9:29

To Build the Members' Testimonies

Therefore, O ye that embark in the service of God, see that ye serve him with all your heart, might, mind and strength, that ye may stand blameless before God at the last day.

D&C 4:2

I grew up in western New York and attended the Hill Cumorah Pageant in Palmyra several times during my youth before meeting with LDS missionaries, listening to their message and joining the Church. Less than a year later, I moved to Utah to attend Brigham Young University, where I met and married my husband and where we made our home. Whenever we return to western New York to visit my family, we always visit Palmyra and the Church sites there.

After one particularly trying period, my husband offered to take me on a vacation and asked where I'd like to go. "Home," I answered. Home to me was still western New York—where I grew up, where I joined the Church and where the Church was restored.

For many years, the Church historic sites in Palmyra remained very much the same. Then when President Gordon B. Hinckley became prophet, he mounted a campaign to more completely restore the various Palmyra Church sites.

The original Smith log cabin where Moroni appeared to Joseph was reconstructed. The Smith family frame house was restored to its original design. The barn and shop across the road from the house were reconstructed. The road was moved. Instead of one path leading into the Sacred Grove, several paths were created that wound through the grove of trees, ending in the field behind the log cabin. The Grandin Print Shop was expanded. A temple was built. Missionary housing was constructed. The old stake center was given to the city, and a new stake center was built near the temple. The old visitor's center at the Hill was replaced with a brand-new one. The Hill Cumorah Pageant was improved. The Martin Harris home was purchased, and a park was built adjacent to it. More work was done at the Peter Whitmer Farm in nearby Fayette. Indeed, what used to take only a few hours to visit now takes a couple of days. (And it's not just Palmyra: the Church is busily improving nearly all its historic sites.)

Because I go home almost every year, and visit Palmyra every time, I have watched with great interest all the new and additional work being done there over the years.

I remember the first time I approached the newly reconstructed Smith family log cabin. Tears streamed down my face as I contemplated what had transpired in that little log house in the western New York wilderness so many years ago. When I entered the upper room where Moroni had appeared to Joseph, I felt the Spirit more strongly than I have ever felt it in my life.

I remember when President Hinckley announced that

the 100th temple in the Church would be the Palmyra Temple. I ran to tell my husband but could not, because I was weeping with joy so much that I couldn't speak. Once I calmed down, I called my LDS brother and sister who still lived in western New York at the time, and we cried with joy together. We never thought we would have a temple so close to our childhood home, let alone in our beloved Palmyra.

I remember the first time I approached the temple site while it was still under construction. Tears welled up in my eyes as I contemplated the significance of a House of the Lord in the very place where Heavenly Father and his Son Jesus Christ first appeared in this dispensation, in the very place from which the Saints had once been driven. Surely Joseph was smiling from on high.

I remember the first time my husband and I attended a session at the new Palmyra Temple. I began crying when we pulled into the parking lot, and I didn't stop until we departed.

Western New York is my childhood home. Palmyra is my spiritual touchstone.

Once when visiting the newly restored Smith family frame house, I asked the missionary conducting the tour how many of their visitors were LDS. "Ninety-five percent," he answered.

"Only five percent are nonmembers?" I asked incredulously, thinking surely all the new work was meant to attract more nonmember visitors, more missionary leads.

"Why would the Church go to such lengths for members?" I asked, assuming members already know the truth and don't need all this to confirm it. I was surprised by the missionary's answer.

"President Hinckley said," he answered with a knowing smile, "it's to build the members' testimonies."

I was dumbstruck.

mattresses and rigged up showers on trees. Most wore makeup, cute clothes and shoes that were never intended for hiking. We usually had a leader that did all the cooking and a priesthood leader who supervised, chopped wood for the fires and set up the tents. We girls spent our time doing crafts, chatting and eating the snacks our mothers packed for us.

This year was different. Before camp we were all forced to certify in first aid, which involved passing a written test administered by a registered nurse. Then when we got to camp we were told we would be sharing tents by age groups, not just in groups of friends, and we would have to pitch the tents ourselves.

There were about six of us Mia Maids, and we were to sleep in a gray, eight-man tent. Our tent was old and had no instructions, but we finally figured out how to pitch it after awhile. We were pretty sure it wasn't supposed to sag like it did, but we were tired and hungry so we quit. No big deal, right? After all, a leader could fix it for us later.

We went to see how the food was coming along and to our horror, there was none. We were told someone needed to chop the firewood while others got the meal started. Thankfully, one girl had spent some time on a farm and knew how to wield an axe. Otherwise, we all might have been forced to subsist on the gummy worms stashed in our backpacks.

As the week wore on, we all eventually got the hang of things. Our food was burned, but thanks to all the work we were doing we were hungry enough to eat it. We were required to actually attend classes and were being tested regularly on the stuff we learned. Miraculously, our tent didn't collapse on us, although we never could get it zipped up. We slept with our blankets over our heads to keep the mosquitoes away.

The last night of girls' camp was traditionally testimony

meeting night. For most of us, it was the one time of year that we spilled our spiritual guts and tentatively admitted we believed in the gospel. Usually, it was an all-night affair with lots of tears and hugs. And, not surprisingly, it was the highlight of the week.

This year, though, like everything else, it was going to be different. After a full day of hiking, a burned dinner and some lazy campfire conversation, everyone was summoned to the base of the nearby mountain. We were told not to bring flashlights or water—just ourselves. We all tromped over and began to sing hymns; the last campers arrived just as the sun was setting. Someone offered a prayer, and we were divided into groups of eight and assigned a leader with a flashlight.

From behind a tree someone produced a stack of PVC pipes spray-painted to look like metal. We were told to proceed in absolute silence and to hold on to the "iron rod." If we let go, odds were that our leader—the only person who could see in the dark and knew the path—would lose us. We all rolled our eyes, snickered and grabbed on.

The various groups of girls were sent off on the trail at staggered times. Our group was one of the last, and even though we knew we weren't really alone, by the time we set off, all of us had a tight grip on the pipe. Our leader started on the trail as stars began to pop out of the night sky. We could see small pockets of light ahead of us on the trail, but that was it. As the darkness increased, so did our solemnity.

We hiked silently for a while, crossed a stream and stopped for a rest. Suddenly, a group of young men from our stake burst out of the trees. They asked us what we were doing, where we were going—and then invited us to go with them instead—tempting us with a warm fire, food and games. We girls kept silent and held on to our length of pipe, absolutely confused.

The longer we stayed silent, the angrier the young men got. They started to call us names and make fun of us. Just as we were about to burst, our leader tugged on the rod and signaled us to begin hiking again. The boys' voices died out after awhile, and we picked up the pace a little bit.

After hiking a little longer, we stopped for another rest. As we caught our breath, a light turned on. In its wash stood one of our leaders, who smiled and told a story about how she had withstood peer pressure. She testified about God's love for us, of his plan for us, and sent us on our way.

We continued holding on to our rod and followed our guide around twists and turns in the trail. Sometimes we could hear other groups and voices in the darkness calling out, but mostly we hiked in silence. With each rest we took, we were greeted with another set of visitors. Some were good stops where we were encouraged. But there were also more provoking stops—like the older girls smoking and drinking and saying that we should, too. It was our body, they said, and we weren't hurting anybody else.

Finally, at one stop one of our leaders came out and offered us a comfy seat, some hot cocoa and some choco-lates. She said it was okay to give up and take a rest. No one really cared what we did. What did something like this matter in the long run anyway? It was okay to give up, she told us. At this point we had been hiking for quite some time, and we were tired and hungry. One girl in the group spoke up, "Are you sure? Guys, the chocolates just look so good, and I am so tired!" We all kept silent.

She looked around. The leader stepped closer and held out the temptation. The girl reached out her hand to take a piece, only to discover the candy was just out of reach. We all watched intently. If she really wanted the candy, she would have to let go of the rod. There, in the moon-light, was the basic question of agency. Each of us, like that girl, would have to choose between holding on to the rod or letting go and taking our chances with an easy reward. Our friend wavered for a few moments and our guide began to tug on the rod.

"Maybe we don't have too far left to go," the girl concluded, leaving the chocolates behind.

Throughout the hike, we were faced with choices. It wasn't enough that we were trudging up a mountain in the dark and cold. We had to constantly recommit to trusting our stake leaders and the plan they had laid out for us.

As it happened, the girl was right, and we didn't have too much farther to go. For a while we had been able to see a distant glow that we hoped was getting closer. Then, I thought I heard music and voices. As we rounded the last bend, a stunning sight greeted our tired eyes. There was a huge, glowing tree right in front of us. It was surrounded by lanterns and people dressed in white—to our tired eyes, they looked like angels. As we walked closer to the tree, we began to see each individual light twinkling and bouncing off little crystals hanging like dewdrops from the branches. The "angels," who were our bishops and parents, came to greet us and led us over to comfy chairs and blankets (and snacks!), all the while congratulating us on our successful journey.

Of course, my parents were there, dressed in white and happy to see me. But the grins on their faces were nothing compared to what I was feeling inside. After that strenuous hike, the joy I felt at seeing my family and the sweet serenity of our surroundings was too much for me. I thought my heart was going to burst. I had no idea the Spirit could fill me so completely. I was full of Lehi's "exceedingly great joy."

When the last group of Young Women arrived, everyone was gathered together for a testimony meeting. It was like no other. Instead of the usual tumultuous and emotional teenaged testimonies, we shared quiet convictions of peace and joy. As each bore her testimony, a leader pulled a crystal off the tree. Each was on its own chain and magnified the lights surrounding us. We were told the crystals served as a tangible reminder of the light and Spirit we had experienced that night. We were challenged to keep that light by holding to the course the Lord had laid before us, always remembering the sweetness of the reward that awaited us.

I wore that plastic crystal for months, until it was lost in my incredibly messy room. Through my difficult first year of middle school, I wore it under my shirt and felt it whenever I was upset. At those times, I remembered with fondness my happiness at seeing my family and their delight at seeing that I had clung to the iron rod. For one brief night that summer, I had felt celestial joy—and I knew it was something I wanted to feel again.

Laura Craner

My Heart Is Telling Me

For as he thinketh in his heart, so is he . . .

Prov. 23:7

I was visiting my old ward for fast and testimony meeting; my heart was bursting as I told the following story:

Our house was a mess, and it was time to clean! I told my five-year-old son, James, that he needed to help me clean. He told me he didn't like to clean. I told him that I didn't like to clean, either (that's why it was a mess!), but that we all needed to help out. He started giving me some attitude, so I told him to go to his room and that he could come out when he was ready to help. He stomped off, and I started cleaning.

About two minutes later, James returned, looked at me, and said, "I'm going to help you clean. Do you know why?"

I rolled my eyes and asked, "No, why?"

He said, "Well, my brain is telling me that I don't like to clean, but my heart is telling me I should anyway."

I explained to him that was what choosing the right felt

like. Sometimes in life we have to do what our heart tells us to do instead of what our brain is telling us to do.

The next Sunday a dear friend pulled me aside and told me of some unfortunate events that had occurred in their home. Over the previous week, one of their children had become suicidal. At one breaking moment, the mother told her daughter they both needed to pray. Each went to her room and prayed. The daughter returned a few minutes later and the mother asked her how she felt. With tears in her eyes, she told her mother that all she could think about was what I had said in my testimony. She said, "My brain is telling me that I don't want to live, but my heart is telling me I should anyway."

I cried at the thought that a simple story could have such impact on a struggling teenager. I am happy that the Spirit prompted me to tell that little story, and I'm even happier that she was listening.

Annaliese Enderle

From Wings to the Temple

And it came to pass that I beheld that the rod of iron, which my father had seen, was the word of God, which led to the fountain of living waters, or to the tree of life; which waters are a representation of the love of God; and I also beheld that the tree of life was a representation of the love of God.

1 Ne. 11:25

Growing up in an LDS family doesn't always guarantee you'll listen to everyone's counsel. As a teenager, I definitely was not a listener—and I rode on the wings of other people's testimonies. That continued until I was an adult, when I decided I was tired of riding and wanted to be the pilot. It was only after a series of not-so-pleasant events and my friend's cutting words about my marriage that I decided to take a serious look at what I really wanted from life.

I began a quest for my own knowledge of the truth through much prayer and scripture reading. For the first time in my life the scriptures were no longer "Greek" to me. Not only did I understand them, but the words came to life as they played out each scene in my head. My heart swelled as I read and finally had a confirmation of their truthfulness. I was now the pilot, and I longed to soar to everyone and share this great treasure I had found!

That experience set my compass on a whole new life course. After some coaxing from my mom, I attended the temple again to perform baptisms with the youth. This turned out to be another pivotal event in my life. As I prepared to go to the temple I could feel Satan trying to get his hooks into me through the ways of the world. I did my best to avoid anything "evil," even if it was just in appearance. Listening to uplifting music during the seven-hour drive to the temple helped promote the Spirit. As we got closer to the temple I anxiously looked for glimpses of Moroni. As we rounded the corner I saw him, high above the temple, shimmering in the sunlight, nobly grasping his trumpet. Tears filled my eyes as I remembered being at the temple as a youth. I was so grateful to be near the temple and feel the Spirit there once again.

It was the greatest feeling to be at the temple, but I literally felt like my heart had been ripped out when I saw all of the endowed chaperones (all of the adults other than me) leave to change into their temple clothes. There I sat in the temple waiting room—and even though the room was filled with youth, I felt alone. I felt like I had been left behind or left out. It was something like being picked last for a sports game in elementary school, but a hundred times worse! Avoiding eye contact was the only way I could keep from bursting into tears. At the time I didn't understand why I was feeling this way. I was at the temple! You're not supposed to feel like that at the temple! The rest of my day at the temple was filled with the Spirit and was awesome as I spent it performing baptisms and confirmations.

A few weeks after my temple trip, I had a vivid dream

that reminded me of those moments in the temple waiting room. In my dream I stood in a dark, smoky room. In the middle was an iron rod that ran from one end of the room through an opening at the other end of the room. On one side of the rod people were gathered around a bar—drinking, smoking and watching those of us by the iron rod. As I held on to the rod and walked toward the door, I saw people from my ward, dressed in white, standing at the door. I was happy to see several recognizable faces. I then noticed that the people around me holding on to the rod were also dressed in white and were allowed to go through the door.

When I reached the door and looked through it, I could see the temple in the distance. The rod led all the way to the temple, and along its path people in white were walking toward the temple doors. There were families. There were couples. There were friends. As I drew closer to the door I could feel the love of all who passed through it, but then I realized I couldn't go through the door. Those who did had a temple recommend. I didn't. I again experienced the feelings of being left out and alone.

When I woke up and began thinking about my dream, I remembered the way I felt in the waiting room at the temple. During the next few months, I had several other dreams with similar themes. Those dreams put into motion the necessary steps I needed to take to receive my own endowment.

When I began working to achieve that goal, I was warned that the journey would not be an easy one. Many obstacles stood in my way—especially as the time drew closer for me to go. This change in me was difficult for my then-inactive husband, and it caused a lot of contention in our marriage. Additionally, I suffered a miscarriage; the engine in our family car cracked, leaving us with a small pickup truck to transport our family of four; our finances were very limited, and the money I had set aside to purchase garments had to be used to buy special shampoos and sprays when our children contracted lice. I lived by the saying, "I never said it would be easy. I only said it would be worth it."

Despite the obstacles, I continued to have faith and refused to give up. Four months after the youth temple trip, I once again took the seven-hour trip and returned to the temple—but this time I didn't feel left out. I finally belonged. I had a temple recommend to receive my endowment.

I received many blessings through my experience. The day before I left for the temple, a check arrived in the mail from a great friend who wanted to be there with me but couldn't. She sent the check to help with the cost of purchasing garments. She never knew the money I had set aside was gone! After attending the temple I became pregnant and gave birth to our third son on the Fourth of July. We were able to purchase a minivan to accommodate our growing family. My inactive husband slowly began attending church again (when I requested this in lieu of gifts for every occasion), and one day decided to start wearing his garments, too!

Although I continue to experience obstacles, I find strength through faith and a growing testimony of the gospel. I know if I had continued riding on the wings of others and had not become the pilot, I would have fallen off—and my parachute at the time was full of holes!

Kirsten Fitzgerald

The Faith of a Child

Behold, verily, thus saith the Lord unto you: In consequence of evils and designs which do and will exist in the hearts of conspiring men in the last days, I have warned you, and forewarn you, by giving unto you this word of wisdom by revelation.

D&C 89:4

Having been raised in a home with an alcoholic, I saw firsthand the problems alcohol can cause in a family. My father was a minister and never apologized for his drinking. In fact, some of his best drinking buddies were members of our own congregation. My parents divorced when I was just seven, and my father met his next wife in a bar. My father died before his fifty-second birthday from complications related to his drinking, and I wondered if there was any group of people that didn't believe in drinking alcohol.

My daughter and I were introduced to the gospel by a neighbor in 1978. One of the things that attracted me to the Church was the Word of Wisdom. I lived next door to my bishop and knew that he not only professed to live the Word of Wisdom, but he really did live it.

As we listened to the missionary discussions, I had a strong impression that we were where we needed to be—and, more specifically, that I was being given this opportunity so that my daughter would be raised in the gospel. At the time it wasn't so much about me as it was about her. The gospel came so easily to her, and it seemed apparent that she was one of those choice spirits reserved for these latter days.

All these feelings were confirmed as time went on. She couldn't wait to go to Young Women. She faithfully attended seminary every day. She received good grades in school, and we often referred to her as our "perfect child." She was a wonderful example in every way, and while I had thought I was there to teach her, she was always teaching me.

Because she was totally immersed in school and Church activities, we bought her a used Ford Mustang. We trusted her to give rides to friends once she had some practical driving experience, but we learned that even if you're responsible, there simply are things you can't foresee happening.

One night she pulled onto an ice-covered driveway to pick up a friend. She left the car running and waited, but the girl didn't come out. She finally got out of the car to go up to the door, but as she did, she fell, and one leg went under the car. The car began to slip on the ice and rolled over her leg. She wasn't hurt—and, in fact, was able to get back in the car and drive home.

When she arrived home and told us what happened, I marveled at how she hadn't been hurt—or killed. She said, "Mom, it's because I obey the Word of Wisdom." Her words were spoken with such complete faith. Whatever reason she had been preserved, she knew the Lord was watching over her. She understood the principle and the promise.

The Word of Wisdom has been a definite blessing in our lives. There was never a moment's worry about our daughter drinking and driving; never the concern of her drinking and losing the ability to make the right decisions. Our daughter knew from an early age that if she was faithful, the Lord would protect her. And He did.

Joyce Moseley Pierce

Three Wheels of Hope

*And see that ye have faith, hope, and charity,
and then ye will always abound in good works.*

Alma 7:24

I had an unusual dream where, as an adult woman, I was trying to ride a child-sized tricycle. I was in a race of some kind, and was trying to balance the awkward little tricycle down a narrow, dark street. The street was a familiar one from my childhood hometown of Charlestown, Massachusetts.

People were hanging out of their apartment windows on both sides of the narrow street screaming down at me, "Just give up, you fool! You'll never make it with that little bike."

I kept telling them repeatedly, "All I have is this three-wheeled tricycle." I struggled to steer and kept tipping to the side, but I kept my balance and ignored the people who were mocking me as I slowly pedaled by.

Then at one point a man left his home and ran out into the middle of the street. He got right into my face, forcefully screaming and mocking me. He raised his hands over his head and yelled, "YOU'LL NEVER MAKE IT, YOU FOOL. JUST GIVE IT UP!" He continued screaming repeated words of discouragement right in my face.

"This bike will take forever at the speed you're going!" he screamed.

I boldly replied, "I must push forward; I must get to the finish line!" With great strength, I awkwardly pedaled past him and ignored all his mocking words, leaving him and his words behind.

I held on as tightly as possible and steered straight ahead with great determination. I had unshakable faith that I would make it! I also knew it didn't matter how long it would take, because I knew it was worth it.

At that point, the dream came to an abrupt end.

I awoke on the chilly November morning and remembered the dream very clearly. I also remembered that the night before I was feeling discouraged—but now I felt happy and peaceful, and my spirit felt alive with hope. The dream had given me inspiration to struggle on, no matter how difficult life gets.

I dressed quickly for work and reflected on the dream nonstop until I got to my desk and recorded it. I prayed earnestly to know its meaning—I knew it was an important dream that I was supposed to share with others.

I think we've all been given small tricycles as adults, and we struggle to balance our lives down the dark, narrow streets of mortality. The world wants us to give up and wants us to think we should have it better than a tricycle. Obviously, I would certainly prefer a ten-speed bike so I could glide easily through life—but then how could I learn to be humble and rely on Heavenly Father?

I now consider the tricycle to be my three wheels of hope, and this narrow path I struggle on will lead me to Heaven someday if I'm faithful and true. The dream has given me courage and hope that I will finish the race inch by inch. I know I must never give up, but press forward always.

Susan Durgin

The Greatest Glory

But blessed are they who are faithful and endure, whether in life or in death, for they shall inherit eternal life.

D&C 50:5

In July 2003, my baby Melynda was suffering from serious heart failure and waiting for an experimental device to be approved for her use. It had been a very hard year as a result of Melynda's numerous hospitalizations, and we decided to take a short vacation that summer to the Smoky Mountains National Park after receiving the cardiologist's approval.

Paul, Melynda and I went on a hike one day up the Grotto Falls trail. The hike was about one and a half miles up a mountain, with three waterfalls along the trail. At the very top was a beautiful grotto cave and waterfall.

It was July. It was super hot and humid—and climbing one and a half miles up the mountain became exhausting. The first waterfall was so beautiful, I considered stopping there and going back down. But Paul encouraged me to keep going. Ironically, he was the one hauling Melynda in a backpack—I'm such a wimp!

By the time we reached the second waterfall, I was exhausted and drenched in sweat. People coming down the trail told me I was only halfway to the grotto. I wanted to quit!

Suddenly I saw an inspiring sight. Thirteen-year-old twin girls and their family had been climbing behind us; when we stopped to rest, they passed us. One of the twins was blind and was climbing that rocky mountain trail on her own, with the use of a cane. I immediately felt humbled. *What am I complaining about?* I thought. *If that young blind girl can climb Grotto Falls trail, then I can, too! Endure, endure! The vision of the great waterfall will be worth it!*

At that moment, the Holy Ghost witnessed to me further: "This trail is like the path to the telestial kingdom. Even though the terrestrial and telestial kingdoms have beauty, the greatest glory is in the Celestial Kingdom. Endure, endure, Marie. Your test of faith will be worth it."

I thought how grateful I was for the fullness of the gospel and the constant companionship of the Holy Ghost, which can teach us spiritual truth at any time. It took the example of that sweet, blind girl climbing the mountain to encourage me.

Grotto Cave and Falls were wonderful, and as I walked down the mountain that day I had a renewed sense of courage to face the trials of Melynda's health with a steadfast hope in Christ. I wasn't alone—and Heavenly Father was communicating a more eternal vision for me that day. Months later I would see my own version of the beautiful Grotto Falls as Melynda's heart defects were miraculously repaired with the experimental device approved for her.

Marie Kirkeiner

The Fast I Have Chosen

Is not this the fast that I have chosen? To loose the bands of wickedness, to undo the heavy burdens, and to let the oppressed go free . . . Then shalt thou call, and the LORD shall answer . . . Here I [am] . . .

Isaiah 58:6, 9

It was the day of the final test before my five-month-old daughter Rachel's scheduled surgery, and I wanted a miracle. I prayed that the cyst that made her head swell would disappear and that she would be happy and healthy again. I had heard of stories of answered prayers, of diseases that suddenly disappeared. Rachel was only a baby, and I couldn't imagine why she had to go through surgery. I wanted a miracle, and I wanted it right then.

I decided I wouldn't eat that day; instead, I decided to fast. It was my one last reach for God, my one last chance for Him to hear me and grant my petition. For the first time, I wasn't fasting out of habit or because I thought I should. I would be fasting with a purpose, a real need. God would hear me; I knew He would. I was frightened at the thought of my baby undergoing surgery, but God would take care of that.

I went to work in downtown Salt Lake City with my baby daughter consuming my thoughts. I still felt uneasy and concerned about my daughter's impending surgery. When it was time for lunch, I decided to go for a walk around Temple Square. I eventually found myself in the North Visitors' Center. On the second floor I stopped and looked at the paintings depicting the life of Christ from Isaiah recording his marvelous visions of the Savior's birth and earthly ministry to the depictions of the Savior's crucifixion and glorious resurrection. I then sat in front of the Christus, that heroic statue of the resurrected Lord. I looked at the piercing in His hands, feet and side. I looked at His arms stretched open wide, inviting all to come unto Him, and I felt the Savior's love enter my heart.

When I returned to my office, I pulled out my scriptures. I turned to Isaiah 58:6, 9 and read:

"Is not this the fast that I have chosen? To loose the bands of wickedness, to undo the heavy burdens, and to let the oppressed go free, and that ye break every yoke?

"Then shalt thou call, and the LORD shall answer; thou shalt cry, and He shall say, 'Here I am . . .'"

Then my burden was lifted. I knew that Rachel would have the surgery, but that the Lord would take care of her. His miracles were the surgeon and the hospital and all the technology that would help her heal. But a greater miracle took place in my heart: Fear was replaced by faith and acceptance. I had the strength to let go and let God do things His way.

My fast was complete. I called on God. And God said to me, "Here I am."

Douglas Brown

An Incredible Calm

In all their affliction he was afflicted, and the angel of his presence saved them: in his love and in his pity he redeemed them; and he bare them, and carried them all the days of old.

Isa. 63:9

I was born and reared in Manitoba, Canada, where I spent many summers as a child in the summer beach town of Gimli. A few years after I joined the Church in Winnipeg, there was a young single adult campout near there. When I heard where the campout was, I was excited: I hadn't visited there in many years. I had some fond and some not-so-fond memories of Lake Winnipeg from my childhood. I loved getting away from the city and having two summer weeks there with my single mom and brother. I also loved the water, and both my brother and I were good swimmers. However, the kindest way to describe what lay under that water is "ten miles of rocks and then a sandbar." Oh, I remember the bashed shins and turned ankles every year!

The campout was on a Saturday; the sun was warm, but the wind was strong and chilled us when we weren't in the water. As much as I loved being with my old friends and making new ones, I wanted to spend some time alone, so I did something I should not have done: I swam out into the deep water by myself, away from the crowd. I didn't tell anyone what I was doing, nor did I ask anyone to look out for me.

As I mentioned, the wind was strong that day, and the waves were high. At that point in my life my asthma was sometimes severe, and I always had my inhaler with me. That day, though, I had left it on the beach. I was floating in fairly deep water, facing the beach, feeling good and watching some of my friends. They were about fifty feet away on my left, playing volleyball in the water and having a great time. I enjoyed watching them and listening to their laughter. One man named Cliff was about thirty feet behind me and to my left, standing on one of the few sandbars and watching the volleyball game.

After a bit, I decided I wanted to play volleyball, and thought I should get Cliff to join us as well. As I turned around to yell an invitation to him, a huge wave slapped me right in the face. I lost my breath, which triggered an asthma attack. I was immediately in trouble, and I knew it. I tried to stay calm and conserve energy, but it was getting more and more difficult to breathe. That's not all: I had to tread water to stay afloat, and that was using energy. I couldn't waste any breath to call out for help, nor could I waste the energy needed to raise my hand out of the water to signal for help. All I could do was try to keep myself afloat.

I looked around. No one was paying any attention to me at all. I started to realize the gravity of my situation. I couldn't keep going much longer, and I realized there was a very real possibility that I could drown.

When I first joined the Church, I had an intense fear of death. Learning about the plan of salvation had helped me overcome that fear. Now, as I looked death in the face, a feeling of incredible calm washed over me. I knew it was the Holy Ghost. I tried to remember everything I had learned, and I knew I needed to trust implicitly in my Heavenly Father. I closed my eyes and said, "Father, Thy will be done." Then there was nothing.

I have no recollection of what happened after that, but when I opened my eyes, I was on the sandbar. Cliff was looking off into the distance, still watching the volleyball game. He didn't even see me behind him until I spoke his name. I didn't detail what had happened. I simply told him I had had a bad experience, and he helped me to shore.

To this day, I know that there is no earthly force that could have taken me to that sandbar, against the current and through the choppy waves, without anyone seeing. I know that I was carried. I know that I have individual worth to my Heavenly Father, that His angels take care of me, and that I have more to do in mortality before I meet Him again.

Cheryl Panisiak

He Will Provide

Or do ye suppose that the Lord will still deliver us, while we sit upon our thrones and do not make use of the means which the Lord has provided for us?

Alma 60:21

I had three children by the time I was twenty-one; money was always tight, and it seemed that week after week I sat with pencil and paper, trying to figure out how we would pay for groceries after our bills were paid. It was a constant struggle, and we were never able to get ahead.

When I was twenty-eight, my neighbor introduced me to the gospel. I knew from the first discussion that what they were teaching me was true, and very early on, I wanted to be baptized. I was finally receiving the answers to questions I'd been asking most of my life.

Everything made sense to me, but the one principle I knew I'd have trouble with was the law of tithing. How in the world was I going to squeeze 10 percent out of a paycheck that was already too small to cover our expenses? I discussed my concerns with my neighbor.

"If you are faithful in paying your tithing, the Lord will provide," she assured me. She said she couldn't promise that we would have any more income, but if I would examine my spending, I would find a way to not only pay my tithing, but to cover our expenses. She said maybe I would become more frugal in my grocery shopping—using coupons, learning to plan meals so that I could use every last morsel. Maybe I would become less wasteful—learning to mend my clothes, or even make them, rather than buying new ones. She bore testimony of how her life had been blessed by being a faithful tithe payer, and she knew for certain that mine would be blessed, too. She challenged me to exercise my faith and make the commitment to always pay my tithing.

I wrote that first check and prayed that the Lord would help me in my efforts. As the years went by, I discovered that there were quite a few things we could do to keep from spending money. I learned to cut back, stretch or do without!

- Instead of taking the kids to an occasional movie, we found things we could do at home. The kids and I loved riding our bikes together. It not only strengthened us as a family, but helped us to be in better physical shape.
- We planted a garden, and my grandmother was delighted to share her experience in preserving the food. This not only taught my children the value of work, but brought me closer to my grandmother.
- I searched for ideas on how to make gifts instead of buying them. Grandma taught me how to sew and crochet, my mother taught me how to decoupage and cross stitch. We enjoyed many hours perfecting our crafts and even sold a few. This helped me develop not

only my talents, but even brought in a little extra cash.

- I got serious about looking for sales and using coupons. Why pay more for the same thing if you can get it at a discount?
- I learned how to make three meals out of a single chicken! I often remarked to my family that Brigham Young would be proud because of his counsel that not one grain of wheat should be wasted.
- I focused more on whole foods instead of buying packages of prepared foods that were filled with sodium and preservatives. I learned that when our bodies were fueled with nutritional foods, we were healthier and happier.
- I learned to repair instead of replace. This helped me appreciate the value of everything that we had been given.

I am grateful for my neighbor and her early counsel. Because she had a testimony of tithing and encouraged me to have one of my own, I have been able to face my bishop each year and answer honestly that I pay a full tithe.

The law of tithing is one principle that is very clear. You're either paying it or you're not—and the Lord blesses those who keep their covenants with Him.

Joyce Moseley Pierce

Generation X comes down from the mount . . .

2

FAMILY

*... Choose you this day whom ye will serve ...
but as for me and my house, we will
serve the LORD.*

Joshua 24:15

The Mommy Store

And he spake unto the multitude, and said unto them: Behold your little ones.

3 Ne. 17:23

I truly cherish the once-in-a-lifetime moments when the world comes to a standstill—when time magically slows to a halt, creating a place where everything seems to move in slow motion . . . those times when the veil between Heaven and Earth seems to become equal, just for a split second. This was one of those moments.

Walking through the crunchy leaves scattered about the earth on an autumn afternoon, my four-year-old daughter slipped her little hand into mine as we walked along the trail. The palette of autumn's color bathed our eyes and enveloped us with wonder, as if every little leaf we gathered became a priceless treasure of discovery for my daughter. As she collected an armful of glorious clutter to toss in the air she squealed with delight and looked up at me with her chocolate-brown eyes and casually exclaimed, "Mommy, I'm so glad I picked you for my mommy." Without skipping a beat, she tossed her treasure of leaves into the air, throwing her head back as nature's bounty came twirling down onto her sunlit laughing face.

I watched her for a moment, sort of caught off guard by her confident statement, and asked, "You picked me?"

Bending over to pick up another armful of leaves, she glanced up at me as if she had forgotten I was there. "From the mommy store in Heaven," she stated, as though I didn't remember.

"You must remind me," I urged her on. "I really can't remember what it was like."

She threw her arms heavenward with an excited squeal, allowing the ritual to enthrall her once again like it was the very first time she had done it.

"The mommy store in Heaven. All of the mommies were lined up, and you were the last one. I picked you because you looked at me and smiled at me, and I liked your smile," she casually stated, persisting in her task of filling her arms, and as if Heaven and Earth had no boundaries in her little world.

She left me standing speechless as she continued in her next repetition of childhood delight. The air about me became silent; I literally could have heard a pin drop. Everything enveloped my soul in slow motion; even the laughter seemed distant, echoing through my head like a faraway dream.

I slowly bent down, facing my little angel, interrupting her next move and gathering her into my arms. "I love you so much!" I whispered, nestling her against my neck. She giggled and threw her head back with laughter as it tickled her. "I am so lucky to have you as my daughter! Thank you so much for picking me in Heaven to be your mommy. I am the luckiest mommy in the whole world!" I told her as I helped her find another armful of delight.

At that moment, I truly saw Heaven in her soul-piercing

eyes, and I knew without a doubt that I would remember this once-in-a-lifetime moment into the eternities. It was a place where Heaven and Earth intertwined as one, just for a split second, allowing us to step into and experience the bonds of an eternal, awe-inspiring connection.

Lisa May

She Has Always Been There

And the mother of the child said, As the LORD liveth, and as thy soul liveth, I will not leave thee. And he arose, and followed her.

2 Kgs. 4:30

Shortly after graduating with my MBA from Brigham Young University, I read Dr. Raymond Moody's amazing book, *Life After Life*. The book is about Dr. Moody's research involving people of all ages, nationalities and religions who had survived near-death experiences (NDEs). Their stories shared many similar elements—these people had passed through a tunnel at death, had been greeted by a being of light and had experienced an instantaneous life review during which their life flashed before their eyes. Without exception, when they returned from the brink of death, their lives were forever altered—often dramatically.

The stories fascinated me. I bought and devoured every book I could find on NDEs. I shared the stories I had read with my Sunday school classes and even in my professional seminars. I couldn't figure out why I was so fascinated by the subject—and it would be almost thirty years before I found out. But I'm getting ahead of myself. . . .

I'll never forget the day someone shared her personal NDE with me. In the late 1980s, I briefly mentioned my fascination with NDEs at a real-estate seminar in Cherry Hill, New Jersey. Following my presentation, a young woman in the audience approached me. She explained that she had been pronounced clinically dead after suffering a serious illness. The medical staff had actually zipped her up in a body bag to transport her body to the morgue. Then something shocking happened—the body bag began to move, and the "dead" person began pounding the inside of the bag. When they unzipped it, they realized the young woman was most definitely alive.

After her recovery, she didn't tell anyone what had happened during the few minutes while she had been "gone." She was afraid people wouldn't believe her—that they would think her crazy. Several years later, she finally told her mother what had happened.

Upon "dying," she told her mother, she saw her body lying "down there" as the medical staff was zipping up the body bag. She remembered being greeted "on the other side" by a beautiful woman who exuded so much love. This "angel lady" told the young woman that her "time" was not yet up, and that she needed to return to life. That's when she awoke to find herself zipped inside the body bag.

Her mother began to ask details about the "angel lady" who greeted her daughter. As the details came, the mother sensed that her daughter was describing a deceased relative. They rushed to the attic and began leafing through a pile of dusty old family albums. Suddenly, the young woman saw a photo that shocked her.

"That's her!" she exclaimed with excitement. "That's the angel lady!" Both mother and daughter stared at the photo in silence. Finally her mother spoke.

"I've never shown you these photos, because they are too painful for me to look at," she said softly. "The woman in the photo is my mother—your grandmother. She died when I was pregnant with you."

As the young woman shared her story, I felt warm goose bumps sweep over me. Perhaps her story touched me so deeply because, just as this grandmother had not lived to see the birth of her granddaughter, my own mother had not lived to see me.

Amy Judd Allen died in childbirth on May 20, 1948—the day I was born. Because of several disappointing miscarriages, she had laid in bed for months, determined that this pregnancy would be successful. I can only imagine how much she wanted to hold me in her arms after having carried me for nine long and painful months. And then, on that most joyous day, she didn't make it through the valley of death. As I came into the world, she passed out of it.

My forty-five-year-old father, sixteen-year-old sister, and ten-year-old brother did a wonderful job raising me, but I missed the warm, tender nurturing that most other babies enjoy. I still do. Mother's Day is always such a strange day for me. Fathers, sons and daughters stand up in church and praise their wives and mothers—then honor them with flowers and gifts. As I watch these ceremonies, I think how fortunate those people are who have had mothers to watch over them, care for them, correct them, nurture them, instruct them and love them. For most of my life, I've felt that I missed something very special.

And then, I had my own NDE.

It was March 15, 2003. I was returning from giving a speech to a thousand people at the Anaheim Convention Center. It was about 9 P.M. on a dark, rainy night, and as I drove home, I listened to the news of dozens of accidents on the California freeways caused by the heavy rain. I don't remember anything about "my" accident. A driver in the sole car behind me on that dark night witnessed my car veer off the road at full speed and smash into a large tree in the heavy brush just a few feet off the freeway. This "Good Samaritan" stopped, immediately called 911 from his cell phone and waited until the ambulance arrived. My car was so demolished that they had to cut me out with the Jaws of Life. If it hadn't been for this single witness, I most certainly would have bled to death in the darkness. I remember none of it.

I was rushed to the hospital with massive injuries. I was put on life support in a medically induced coma as they assessed the damage. I don't remember a thing. When I came to my senses a few days later, with my wife and two of my children at my bedside, I was shocked to learn how close I had come to dying.

I experienced only a few of the elements of a "classic" NDE. I don't remember seeing my body through spirit eyes. I don't remember a tunnel or a being of light or a life review. But, without doubt, my life has been forever altered. And the strangest thing happened as I came "back to life." I knew that my "angel mother" had been there that night— that she had been watching, letting me know that it wasn't my time. In ways that are hard to explain, I now realize that she has always been there—watching over me, caring for me, correcting me, nurturing me, instructing me and loving me, even though I couldn't see her.

It's been two years since my NDE, and I still feel her presence. I often find myself driving down the freeway, whispering under my breath, "Thanks, Mom—for the life you gave me and the life you gave for me. Thank you, thank you, thank you, thank you . . ."

Robert Allen

Green Power

But Jesus said, Suffer little children, and forbid them not, to come unto me: for of such is the kingdom of Heaven.

Matt. 19:14

When I arrived to retrieve my two granddaughters Halle and Maddie for a sleepover, Halle was in "time-out" in her bedroom, while Daddy was playing with Maddie in the family room.

Hearing my arrival, Halle began begging Daddy through the air vent in her bedroom floor, which connected with the air vent above Daddy's head in the family room, "I love you, Daddy; I'm sorry I kicked Maddie, Daddy; I won't do it again, Daddy; is my time-out over, Daddy?"

Had Daddy not needed me to take his daughters overnight so he and Mommy could both make early-morning meetings, I would have been forced to leave without Halle. As it was, Daddy released Halle from time-out and counseled with her.

"Why did you kick Maddie?" Daddy asked four-year-old Halle about her one-year-old sister, Maddie. "Because she bugs me," Halle answered matter-of-factly, as though her actions were perfectly justifiable and Daddy's question was too stupid to answer.

As an involved and observant grandmother who often takes care of my two granddaughters, I can vouch for Halle's claim. Maddie bugs her all the time, mainly because Halle is not yet used to sharing her world with a new baby sister.

I have a younger sister who grew up in my shadow, which was never easy for her. When Maddie was born, I very much feared she would experience the same thing growing up in Halle's long and large shadow, Halle having been the only child of her parents and the only grandchild in our family for three whole years. But from the beginning, Maddie let us know that she is her own woman. As soon as she was able, she was crawling over the top of Halle to get at whatever she was pursuing, not to mention slapping Halle's face and pulling Halle's hair for the sport of it, I hoped, but sometimes wondered.

Halle, on the other hand, having had her own life, toys and schedule for three years, was having a very hard time sharing anything with Maddie, particularly Bama.

I never held Maddie that Halle didn't also demand to be held. (Fortunately, I have a lap and arms big enough and a back strong enough to accommodate both.) I never fussed over Maddie that Halle didn't also demand some fussing (which I never failed to provide). But, no matter how equal I kept things, Halle regularly complained, "You don't love me anymore, you love Maddie more."

So, when Maddie crossed her path, Halle would sometimes kick at her, for which she was always punished.

Daddy asked again, "Why do you kick Maddie?" Halle answered again, "She bugs me." Daddy counseled, "She is not bugging you, she wants to play with you," to which Halle replied, "Well, I don't want to play with her," to which Daddy counseled, "You have to play with her; she's your little sister and it's your job to take care of her."

The counseling session could have gone back and forth for some time because Halle is not one to admit she's wrong or to be told what to do, but Halle wisely knew her responses were tied to going home with Bama, so she let it go.

While we were driving home, we paused to admire the various Halloween decorations along the way. One yard had a giant-sized, inflated and lighted green-faced Frankenstein monster, something Halle had never seen before. "What's Frankenstein?" she asked. Knowing she was not ready for the deep psychological story of the famed literary character, I answered simply, "Oh, just a Halloween monster" and we drove on.

Always wanting to reinforce Mommy's and Daddy's teachings, I asked Halle, "Why are you mean to your baby sister Maddie, who loves you?" She thought for some time before replying, "It's the 'green power' in me."

One of the things I enjoy most about being a grandmother is seeing in my grandchildren what I was too young and inexperienced to see and appreciate in my own babies and children. In fact, I have been so fascinated by my first grandchild that I have recorded her every word and action since birth, filling 700 pages before her fourth birthday. The thing that fascinates me the most is Halle's "take" on life, her "theories," her "logic," her own unique way of looking at and understanding the world around her.

Halle has very long hair that she has never liked having shampooed or rinsed. The older she gets, the better she gets at rinsing it herself, but she never quite gets the bubbles out without help. When I offered to help her recently, she snapped, "No, you can't help me." When I asked, "Why not?" she replied, "Because you don't have girls, you have boys." (I am the mother of four sons, while her mother is the mother of two daughters.) "If you had girls," she chattered on, "you could help me, but you have boys, so you can't, only Mommy can, because she has girls." *A strange, but reasonable theory*, I thought. But she didn't stop there.

"That's why you're fat, because you had boys; Mommy's skinny because she had girls; if you had girls, you'd be skinny, but you had boys, so you're fat." I roared with laughter.

Not only did Halle's frankness delight me, but her "logic" fascinated me. If Bama has boys and is fat, and Mommy has girls and is skinny, then surely when it comes to weight, the deciding factor is the gender of your children. (Had I known, I would have prayed for all girls.)

And so go countless of my conversations with my delightful four-year-old granddaughter.

When Halle made reference to "the green power" inside of her, I knew I was in for another one of her delightful "takes" on life.

"What green power?" I asked.

"The green power inside me that makes me do bad things," she replied absently, having already moved on in her thoughts.

Thinking now would be a good time to introduce the concept of Satan, I launched in, only to remember that Satan has no power over children until they are of the age of accountability, so I shelved that thought and asked more about the green power.

"You know, Bama," Halle impatiently replied, as though I should already know what she was just figuring out, "like the green monster. When I do bad things, the green power's in me."

Once again, I was amazed by her logic. If that inflatable,

lighted, green-faced Halloween decoration is a monster, and monsters are bad (she had seen, after all, the Disney movie *Monsters, Inc.*), then Halle must have that same green power inside of her when she's bad.

Odd concept though it was, it was also pretty darn smart and logical for a four-year-old and a far better explanation than I could have come up with on the spur of the moment.

But Halle was way beyond me. While I was still contemplating green power, she was vowing that she would never kick Maddie again, emphasizing her commitment with a concluding and dramatic "ever."

Oh, that we all had such logic and discipline.

Peg Fugal

Stopped at the Gate

My grandchildren from Tennessee come to visit me every summer; we love the time we spend together and the wonderful talks we have. When they came to visit this past summer, we took a trip to the Chicago Temple, which is about forty-five minutes away.

During one visit, my husband and I took the kids to the temple on a nice sunny day so we could spend time walking around the grounds and talking about our family being together forever. As we drove to the temple I asked Heavenly Father what I could do or say to make our experience at the temple a lasting one. We arrived and walked around the temple grounds, and nothing specific came to me, though I continued to pray for inspiration.

Suddenly the door to the temple opened as someone was coming out, and right then it came to me, as if God was whispering directly to me. I asked a temple worker who was at the door if I could step in with my grandkids so they could get a glimpse at the inside of the temple and could feel the comforting Spirit that was there. The temple worker said we could go inside, but we needed to stay in the foyer area in front of the recommend desk.

As we entered, I explained that we needed to whisper because we were in the Lord's house, and we needed to be reverent. As I started to talk about the beautiful pictures on the walls, I felt that my conversation was now being guided by the Holy Spirit.

I told Meagan, Drew and Morgan that we could not go past the desk in the foyer unless we had a temple recommend. They looked at me with great curiosity and asked if I had a recommend. I was so happy to be able to tell them that I do. I further explained that I have to be found worthy to have a temple recommend.

"When you think about our visit to the temple, I hope you will always remember what it is like in Heaven," I told them. "You can be good in this life and just get by, without really growing and changing inside to help you become more like Jesus. If you did that, you would make it in the front door of Heaven, but you couldn't get past the guard to all of Heaven so you could be where the Lord dwells.

"Or," I continued, "you can do your very best to get to know and understand the Lord, and ask for His guidance and forgiveness in your life. He will direct you, and the Holy Spirit will show you the way to go. When you reach Heaven the angel will say, 'You are worthy to enter. Welcome home.' You can either walk in and live with your family forever, or you can enter Heaven but be stopped at the gate, and told that's as far as you may go. The choice is yours."

I saw the Spirit touch their hearts as we hugged tightly. That moment in the temple with my grandchildren will stay with me forever, as I hope it will them. I thank the Lord for my family, and for His wonderful plan for our happiness.

Betty Bayne

Pizza, Soggy Cereal and the Atonement

And even if it were possible that little children could sin they could not be saved; but I say unto you they are blessed; for behold, as in Adam, or by nature, they fall, even so the blood of Christ atoneth for their sins.

Mosiah 3:16

When my youngest daughter was only three years old, she loved to mimic her older brother by asking to have two bowls of cold cereal for breakfast in the morning. Each day, the same ritual occurred: She would ask for her first bowl of cereal, eat it, and then request the second bowl. She would then take one bite, say she was full, and refuse to eat the rest.

On one particular morning, I had finally had enough of her wasteful practice. When she asked for the second bowl, I explained that if she didn't eat all the cereal she asked for, she would have to eat it at lunchtime before she could have her "real" lunch. Of course, being three, she agreed. Even after our discussion of what would happen, she ate only a single bite of the second bowl, and then said she was finished. I firmly reminded her that she needed to eat the cereal before she could have what was for lunch. As I put the cereal in the refrigerator, I turned to her and asked, "Are you sure you don't want to eat this now?" Her refusal was clear. As promised, the bowl of cereal went into the fridge to wait for lunchtime.

That afternoon when my son arrived home from kindergarten, the three of us sat down for leftover pizza. I reminded my daughter that she needed to finish her cereal before she could have pizza. I took the soggy bowl of cereal from the refrigerator and placed it in front of her. She took one look at the mushy mess and ran from the table, screaming and wailing.

My tenderhearted son, who had been watching attentively, looked at the slice of pizza in front of him. He then looked at the soggy cereal in front of his sister's place as her cries echoed from the other room. His eyes met mine, and he said quietly, "I'll eat her cereal."

My heart was so full when I realized the sincere love he had for his younger sister. His only thought was to take away her pain, make her happy and have her return to be with us at the table.

This simple, tender statement of my young son taught me a powerful lesson about the infinite atonement of our Savior, Jesus Christ. As the Savior has done for us, my son fulfilled both the law of mercy and the law of justice for his sister in this one simple act of love. Throughout our lives, all of us get ourselves into predicaments that we can't resolve on our own. Our loving and kind Savior hears us weep and offers regrets. Then, with great love and patience, He lets us know that He has already paid the price being demanded for our folly. The display of love my son showed for his sister was tremendous, but it represents only a fraction of the love our Elder Brother so freely gives to us.

Deborah McIff

A Family for Me

*And it came to pass that Enoch looked; and
from Noah, he beheld all the families of the
earth; and he cried unto the Lord, saying:
"When shall the day of the Lord come? When
shall the blood of the Righteous be shed, that all
they that mourn may be sanctified and have
eternal life?"*

Moses 7:45

I grew up in a dysfunctional family with not enough
money to go around. Mom shielded my siblings and me as
much as possible, but the reality of the situation began to
hit me when I was about twelve. I had brown eyes when
both of my parents were blue-eyed. My father always
treated me differently, but I had assumed it was because I
was the eldest.

When I was thirty-two and expecting my first child, my
mom confessed that I had been adopted. After the shock
wore off, I was able to gather the important information—
my real father's name—and come to terms with the

knowledge that I had a whole new family out in the world. I tried to find them, but to no avail. The Internet was a great tool, but it yielded no names for the geographic areas where I looked. I gave up looking, but life dealt a cruel blow when my mother passed away two years later.

In the greatest sorrow I had ever felt, I searched for answers about life, death and the presence of God. My search led me to the Church of Jesus Christ of Latter-day Saints. I was baptized with my husband in February 2004. After my baptism, I had a burning desire to find my family. Logging on to the Internet, I performed the exact search I had before, and a list of names appeared on the monitor. I sat in shock, realizing that this was Heavenly Father's gift to me—and I was scared to open it.

At 10 A.M. on March 30, 2004, I dialed the first number on the list and got an answering machine. I left a message for an Ernest Butler, asking for information about an Olin H. Butler. I then called the other numbers on the list and got either no information or "out of service" recordings.

After work that day, I came home to a message on my answering machine from Ernest Butler. My heart was pounding. I couldn't breathe, and I knew that this was real. When I called, he told me that he was my brother—and that my family had been looking for me for thirty-five years. We stayed on the phone from 8 P.M. until 3 A.M. With tears of joy, I felt such relief that I had finally found my family. I was also very uncertain whether they would accept me.

We met two weeks later, and the relief I felt was staggering. I looked like them, they looked like me, and they were my family. I am blessed because I now have nine brothers and sisters, including the brother and sister from the family I grew up in. But I am even more blessed because I was able to share the gospel with my brother Ernie, and he was baptized in May.

Some people ask whether I am happy knowing that my mother had me out of wedlock; I reply that she was the strongest woman I'll ever know. She chose to keep me and lived a life of literal hell on Earth to raise me with a man who hated me and all I represented to him.

I know that Mom is waiting for me to be baptized for her, and I know without a doubt that she has accepted the gospel. Our Heavenly Father's plan has worked out perfectly for me. Because of obedience to His commandments, I now know my family and what we are here on Earth for. It is my destiny to unite my family and a lost lineage to our Heavenly Father.

This whole experience was akin to sweet pain for me, because I always doubted who I was and why I never seemed to fit in with anyone. I was meant to live the life I did because it prepared me to accept and be a part of a much larger picture. I may not understand or agree with my newest siblings, but I know that I will always love them unconditionally, the way that Heavenly Father loves me. We are, after all, a family.

Ruth Moore

Satan and My Car Keys

And the God of peace shall bruise Satan under your feet shortly. The grace of our Lord Jesus Christ be with you. Amen.

Rom. 16:20

It never ceases to amaze me how clever Satan is. How he will seize any and every opportunity, no matter how small or insignificant, to force his way into our lives—to keep us from living and sharing the gospel.

Such was the case almost every Sunday morning with me and Satan.

Missing church shoes. And socks. And belts.

Church clothes that needed washing. Or ironing. Or mending. Or replacing.

Church materials I was so sure were ready at hand. And weren't.

Car keys that were never where they were supposed to be.

And a husband who always left early for one meeting or another, leaving me without adult help to prepare myself, four kids, and, more often than not, a lesson.

Sunday mornings were a nightmare filled with me scrambling and screaming. As a result, the kids feared both me and Sundays, and the Spirit flew out the window.

I had to do something. I had to make some changes.

I started gathering and preparing church clothes the night before.

I started preparing my lessons a week in advance.

I started putting my car keys in the exact same location every time I came into the house.

Problems solved. Peaceful Sunday mornings. Happy kids. Rich Sunday Spirit. For many weeks running.

Then a shoe disappeared again. I panicked. But the kids found it in the toy box before I exploded.

My lesson materials were nowhere to be found. Oh, I had already put them in the car. Disaster averted.

The car keys were not in their usual place. The kids were not going to wait for that scene. They walked to church. It was too far for me to walk with all my church materials.

Having successfully made it through every other disaster that Sunday morning without losing my cool, or the Spirit, I was determined to find my keys with the same calm resolve.

It was then that the Spirit whispered to me, "Family room window."

"Family room window?" I questioned. And then argued, "Why on earth would my car keys be in the family room window?" I ignored the prompting and began my usual routine search.

Ignition? No.

Purse? No.

Coat pocket? No.

Dress pocket? No.

My calm was slipping.

The Spirit whispered a second time, "Family room window."

Again, I ignored the prompting, knowing better.

Kitchen? No.

Bedroom? No.

Bathroom? No.

Closet? No.

Office? No.

Rage was creeping in.

The Spirit whispered a third time, "Family room window."

Exasperated, I tromped to the family room window, and lo and behold, there lay my keys.

How they got there, I do not know. Nor did I care. I left for church with the Spirit still intact.

I learned a very important lesson that morning: that the Spirit is as interested in me keeping the Spirit on Sunday mornings as I am.

And I have relied on its help every day since.

Much to Satan's chagrin.

Peg Fugal

Jesus in the Sky

Behold, you have had many afflictions because of your family; nevertheless, I will bless you and your family, yea, your little ones; and the day cometh that they will believe and know the truth and be one with you in my church.

                                                    D&C 31:2

It was a beautiful crisp Sunday afternoon when my three children and I left late for our usual meetings at our modest little chapel in the small town where we lived. Our meetinghouse is a small white building just off the highway. Even though it has been added on to three times, it would probably fit inside a typical meetinghouse twice! We have only one ward in town, so the summers and holidays here are always cozy with lots of visitors—and even though we were only ten minutes late, the parking lot was almost full, as was the chapel.

It was difficult to find seats for all of us. Normally, we stay in the foyer when we arrive late, but the foyer was already filled. My frustration grew as I headed for the back doors to the chapel, knowing my husband was at work and I was going to have to keep my children quiet and in their seats on my own.

We waited for the prayer to end before we entered the chapel and tried to find three seats on an aisle. My youngest was only a few months shy of a year, so I carried him in his infant car seat. His older brother was two—and certainly lived up to the title of "terrible twos." My oldest had only one thing on her mind: the upcoming sixth birthday party for her and a few of her friends. As we walked in, she was chattering about what she would get and who would come to the party and what dress she would wear.

My two-year-old made sure we were noticed as we walked to our seats by shouting, "I no wanna sit here, Mommm!" Then he did what we affectionately call his "limp noodle"—he collapsed to the floor, face down, still clutching my hand tightly. A few people chuckled softly as I scooped him up with one arm, still carrying the car seat with the other. Finally, we found a spot and sat down.

I handed out crayons and coloring books, hoping to keep my two children occupied as long as possible—but knowing in my heart it would only work for a few minutes. I gave the baby a bottle. As the sacrament was passed, the children were spread out on the floor, coloring in the hymn books. The baby drifted off to sleep.

Soon after the first speaker stood up, my two-year-old no longer wanted to color. I figured he wanted to run around—and feared he would wake the baby. I was mentally prepared to drag the entire crew out to the hall.

As I started to wrestle with my two-year-old, my mind raced. Were the children even getting anything out of these meetings? Was I doing the right thing by bringing them week after week—or was I just distracting everyone else?

I picked up the crayons and put the coloring books

away, and persuaded my two-year-old to sit on my lap for a few minutes. Then he wanted to lay down, so I held him in my arms. Suddenly he pointed to the ceiling and said, more clearly than I had ever heard him say anything, "Look, Mommy, in the sky! Jesus! Look, Mommy!"

I immediately looked up—half expecting to actually see the Savior there. Instead, I saw only the ceiling fans. After that, my little boy sat quietly on my lap through the rest of the meeting.

I will never forget the way I felt that day. I know my son saw something I clearly could not, and that the Savior really does watch over us. How grateful I was that I made the effort to bring them all!

Jennifer Gowans

Brothers by Chance, Friends by Choice

And the Lord said unto Cain, "Where is Abel thy brother?" And he said, "I know not: Am I my brother's keeper?"

Gen. 4:9

Being a stay-at-home mother of three children brings me daily trials, but the joys I experience each day more than make up for those trials. Our two oldest children—three-year-old Levi and two-year-old Carsen—can sometimes be quite a handful. They do occasionally fight, more so as they get older, but most often they are the best of friends. Together, they can come up with some mischievous ideas—and when they do, it's guaranteed that they will double-team me and cover up for each other.

One day as I was changing Lissy's diaper, things got unnaturally quiet. I quickly finished, and as I started back to check on the two boys, I heard Levi yell, "Come on, Carsen—run! Quick, RUN!" With that, they were off, giggling all the way! I knew I was in for a special treat.

Reluctantly, I went to check out the damage. To my

pleasure, I found that Christmas had come early! The room was literally white. Those two monkeys had ripped what seemed like a dozen rolls of toilet paper into tiny pieces and had strewn them all over the living room floor, couches, piano and entertainment center. They even managed to somehow get toilet paper "flakes" at the very top of my artificial tree. How those two little boys planned and carried out that brilliant plan, complete with all its "tiny" details, in such a short time is still a mystery to me.

I try to overlook most of their joint mischief, telling myself that I'm so glad they are playing together instead of fighting. We have a specific quote we use to describe their relationship: "Brothers by chance, best friends by choice." Levi and Carsen can entertain each other for hours wrestling, building forts and fighting off the bad guys in their superhero outfits. Every morning they snuggle up under a blanket with their arms around each other to watch cartoons and drink their sippy cups of milk. On Sunday mornings, their favorite cartoon is "Nephi and the Boat"—Nephi has always been Levi's favorite Book of Mormon hero!

I used to worry about the boys watching how cruel Laman and Lemuel were to their younger brother Nephi. But after constant repetition I learned that I had succeeded in teaching my children that "hands are for loving." While watching Nephi being struck with sticks, Levi often explains to us that "They're being naughty. It's not nice to hit." Sometimes he gets really worked up and starts to yell at Laman and Lemuel, trying to persuade them to stop and telling them, "Hands are for loving!"

Being two years old, Carsen naturally takes what he wants, when he wants it. Levi has always been so patient with his younger brother, calmly explaining in a sweet voice, "We don't take toys away." Sometimes he is a peacemaker, giving Carsen what he wants and finding something else to play with. And, of course, he likes to remind Carsen that his "hands are for loving."

One summer day, Levi was invited to play at the house of Todd, an older friend who had no younger brothers or sisters. From experience, we knew that Todd didn't get along with Carsen, so when Levi asked if Carsen was going, too, I understandably told him no. He immediately pleaded, "But, Mom, it's just no fun without a brother!" My heart was deeply touched to see their bond as brothers, and I was saddened to separate them for even a few hours. I gently explained, "Levi, Todd yells at Carsen and hits him; he doesn't understand that he is just a little boy who doesn't yet know how to share. We don't want Carsen to get hurt—so when he is older, he can come, too."

Levi's eyes lit up with fire. He stood a little taller, stuck his chest out, pointed his finger, and in an intimidating voice said, "Mom, don't worry—if Todd tries to hit Carsen, I will protect him. I will just tell Todd, 'Don't touch him: I am filled with the power of God!'" I was speechless! He was absolutely serious, and it was all I could do to keep a straight face. I always wondered if those Book of Mormon movies were sinking in. Now I am positive that they were—and that my boys even know how to apply those Book of Mormon lessons in their daily lives!

April Homer

Missing, but Not Forgotten

Have we not all one father? hath not one God created us? why do we deal treacherously every man against his brother, by profaning the covenant of our fathers?

Mal. 2:10

I last saw my brother Mikey in 1989. I last talked to him in 1999. I do not know where he is, what he is doing or why he has chosen to disappear.

Mikey was born on my younger sister Tina's sixth birthday, a week before my seventh birthday. He was what my mother referred to as "a later-in-life surprise." When she brought him home from the hospital, I put away my dolls, and he became my doll. I all but raised him until the day I left for college. I bathed, dressed, changed and fed him. I played with him and put him to bed. I read to him, sang to him and prayed with him. I was his only babysitter. When he was older, I took him to and from school, helped him with his homework and helped him practice the piano.

We four older children were born within one year of

each other, leaving home one after another, leaving our baby brother alone with our parents for several years. Having no one left to play with, he began to make up imaginary friends, which later evolved into an entire imaginary life.

Because he was eventually the only child at home, my father put him to work in his business. He married a sweet girl straight out of high school and they had two children together. My father helped them buy a home. And they began to live what appeared to be a charmed life.

Carelessness on his part led to divorce. When his wife remarried, he foolishly allowed her new husband to adopt his children. I have not seen them since they were babies. They are adults now, probably with babies of their own and probably with no idea that they have a whole other family elsewhere that has never forgotten them and longs to see them.

My brother remarried.

He was still working for my father at the time, but not performing up to par. My father called and asked my advice. I asked what he would do if Mikey were an employee.

"I'd fire him," he answered.

"Then, you have to fire him," I advised.

Little did I know the eventual effect of that advice.

My brother did not work again for many years.

His wife eventually joined the service, and they moved from base to base.

In 1986, he came home for my father's funeral. My mother sent him to the airport to retrieve me. He had his wife waiting in full dress uniform with a sign, much to both my and her embarrassment. On the drive home, he regaled us with tales about the Mafia providing the limousines for Father's funeral because Father had done so much business with them over the years. My father never knew, let alone worked with, the Mafia, but I let it pass, knowing his childhood imagination was still at work.

In 1989, he came home for Mother's estate auction, claiming he had been sent by the service to see what he could secure for the government, his imaginary life still in full swing.

I went home for the estate auction, too, taking with me my then teenaged son. Mikey kept my son up late one night regaling him with tales of service as a helicopter pilot during the Vietnam war, much to my son's delight. Later, when my son began to repeat the stories to me, I stopped him and confronted my brother.

"Why do you tell such stories?" I demanded. He threatened to kill me. I have never seen him since.

Later I received a call from the LDS missionaries serving on the base where my brother was living. They had taught Mikey the gospel and were preparing to baptize him. Rather than being overjoyed, I was hesitant, questioning my brother's intent. I was afraid he was joining the Church only to make himself more acceptable to our predominantly LDS family. The missionaries assured me that his intent was pure. I rejoiced at the good news.

While his wife worked hard in the service, Mikey sat home in base housing watching TV. She eventually divorced him.

The next thing I knew, he was working in a factory. A vat fell on him and he went on workman's compensation for quite some time, living in a motel with no phone and only a post-office box. I faithfully wrote to him, never forgetting a holiday or his birthday, always sending graduation, missionary and wedding announcements, sometimes enclosing a check.

The next thing I heard, he was working at a hospital. He started calling all of us regularly and convinced us that he was earning a surgical nursing degree, much to our delight. Though we welcomed his calls, we tired of his hospital stories, questioning their veracity.

During that time, he claimed to be active in the Church, much to our relief.

One day I called the hospital to talk to Mikey. The operator, who knew me quite well by then, informed me that he no longer worked there. I asked if he had been hired away. She asked what I meant. I said, "Well, I know surgical nurses are in great demand. Did another hospital hire him away?"

She laughed and replied, "He was our bed-maker: Maybe the linen company hired him."

I was so incensed that I wrote him a letter, demanding to know why he kept telling stories, assuring him that we do not care what he does for a living, begging him to change. That was in 1999. I have not heard from him since.

A couple of years ago, my older brother called the state police and asked for their help in locating Mikey. They found him. But, without his permission, they could not reveal any information about him; permission he denied.

A little while later, I received a call from an elderly Church missionary asking me for Mikey's address. I asked who he was and why he was looking for Mikey. He explained that he was a Missing Church Member Missionary, assigned to locate missing Church members. Mikey's membership records, he explained, had been floating since he left the last base he had lived on (which indicated that Mikey was not active in the Church, yet another tale).

A member of the Church my whole adult life, I had never heard of Missing Church Member Missionaries. I was impressed—and hopeful that they would find Mikey when his family could not.

They called again the next year with the same question: "Where's your brother Mikey?"

Again, I answered, "I don't know."

"How can you lose track of your own brother?" the missionary asked.

"It's not by choice," I replied.

The Missing Church Member Missionaries continue to call me—as well as my LDS mother, brother and sister—every year looking for Mikey. Every year we tell them the same thing. "He's disappeared."

They keep looking.

We keep praying.

For a miracle.

Recently, I watched an LDS family turn their back on a homosexual family member, which enraged me. I confronted them. "I haven't seen my baby brother in sixteen years," I said, "or talked to him in six years. I wouldn't care if he was gay or insane. I just want to know where he is and that he's all right. I want him to know that I love him, miss him, and want to hear from and see him." It must have done some good. They have since re-embraced that gay family member.

If my baby brother were to miraculously contact me today, I would send him a ticket to fly to my home for a visit. I would listen to his crazy stories and love him anyway. I would try to help him get back into the Church. I would try to get him some therapy. I would try to help him begin to deal with reality. I would re-embrace him and love him unconditionally.

But I may never get that chance.

In fact, I may be the one responsible for his disappearance.

Maggie May

(Details have been changed for privacy.)

In Memory of Our God and Our Children

And it came to pass that he rent his coat; and he took a piece thereof, and wrote upon it— In memory of our God, our religion, and freedom, and our peace, our wives, and our children—and he fastened it upon the end of a pole.

Alma 46:12

It is not a surprise that during the teen years many youth challenge family values and become somewhat rebellious. We were relieved when our youngest son finished high school and enlisted in the Marine Corps. When he reenlisted, we felt the joy of knowing he had some direction in his life.

While in the Marines, our son was ordained an elder. He also got married during that time, and has become a responsible father.

When his second tour of duty was completed, he and

his wife decided to return home, where he could begin a career and they could create permanent roots. Expecting their second child and seeking ways to financially support his family, he signed up for the reserves and registered for college.

I will never forget the empty feeling I experienced a few months later when the phone rang.

"Dad, I have been called up," he told me. "I am going to Iraq. I need a priesthood blessing." In that blessing, he was promised that if he lived the gospel, he would return home safe.

We felt some relief as a result of that blessing, knowing our son was headed for the uncertainties of a war in Iraq. When his mother questioned, in maternal desperation, why he had to go, he responded in a way that surprised both of us.

"I am going in memory of our God, our religion and our freedom," he told us, "our wives and our children." In the back of my mind I rejoiced in the fact that our son remembered family values and had recalled family discussions and teachings.

While he was in Iraq, his group was camping just outside Baghdad, where he was washing his clothes. Trucks were passing by. He was hanging his shirt on a clothesline when someone shouted, "Hit the dirt!"

When it was safe and the sniper had been removed, he found two bullet holes in the shirt he had just hung up to dry.

As I write this, I glance at that shirt. It has become our new trophy. I realize our boy had become his parents' hero. When he returned to duty, we did say good-bye— but we also told him, "God be with you till we meet again."

John Nield

The Greatest Sacrifice

Greater love hath no man than this, that a man lay down his life for his friends.

John 15:13

I have seen the Church TV commercial for LDS Family Services many times. The young pregnant girl who cannot marry, cannot raise a baby alone, a baby who deserves two parents.

"I'm not giving her up," the girl says, "I'm giving her more."

It makes me cry every time I see it.

So young, so brave.

And the adoptive parents. So happy, so grateful.

I would never have guessed that one day my own family would find themselves living that commercial in real life.

When our son Richie received his patriarchal blessing just before departing on his mission, the patriarch said something that concerned us greatly: "You will know tragedy in your life."

What tragedy? my husband and I questioned over the years.

Richie was the perfect son. Always loving, always obedient, always helpful, always a good example to his siblings and friends. A good student, a good athlete, who also played the piano. A great scout, an excellent missionary, who married his teenage sweetheart, Joni.

No tragedies there.

A couple of years into their marriage, Richie and Joni decided to start their family. It was then that the prophesied tragedy came to light. They were unable to have children.

After years of fertility work, and one heartbreaking failure after another, they gave up and moved to Chicago where they began a new life without children.

Meanwhile, another son Jack and his wife, Stefi, gave birth to our first granddaughter, Lily, who became the darling of the family.

When Joni learned of Stefi's pregnancy, she cried all night.

I cried a lot, too. I am a take-charge mother who makes sure my children have what they need. But I could not fulfill this need.

So I prayed a lot.

And I got mad.

Every time I read or heard of an abused or neglected child, I questioned God, "Why didn't you send that baby to us where it would have been loved and safe?"

There was no answer.

One night I prayed, "I want you to send a baby to Richie and Joni, *and I mean it!*"

My husband warned me about counseling the Lord.

Sometime later, Richie and Joni decided to adopt, but told no one, not wanting to get anyone's hopes up, least of all their own.

They met with LDS Family Services, filled out all the paperwork, did all the interviews and inspections, and made a portfolio of their lives that Family Services would use to introduce them to birth mothers.

They began budgeting and saving.

Once everything was in place, they took a long overdue and much-deserved vacation to France, where Joni had served a mission.

Ten days later they returned. It was late Sunday night. They checked their phone messages. There were four from Family Services. They returned the calls immediately, awaking the agency director.

"We just retrieved your message," Richie said, "and we're not waiting until tomorrow to learn what you have for us."

"Well, we have a baby boy for you," replied the director. "He was born Friday afternoon and has been waiting for you to turn up. Where have you been? And can you be in Minnesota by Tuesday at 1 P.M.?"

Richie and Joni had only recently passed Family Services' inspection before leaving on their trip. They had not expected to hear from them for weeks or months, maybe even years. Then suddenly, they had only thirty-six hours to prepare for parenthood, without a diaper or a bottle to their name! Because they live in Chicago and use public transportation, they don't even own a car or a car seat!

They called their bishop whose wife loaned them a car seat and some baby essentials. They rented a car and started the long drive to claim their son from a town very near where I grew up.

Still, they told no one.

As is sometimes the procedure with Family Services, they met the birth mother, as well as her parents, when picking up their son at the home of a stake president.

They learned that both the birth mother and father had separately viewed all the available portfolios and had separately chosen Richie and Joni to parent their baby. Surely, it was inspiration.

Even more interestingly, the birth mother and her parents had kept the baby while awaiting Richie and Joni's return, refusing to give the baby to anyone else.

"Why us?" Richie asked.

"Because you've lived an adventurous life," the birth mother answered, "and I want my son raised by adventurous parents."

"We've led an adventurous life," Richie laughed, "because we didn't have kids!"

"Now, we'll never do anything adventurous again," laughed Joni.

They left with their four-day-old son and stopped at the first baby store they passed, buying everything in sight.

After driving for four hours while the wondrous event sunk in, they stopped at a hotel to hold their new son and to call family with the miraculous news.

Richie found me at Jack and Stefi's house, holding my three-week-old granddaughter Annie Leigh (named after me).

"I'm so sorry I haven't called and asked about your trip," I apologized, "but we've been preoccupied with the birth of Annie. . . ."

"Mom," Richie interrupted.

I could tell by the tone of his voice that something serious had happened. Having fasted and prayed for a baby for them for years at that point, naturally I assumed that's what he was calling about.

"Did you hear from Family Services?" I asked excitedly. "Did someone pick you for parents?"

"I'm holding my new son," Richie answered.

You could have knocked me over with a feather.

Stefi grabbed the phone, listened to the news and burst into tears.

Three-year-old Lily groaned at the thought of having to share her grandma with yet another new baby.

Between the two of us, Stefi and I pieced together the miraculous story.

When we prayed that night, we wept with joy and gratitude for the grand and glorious blessing of a baby *finally* for Richie and Joni.

And then we thanked God for the birth mother, who could have aborted the baby, but who chose instead to give him life and then to give him a family. What a brave girl. What a splendid spirit. What a noble sacrifice. How very grateful we are for her and will be eternally.

We think of her often: wondering how she's doing, how she's feeling, how she's coping with her loss. Wondering if her arms and heart feel as empty as ours feel full. Wondering if she will ever understand and appreciate what she has done for our family, giving us a baby we could not get any other way. A son. Our first grandson. Our namesake. Giving him life when it is so easy these days to take life away. Giving him a family in a day when family is waning. Making the greatest sacrifice of her life, while granting us the greatest blessing of our lives.

We think, too, of her parents, wondering how they're feeling, if they're at peace with their daughter's decision, if they're missing their grandson as much as we're loving him. And we feel as grateful for them as we are for the birth mother.

LDS Family Services is one of many adoption agencies in this country, with a twist. They match LDS babies with LDS families, so that baby can have the blessing of the restored gospel and Church in his life, the blessing of endowed parents, the blessing of a big, connected family sealed for eternity.

We visited two weeks later. After holding him for a minute, my husband, Jack, said the sweetest thing: "He doesn't feel any less like mine just because he's adopted."

"Good," I replied, "that's exactly how you're supposed to feel."

It was some time before Richie and Joni named their son Andie, a spelling they made up, wanting the "ie" in Richie's name to also be in Andie's name.

At this writing Andie is eighteen months old. His adoption was finalized two weeks ago and we took him to the temple this past week. Despite the delays, he has felt like ours since the moment we learned of him.

Interestingly, Andie is very much like his father, Richie, was at the same age. Anxious to walk and talk. Cheerful. Inquisitive. Lovable.

How can that possibly be?

God so orders the universe.

Richie used to work for me. His move to Chicago was very hard on me and my business. But Joni is convinced that they had to move to Chicago because that's where they would find their son.

I think she's right.

It's no coincidence that Richie and Joni were living in Chicago when their son was born just north of there.

It's no coincidence that my grandson comes from my hometown, something we will always have in common.

It's no coincidence that Joni's sister Mary, Andie's aunt, was adopted, a special relationship they will always share.

It's God putting together a family that He ordained in the eternities.

As He does, in my opinion, with every single adoption on Earth.

Leigh Baugh

(Details have been changed for legal and privacy purposes.)

Years of Pent-Up Emotion

"One day your dream to be sealed to your husband in the temple of the Lord for time and all eternity will come to pass," my patriarchal blessing assured me. I remember telling her that there must be another husband in my future because there was no way Eddie Pierce would ever take me to the temple! Over the years it became a joke—a way to relieve the stress of living with a husband who seemed to fight me over anything that involved the Church. I tried my best to fulfill church assignments while he was out of town on business. It was just easier to "hide" my callings than deal with the contention they caused.

My daughter and I had been baptized on the same day in 1978. It all started with Donny Osmond's marriage, which spurred a conversation with the bishop's wife next door. The next thing I knew, she was inviting us to take the discussions, and I agreed. I felt the Spirit at our first meeting, and I couldn't wait to be baptized. Eddie didn't come to the baptism and told us not to talk about church in front of him. He said he didn't need organized religion, and he certainly didn't want "some old man in Salt Lake" telling him how to live his life. He liked his coffee and wasn't going to give it up for anyone.

Starting with my baptism, the Church—or rather, my involvement in the Church—became a huge obstacle in our marriage. Eddie felt the Church took time away from him. It was the direct opposite of what the Church taught, with its emphasis on the importance of the family. The problem was that we weren't sharing the same things. Talks and lessons at my meetings inspired me to love Eddie into the Church, but it seemed Satan was waiting for me when I got home. I prayed to know what the Lord expected of me. I prayed to know if I was where I belonged. Each time I received the same assurance that I was. For some reason unknown to me, I was right where the Lord wanted me—married to someone who seemed to test me every day.

In April 1998, I decided I'd waited long enough to receive my endowment. Once I made those covenants in the temple, the windows of Heaven were literally opened to me. It was as though the Lord was waiting for me to take that leap of faith before He was ready to bless me with anything else.

In August of that same year, twenty years after my baptism, it became apparent to me that things were not improving between us. I had friends who knew my spiritual side, but it was something I had to continue to hide from him. I prayed about it again, and this time the Spirit confirmed that my decision to leave was the right thing to do. I can't tell you what made it acceptable then when it had been wrong for twenty years, but I couldn't deny that it was the answer I received. I prayed again, pleading, "Heavenly Father, if I understand you correctly, you approve of my decision to move out. But I don't know where to go or what to do. If this is right, you're going to have to open some doors for me."

That night I went to bed not knowing how I was going to accomplish this change, but I woke up out of a sound sleep at 4 A.M. and was given the first piece of the puzzle. A good friend of ours owned a rental house, and I remembered that his renters had just moved out. I could hardly wait until 8 A.M. to call and ask if he would rent the house to me. He said yes, without asking any questions.

I prayed for continued guidance, and the Lord was there with me every step of the way. I went to the bishop and told him of my decision. I assured him I wasn't even considering divorce—I just needed to get away to clear my head and figure out exactly what I wanted. He asked if there was anything he could do to help. "Aren't you going to try to talk me out of it?" I asked. He told me it sounded like I'd already thought it through and gotten the confirmation I needed. He suggested I ask the elders quorum for help moving my things.

Everything was in place, and I planned to move over Labor Day weekend. I decided not to tell Eddie I was leaving because I didn't want the fight. A death in the family postponed my moving from Saturday to Monday, and I wondered why the Lord had added that test to the growing list of challenges, but everything worked out. In fact, going to that funeral confirmed again that moving was the right thing to do. The brethren in our ward were there to help me move; sisters came to help pack and unpack. I was out of the house before the end of the day, and around 4 P.M. I called Eddie at work to tell him I wouldn't be there when he got home. All he said was, "It's probably for the best." I gave him my phone number and told him if he wanted to talk about anything, to give me a call. He assured me that he wouldn't need the number. I hung up thinking it had all gone far too smoothly!

Once he spent a day or two in the house alone, he changed his mind. He called me at work. He called me at home. He sent flowers. All I really wanted was some time to think. In twenty years he hadn't wanted to talk, and now that's all he wanted to do. He told me he would never join my church, but he was willing to learn more about it so he would understand.

I agreed to have dinner with him. Again, he told me he wanted to learn more about the Church. I told him if he really wanted to know about it, President Gordon B. Hinckley was coming to town for a regional conference, and he could hear about the Church directly from the prophet. He said he'd like to go, but as soon as I invited him I felt uncomfortable about it. This would be my first opportunity to see the prophet, and I wanted to go there fasting, to invite the Spirit. I told him if he planned to go and make light of it, or just find things to argue about, I didn't want him to go. I really wanted to go by myself, but he was so convincing in wanting to learn more that I agreed to take him with me.

President Hinckley came to Houston and spoke to a crowd of about 25,000 at the Astrodome on September 26, 1998. While other speakers took their turn, there was a lot of moving around, but when President Hinckley stood up to speak, people took their seats and a quiet calm fell over the stadium. The Spirit was strong, and I was filled with the knowledge that President Hinckley is a prophet of God. The first thing he did was joke about our sound system. "I don't know what you Houstonians paid for this sound system, but I believe you were cheated." Everyone laughed. Apparently, people had been moving around earlier trying to find a spot where they could hear. I can't remember what President Hinckley said after that, but my heart just broke when he walked off that stage. I could never get enough of our dear prophet, and I wanted him to stay there forever.

On the way home, I asked Eddie if he felt anything. He

said he felt peace and calm. I told him that was the Spirit. "What's the Spirit?" he asked. I told him the Holy Ghost was telling him that President Hinckley was a prophet and that the things he heard were true. There was no arguing or contention. When we got back to the house, I asked if he wanted to watch a church video with me. He agreed, and we watched "On the Way Home." At one point, Eddie broke down and sobbed. Thirty years of pent-up emotion came pouring out as his now-softened heart had felt the Spirit.

That week we had the missionaries over for dinner. Elder Rehling made a distinct impression when he asked, "Brother Pierce, how long have you been a member?" When Eddie told him he wasn't a member, this young missionary was at first speechless, then rebounded with, "Well, would you like to take the discussions?" Eddie told him no, he didn't think so, and that was that.

A few days later Eddie called me and asked for the missionaries' phone number. I gave him the number and tried not to think much about it. He did call and schedule a meeting with them. After the first discussion they challenged him to read from the Book of Mormon and pray about whether it was true. I wasn't there for the discussion, but when he told me about it, I explained to him that his confirmation might come in many different ways—he might feel peace, he might feel a burning in his bosom, he might just have the feeling that it was true. I told him that he would know. He read Moroni 10:3-4 and prayed about it, and decided that when they asked him about baptism, he would tell them no. However, when the elders challenged him at their next meeting, he said yes, and then started to laugh. He said, "I guess I'd better explain why I'm laughing. It's just that I was all prepared to tell you no, and when I opened my mouth, 'yes' came out!"

Giving up the coffee wasn't a problem once he committed to it. He continued the discussions, and baptism was scheduled for October 24, 1998. A friend who was our former branch president came to visit and asked Eddie if he was joining just to get me back. Eddie assured him that as much as he loved me, he wouldn't join the Church just for me.

The day of Eddie's baptism arrived. His sister Barbara, who had joined the Church after her daughter and son-in-law were baptized, was there to see it for herself and offer the opening prayer. The Relief Society room was packed, and there wasn't a dry eye in the place as our friends and family witnessed this life-changing event.

One of my friends told me I shouldn't expect a baptism to change him or our marriage. It's true that we are both very different people and have our own strengths and weaknesses, but the most important thing we share is our love of the Lord and our commitment to the gospel of Jesus Christ. We were sealed as a couple and to our daughter in the Dallas Temple with a room full of friends there to support us. We served as temple workers when the Houston Temple opened. He was there to support me every step of the way in my calling as Relief Society president. I support him in his calling as high priest group leader. It is such a joy to be able to serve the Lord together—no more hiding my light under a bushel, but sharing it along with my husband and looking forward to the day when we can serve a mission together.

Others told me that one day he'd come around, but my faith wasn't strong enough to believe it. The Lord kept the promise He made in my patriarchal blessing so many years ago. I know with all my heart that He was waiting for me to covenant with Him in the temple. Once I did, the blessings poured out, and my marriage, which was once only for this life, is now for time and all eternity.

Joyce Moseley Pierce

God Didn't Bless Me This Week

Our youngest son, Jer, was born with a sweet, but sometimes contentious spirit, which first became apparent when he was about eight years old.

One Sunday morning when we were all preparing for church, he announced, "I'm not going to church this week."

Surprised, I asked, "Why?"

"Because God didn't bless me this week," came his matter-of-fact reply.

Knowing the handling of such matters could have a life-long effect, I immediately appealed to the Spirit for direction and learned the Lord has a quick wit.

As fast as I had the thought, an answer came to me.

"Are you breathing?" I asked.

Perplexed, my son looked at me and slowly answered, "Y-e-s."

"Then you've been blessed," I announced. "You're going to church."

Sherm Fugal

Confessions of a Scrapbooking Skeptic

Write and keep a regular history . . .

D&C 47:1

I've never really taken the time to become very involved in the scrapbooking craze. To tell the truth, I've had difficulty understanding the hype surrounding the hobby and why so many droves of women have recently felt they want to join in. For me, the prospect of sitting down with boxes of old photos to start such a project is overwhelming, to say the least—especially when it seems a standard photo album would serve my purposes just fine. However, my sister Bobbi invited me to a scrapbooking party one evening and I somewhat reluctantly decided to join her. I thought, if nothing else, that I could treat the evening as a research project and hopefully learn more about why this is such a phenomenon.

It would be misleading if I didn't admit that I approached the party with plenty of prejudice and skepticism about the craft. But, I like to think of myself as an open-minded person, so I decided that in order to free myself of my prejudices, it was only appropriate to become more educated.

The Carryall of Carryalls

I was at home visiting my family in Idaho when I was asked to go to the party at a local scrapbook supply retailer—which started at 10 P.M. *Why so late?* I complained to myself. But I decided to quiet my criticism and just play along—for the sake of research. I brought with me several old photos, reminding myself that I had the negatives if all of this ended up being a big mistake.

Then, once at my sister's house, I saw it. A rolling toolbox larger than a carry-on suitcase, overflowing with scissors, punches, papers, and yes, plenty of die cuts. Feeling immediately overwhelmed and underprepared for the night's events, I tried to pass off the mobile tackle box as an over-the-top exception to the rule, assuming that the supplies of other attendees would be much more conservative.

We arrived at the supply store and wheeled ourselves through the door. I immediately noticed a distinct change in my sister's demeanor. Part five-year-old on Christmas day, part Energizer bunny, the determined look in her eyes told me that I was about to see a side of my sister that I had not yet experienced.

Bobbi headed first to the stickers, where there were rows upon rows upon rows of little paper accents. She began talking to herself as she wandered from area to area, ". . . Look at all of the letter fonts! . . . Oh wow! New textured paper . . . Ah! I need these eyelets! . . . Oh no, the die cut line is too long." She had a language all her own, and I suddenly felt as if I was sneaking in on a private club, with all of its predetermined lingo, rules and code of conduct— and I didn't have a handbook.

The Welcoming Committee

"Oh, Bobbi! Is this your sister?" asked one inquisitive club member. "Why haven't we seen you here before, Bridget? You live in Utah? You're so lucky! You all have so many great scrapbooking stores down there!" . . . "You'll have to show me your stamp collection. The latest and greatest always seems to come from down south. . . .What? No, I don't collect postage stamps either—I meant your rubber stamps, like the kind you decorate with, silly!" . . . "This is your first time scrapbooking? You're kidding! You've got a lot to catch up on! Well, we'll get you started right away and make you feel right at home here."

In my head I cynically imagined a deep, sneering, "Ha, ha, ha . . . now we've got you!" after that last phrase, but I took a few deep breaths and tried to imagine I was spending some time in a foreign country and this was just a bit of culture shock.

Then we entered the back room where the party was underway. The doors to the retail portion of the store had been locked, and there I was, surrounded by about twenty women, all of whom had a large entourage of scrapbooking gear. I thought my sister's mobile scrap unit was amazing, but quickly discovered that her gear was actually quite moderate.

After pacing the retail store with my sister, trying to find the best accompaniments to her "Homage to Kindergarten Graduation," I finally sat down and was handed several pieces of very lovely pastel cardstock. Bobbi suggested that I take a look at some of the pages she had done to see if I liked any of the ideas. At this point I was just about ready to run out the door and into the Taco Bell next door to claim "sanctuary!"

But, I didn't.

Amidst all my nerves and bewilderment, I remembered

that I came to this event so that I could share an evening with my sister and perhaps gain an understanding, if not respect, for this funny new tradition. I sat down and started to observe these women, at 11 P.M., as they began to create their masterpieces.

Gazing at Caked Spaghettios

It was at this point that I started to make some interesting observations. As I mentioned before, much of my hesitation in this whole process was due to a lack of understanding about why they did it. Why the obsession? Why this? Why so much time and money? To me, if I want to display a picture, a photo album works fine—and if I want to express my creativity, then I can take a painting or pottery class. I skeptically wondered if a lot of the reasoning behind the scrapbooking phenomenon was that some women thought it was something they *should* do—not necessarily something they *wanted* to do.

I sat in my chair and started watching what was going on around me. I looked at all of the tools and papers and photos. I was amazed at all of the resources available for these projects. After a few minutes of observation, however, it wasn't the product that most interested me, but the process. I began to see how these women were working away with smiles on their faces, and I saw the way they were able to relax into a new role, apart from the one they played all day long. They were laughing, they were snacking, they were telling stories, and I got the feeling that for a little while they were happy to be able to forget that Jane had been teased at school or that Tom was struggling in math or that they had had an argument with Bill. They were still loving wives and mothers, but they were also just women, enjoying a hobby they had been introduced to through the help of a friend—possibly at a scrapbooking party in the middle of the night.

My heart softened just a bit, and I began to understand some of the "whys" a little better. But I still didn't quite understand why it required all of these funny little embellishments and papers and ribbons and wire. Why not stick with a photo album, save yourself some time and money, and read a book when you need some time to escape? I think maybe this is one of those times when I hear my mother's voice in my head saying, "When you have children, you'll understand."

I don't think all women with children understand or subscribe to this phenomenon—or that all single or child-less women are as perplexed by scrapbooking as I am. However, from my observation, I don't think it's assuming too much to say that the hobby definitely lends itself especially well to moms with kids. At one moment during the night I looked down the long table at the other end of the room. I saw a woman working away with her acid-free paper and glue pen who paused for quite a while as she held a photo down below the table in her lap. She was just sitting and smiling quietly while the other women gabbed around her. I got up and casually walked to the other end of the room where I could see the woman more clearly. She was looking at a picture of her toddler in his high chair, caked in Spaghettios.

My Findings

I was starting to understand a little bit better. To her, and probably to most of the women that night, these photos represented their biggest accomplishments and their largest sources of pride (and rightly so). I started to see all of the doodads as a way for them to show the world (or at least those looking at their scrapbooks) just how special the people in their lives are—so special that a simple picture doesn't quite do it justice. To them, a little—okay, or a lot—of flair and framing serves as a much better medium to showcase the masterpiece that is their families.

Amidst all of my bewilderment and joking about that night, I think I finally got it. This was a way to enjoy friendships with other women while looking back on events and people that mean much more to them than even their hearts could hold—much less a plastic photo sleeve. If the purpose of my evening was to learn why scrapbooking is so popular, I succeeded—because I now understand that it is less about the materials and more about the people.

For now, at least, I'm going to stick with writing as my method of creativity and expression. I learned a lot from my research project, including the fact that I don't have much of a talent for putting together a very nice scrap-book page. I think I'll leave that to my sister and the other women I met that night. Maybe I'll take Bobbi to a pottery class someday and have a new story to tell. I do keep in mind, though, that the prodigal son did eventually return, so if you see me one day picking out vellum in a specialty store with a shopping basket full of decorative punches and grommets, you'll know I've had a change of heart and am ready for another party—this time not just for research.

Bridget Rees

(Originally published in LDS Living *magazine, July/August 2004; reprinted with permission.)*

Jesus, Joseph and Halle

For ye are all the children of God by faith in Christ Jesus.

Gal. 3:26

My first granddaughter, Halle, is an unusually articulate child. She was toying with words at the age of eight months, mimicking everything she heard by the age of one, and fully conversant by the age of two, which I am told by more seasoned grandmothers is most unusual (much to my pride).

One day when Halle and I were driving past the Mt. Timpanogos Temple, she said, "That's where Jesus lives." She was about two and a half years old at the time.

"That's right," I said.

"He held me before I came here," she said.

Knowing the veil is still thin at that age, I listened intently.

"He loves me," she continued.

"I'm sure He does," I quietly assured her.

"And He misses me," she added.

"I would, too," I whispered.

I loved the picture her sweet little memory painted in my head of Jesus holding each baby before He sends them into mortality; letting them know that He loves them, that He will miss them.

"I saw Joseph, too," she said. "And he smiled at me."

I loved that mental picture even more. Joseph Smith personally saying good-bye to every Latter-day Saint before he or she begins her mortal ministry. Encouraging each one with the same smile that warmed so many hearts when he walked among us.

Halle is four now. She has no memory of that conversation. But I will never forget it. Just as her Heavenly brothers will never forget her. Or me. Or you.

Peg Fugal

A Simple Sheet of Paper

Which our forefathers have awaited with anx-
ious expectation to be revealed in the last times,
which their minds were pointed to by the angels,
as held in reserve for the fullness of their glory.

D&C 121:27

When we moved to a smaller home, I lost my separate
office—so I dutifully set up an office space in the end of
my new family room. Next to my computer table I used a
two-drawer wooden filing cabinet to hold all my office
supplies, and I carefully loaded it with the things I knew
I'd use most often. The top drawer, which I accessed many
times a day, held essentials like paper clips, tape, a stapler,
pens, pencils and markers.

I was working hard on family history research, and was
trying to extend several lines on my father's side of the
family. My father died when I was ten—and his father
died six months after that—so I couldn't go to either of
them for help. I had exhausted all the usual sources of
information, and had even spent several long days at the

library searching census and parish records. Still there was nothing.

I couldn't understand how an entire family could just drop off the face of the Earth! There *had* to be a clue, somewhere. I suppressed the temptation to move on to other, infinitely easier, lines of research on my mother's side of the family. Though I couldn't locate my father's ancestors, I knew beyond any doubt that they had accepted the gospel and were anxiously waiting for the saving ordinances to be performed on their behalf. As the only member of the Church in my father's line, I knew I had the responsibility to see that those ordinances were performed.

Sitting at my computer that morning, the responsibility weighed on me. If I didn't follow through on these lines— only a generation or two removed from me—I knew no one else would. I knew, too, that on the other side of the veil those family members had been patiently taught the gospel and were prayerfully waiting for the work to be done. Yet I had done all I could.

Or had I?

Humbly I closed my eyes, bowed my head and petitioned my Heavenly Father from the depths of my soul. "Oh, Heavenly Father," I pleaded, "I know these people have accepted the truth. I know, too, that it's up to me to find them. I have tried so hard. I have done everything I know to do. It is with great faith that I place this task in Thy hands, and plead with Thee to lead me to the information that will unlock the door. In return, I promise to do everything in my power to be receptive to the promptings of Thy Spirit."

I finished my prayer, then stared at my computer monitor. Still nothing. Knowing my prayer had been heard and would be answered in His own way, I began gathering up the papers I had been working on. I opened the top drawer of my wooden filing cabinet to get a paper clip.

Sitting on top of my dish of paper clips was a carefully folded piece of onionskin paper. I was puzzled. The paper had not been there earlier that morning. And that's not all: I hadn't seen paper like that since I was a child, when my mother had used it for carbon copies on her old manual typewriter. But here it was, in my top drawer, crisp and white as though it was brand-new.

I unfolded it and stared in stunned amazement. It was a hand-drawn pedigree chart. In the first space was my father's name. Written across the top of the paper in my mother's precise handwriting was the simple instruction, "Just fill in what you can, Dad. Thanks." She had mailed it to my grandfather in Miami more than forty years earlier, but he had never returned it to her.

I scanned the paper eagerly. Scribbled across the lines of the pedigree chart in my grandfather's halting handwriting were the names—the precious names for which I had so diligently searched. Penned in beneath the names were dates and places, more information than I could have ever dreamed possible.

My grandfather *had* returned the paper—more than four decades after his death, to a granddaughter who was doing everything she could to bring the saving ordinances of the gospel to his family. I can't begin to imagine where he had kept the paper, so carefully creased and folded so the fountain-pen ink wouldn't smear or run—but he had kept it in flawless condition until he could deliver it to me that morning.

What joy filled my soul as I completed the research and submitted the names for temple ordinances. And what joy I feel each time I attend the temple with one of those names, knowing that he may have helped deliver to me the paper that unlocked the door to salvation.

Kathy Frandsen

My Search for Roots

I thank God, whom I serve from my forefathers with pure conscience, that without ceasing I have remembrance of thee in my prayers night and day.

2 Tim. 1:3

In a small town about one hour north of Mexico City, my mother lived with her loving parents. My grandfather was a very successful merchant, and they owned the largest stores in the area. When my mother became an "adult" (over the age of eighteen), she decided she wanted to go with one of my aunts to live in Mexico City—the big city of every provincial kid's dreams. Naturally, my grandfather vehemently opposed the idea and could not comprehend why they wanted to go to a city where they would be exposed to many dangers, especially since all their emotional and financial needs were being plentifully met at home. They did not need to work at all, and they had many servants and the nicest home in many of the surrounding cities.

But, like many young people, my mother and aunt thought they were very smart and had everything figured out, so they left for Mexico City. They indeed found it very exciting. They met many interesting and sophisticated people; among them my mother found an especially dashing man. He was a very promising lawyer with whom she promptly fell in love. As a result of that love I was born, but my mother found out that this man was already married—so, her heart broken, she tried to forget him.

When I was born I was sent to live in my mother's hometown with my grandfather and grandmother, whom I called Mom and Dad, until I became six years old. At that time my mother came to reclaim me and take me to live with her and my aunt in Mexico City. I was instructed at that time to stop calling my mother by the name of "aunt," as I had been doing up to this time, and to start calling her Mom. Of course, that was very confusing to a young child. To make matters worse, whenever I asked about who my father was, I was dismissed and told not to ask any questions about him.

As I became older my curiosity about my origins and my father increased tremendously. That was especially true because in Mexico, we use both our father's and mother's last names in addition to our given names—but I had only my mother's last name. To answer my questions about my father's last name, I was told to use a last name that turned out to be the same as the man who was then president of Mexico. That worked until the time I had to enter junior high school. My mother told me I was old enough to go register myself. I filled in the application and put my "father's" and mother's last names in the indicated places. I handed the application, along with my birth certificate, to the ladies doing the registration. After checking it, they gave it back to me and told me it was wrong, because there was no such name as my father's last name registered on my birth certificate. I called my mother and asked her about it; she came to the school, filled in the application herself, and simply told me not to put my "father's" last name on anything again!

In those days, my thoughts ran the gamut: *Was I adopted? Was I from another planet?* I couldn't get information about my origins anywhere; my mother was even secretive about her side of the family.

I guess my search for that exterior identity guided me to look inside for an answer. This led me even as a young child to have a deep interest in religion, and as I grew up I started thinking seriously about becoming a Catholic priest. I started studying in-depth the religion that had been practiced by my ancestors for many years. But the more I studied, the more disenchanted I became, because I could see that things had changed so much since the church had been established by Jesus Christ. At the same time I felt very ambivalent about the Protestant churches, since I felt they were just part of that original fallen church. But since I did not have any other alternative for my beliefs, I continued exploring the possibility of joining the seminary to take a deeper look at the Catholic church.

I was attending high school in a downtown location in Mexico City. As a result, I was able to make the acquaintance of many tourists from the United States who visited the area. This helped me to learn English and to know more about the United States. At the same time, I was writing to pen pals all over the world so I could improve my written English. One day, as I was going to the post office to send some letters, I saw a lady with a pretty daughter; the two of them were obviously lost. I approached the lady and asked her what she was looking for. She told me she was looking for the post office. I told her I was going that way because I needed to mail some letters, and that I would show her the way.

As we walked to the post office, this lady asked me what my religion was. I told her that I was a Catholic, but that I really did not feel like it was the actual true church and that I did not believe in Protestantism either. When she heard this, her eyes sparkled, and she told me she wanted me to come with them to their hotel so I could meet her son, who was returning from a so-called "mission" in Argentina. They told me about their church, which was called the Mormon church—but, since they had to leave the next day, they were only able to give me the address of the local Mormon meetinghouse so I could attend and learn more about it.

Three weeks later, I did attend the Mormon Church meetings, where I met a couple of "missionaries." I made an appointment so they could come to my home to teach me. After the first lesson I was so impressed that I asked my best friend, who was going to enter the Catholic seminary in just a few weeks, to come and take the discussions with me. At the end of the six discussions we were baptized.

With this newfound faith I had renewed hopes in my present and future, as well as my past. And it was because of this newfound belief that I decided to renew my efforts to find out who my father was so I could do my genealogical work. Up to this point I had been working on my mother's side with little success, due to my mother's reluctance to provide me with any information. Needless to say, my overwhelming desire to get information about my father slammed against the immovable will of my mother, who continued to refuse to give me any information at all. I did not know anything at all about my father—not even a first name, a date, or an address . . . nothing!

At that time I decided to come to study in the United States, and I picked Ricks College (now Brigham Young University Idaho). When I got to the United States, a friend I had in Logan told me that their foster brother from Finland had been in the same situation. He had given his mother an ultimatum: "Either you tell me who my father is, or else I am going to put an ad in the newspapers saying that I am an illegitimate child and that I need to find out who my father is. If you are my father, please let me know." I explained that I didn't think that strategy would work in my case. First of all, my mother would probably punish me severely if I gave her such an ultimatum. Second, in a city as large as Mexico City it would be almost impossible to get someone to read such an ad—let alone to get him to admit to such a deed. Finally, the number of illegitimate children in Mexico is very high. So I decided to take advantage of the fact that I was in the United States, and kept digging for information about my mother's side of the family at the Genealogical Society Library in Salt Lake City. Somehow I felt that if I did as much as I could on the things that I knew, I would eventually learn who my father was and would be able to do the genealogy on his side also.

I stayed at Ricks one year, and then returned to Mexico City to work for a year to earn the money to go on my mission. I was called to go to the Mexico North Central Mission, where I spent most of my time in a city called Ciudad Juarez. Even there I tried to get more information on my mother's family wherever I could by checking with anyone who might know about my last name, since it is a rather uncommon last name.

At the end of my mission I went back to Ricks, and the first thing I did was visit one of my former professors, who told me that there was a girl from Mexico at Ricks who was an excellent dancer. That was an exciting piece of news I could not resist—a girl and a good dancer, even! I decided I had to visit her right away, so I did. I went to her house, and while I was there she suggested maybe we

should go register together. She said that when we finished, her mother, who was not in at the time, would come
and pick us up so I could meet her as well.

We did as she suggested, and when we finished with
registration, her mother was waiting for us in her car. I
approached the car from the driver's side while this girl
went to the passenger's side. She told her mother through
the window: "Mom, I want to introduce you to my new
friend," and then she repeated my full name.

As soon as her mother heard my name, she asked,
"What's your mother's name?" When I told her, she then
asked, "Where is she from?" As soon as I finished telling
her, she literally collapsed onto the steering wheel and
started crying uncontrollably. I was taken aback by her
reaction and could not understand what was happening—but I didn't think she was crying out of happiness at
finding a prospective husband for her daughter. I got my
answer when they took me to their home and there
explained the reason for her tears: SHE WAS MY
FATHER'S SISTER!

Then it was my turn to cry. How can I possibly explain
how I felt when, for more than twenty-five years, I had
been trying, without success, to find out who my father
was—and then, after traveling two thousand miles to
another country and in a small town in Idaho, I finally
found out! My aunt also explained another reason for her
tears: My father had made her promise that she would
continue to search for me, as they had been doing for a
long time. Even though my father visited the little town
where my mother was from, he had not been received
well—and her family had refused to give him any information about my mother's whereabouts. So my mother,
for all intents and purposes, "became lost" in Mexico City.
They had tried in vain to contact her and me. My "aunt"
was now comforted in the knowledge that she had finally

fulfilled the promise she had made at my father's deathbed to find me.

I was sorrowed to learn that my father had passed away, so I would not be able to meet him on this Earth. But there was good news: I learned that all the family on my father's side had become members of the Church. This is quite remarkable, since in those days there were not that many members of the Church in Mexico. My father had become a member of the high council in the only stake that was then organized in Mexico. When they had the first-ever stake conference in Mexico City, both my father and I had been present—but we didn't know each other, of course.

There was still more good news: My father's family had done a lot of genealogical and temple work, so I was able to get a thick pile of pages already filled out with information about my father's ancestors! My dream to have the genealogical and temple work done on my father's side was fulfilled overnight!

When I got married my half-brothers and half-sisters attended my reception, and I finally found closure to my quest to find my roots. But even this closure did not bring all my questions to a halt. How could I explain the fact that out of the millions of people in Mexico, two had decided to join the true church—and that I had then gone to a college where, besides me, there was only one other student from Mexico City, and she just happened to be my unknown cousin? When I analyze all the implications of my case, I realize more and more that God's ways are indeed incredible.

Julio Arciniega

Unspoken Names

*F*oreshadowing the great work to be done in the temples of the Lord in the dispensation of the fulness of times, for the redemption of the dead, and the sealing of the children to their parents, lest the whole earth be smitten with a curse and utterly wasted at his coming.

D&C 138:48

My mother was baptized, but never active in the Church. I was baptized, active, and with my husband, raised four sons in the Church, two of whom have married Church members and are raising children in the Church.

My mother was never active in the Church because my father was basically anti-Mormon. For many years, he allowed the missionaries to visit Mother, until we children began identifying ourselves as Mormons. Then he banned them.

Once when Mother was very ill, the missionaries saved her life with a priesthood blessing, at which point my father welcomed them back into our home.

Though he would not listen to their message or go to Church with them, he was always willing to feed them and to accept their help on our 265-acre dairy farm on their preparation days. Sometimes, he played pool with them in our basement or rode snowmobiles with them in the winter around our farm property. Sometimes, he slipped them a little extra cash. The missionaries loved my dad, who hated Mormons.

After Daddy died, my only LDS brother, Barney, did his temple work, but wasn't sure whether Daddy had accepted it or not.

A few years later, my mother called me one day and announced, "I want to go to the temple; can you help me figure out and catch up my tithing?" I was bowled over. I never thought I would live to see a parent in the temple.

I immediately called the missionary who had baptized me, and with whom I had stayed in touch over the years, who also happened to be my father's favorite missionary, and told him about Mother's call. He listened while I cried with joy and then asked, "Do you know what I think happened?"

"What?" I asked.

"I think your dad got over on the other side and discovered we were right," he said, "and now he wants his family."

I cried even harder to think that my hard-nosed, anti-Mormon father wanted me (and the rest of my family) eternally. I think it was the very first time I ever really felt wanted.

I arranged to meet my mother as well as my LDS brother and sister at the Toronto Temple, which was their temple.

A couple of days before I departed for Toronto, my mother called. "I think my mother and father were baptized once," she announced.

"What?" I exclaimed.

"The Church should have their records." Once again, I was bowled over.

I called my genealogist friend and told her about Mother's call. "Well, we can find out," she said. "Meet me at the Church history office tomorrow morning." I didn't even know the Church had a history office, but I did as I was instructed.

When we arrived, my friend quizzed me. "About what year would they have been baptized," she asked, "and where?"

I related what few details my mother had shared. She went to the front desk and requested specific rolls of microfilm. Then we went into a reading room, loaded the rolls of film and began scanning for my maternal family's name.

I didn't have much hope of finding them, but my friend was confident and, sure enough, we found them. Grandma, Grandpa and their two oldest children had indeed been baptized, which meant we could do their temple work on the same day we took Mother to the temple. I was ecstatic.

Looking into the reading machine, I saw the very cards the missionaries had filled out prior to their baptisms all those years ago. And then a miracle happened.

I had been searching for years and years for the names of my maternal great-grandfather and my maternal great-great grandfather, names no one in the family ever spoke because both my grandmother and great-grandmother were born out of wedlock. But there they were, hand-written by the missionaries on the baptism information card they had filled out so many years ago.

I guess Grandma decided just that once that she would reveal the names, ending years of frustrating research for me so many years later.

The cards also contained the complete names and birth-dates of all my mother's siblings, two of whom were dead, information I had never been able to complete.

I marveled that the Church took such detailed notes, let alone saved them, let alone had them ready at hand when I needed them, a sign of the true church to me.

When we took Mother to the temple, an office worker looked at all the information finally fully filled in on our family sheet and asked, "Would you like to do all these people today?"

"Can we?" I asked.

"Yes," she replied. "In fact, we have youth here doing baptisms for the dead; we'll send your names down to them first."

Along with taking Mother through the temple, we also did the temple work for twenty-eight other relatives on both sides of our family that day.

It was one of the best days of my life. It was the day I felt for the first time like I belonged to an eternal family unit. And I could feel my father's presence in the room and imagine the smile on his face. He finally had his eternal family.

Ilar Rhodes

3

GRATITUDE

I say unto you that if ye should serve him who has created you from the beginning, and is preserving you from day to day, by lending you breath, that ye may live and move and do according to your own will, and even supporting you from one moment to another—I say, if ye should serve him with all your whole souls yet ye would be unprofitable servants.

Mosiah 2:21

Heavenly Treasures

But lay up for yourselves treasures in Heaven, where neither moth nor rust doth corrupt, and where thieves do not break through nor steal.

Ne. 13:20

I remember the experience with gratitude. It was a Sunday afternoon, and the stake APYW committee—both youth and adults—were gathered and waiting for the high council room to empty so we could hold our monthly meeting there. We all "fit" around the large table, and it was a very good place to hold our meetings. As we waited, Patriarch Richard Larson was giving a patriarchal blessing to someone inside that room. He was giving the blessing from Heavenly Father, through the gift of the Holy Ghost, and by the power of the priesthood.

In due time, the door to the high council room opened, and Patriarch Larson and those in the room with him left; our group went in. As I stepped over the threshold into that room, I felt the Spirit there so strongly that it caused me to stop suddenly as I realized what had just enveloped me. In that instant my testimony of patriarchal blessings, of the power of the priesthood, of a loving Heavenly Father and of the Holy Ghost was confirmed and strengthened. As I took my seat at the table, I was filled with a wonderful feeling of the presence of the Spirit. It was so great it was as though I could reach out with my arms and gather it in close to me and keep it with me in that abundance always.

The room around me was busy as people took their seats and prepared for the start of our meeting, but I sat in my chair and savored those few moments. I offered a silent prayer of thanksgiving for that sweet experience.

My next thought was that I hoped others around me had felt that concentrated presence of the Spirit. I could feel the intensity of the Spirit in the room diminishing, and I turned to the person next to me. "Did you feel the Spirit when we entered this room?" I asked. Her answer indicated that she hadn't, but a brother nearby heard my question and answered a simple, "Yes."

I was grateful that someone else had recognized the presence of the Spirit during those few moments, because it truly was my wish that every person in the room could have had the same sweet experience that I had just enjoyed.

Treasured moments similar to this one can come to us at any time. Moments like these are gifts. They are like little Heavenly treasures that can be stored in the treasure box of our minds, and we can open that treasure box at any time to once again savor our Heavenly Father's love. We can open that box and look at the treasured experiences that have added to our testimony. And we can, once again, offer a prayer of thanks for the gifts that come from a loving Heavenly Father.

Vickie Mattson

To Help Those Less Fortunate

Blessed are the meek: for they shall inherit the earth.

Matt. 5:5

At the age of twenty-five, I finally prepared myself thoroughly to receive my patriarchal blessing. I was eager to hear the words that would be pronounced upon my head and to learn of the blessings Heavenly Father had in store for me!

It was a wonderful blessing, and it provided many answers I had been seeking. But I was very curious about one gift the blessing described: that I would live a long and useful life and help those less fortunate than myself. I was excited about this gift, and I decided exactly what it meant: I would be rich, and could give people cars and other nice things, like Elvis Presley had done. I was so excited to see the smiles I would generate!

Was I ever wrong!

In 1989, my son Caleb was eight years old. He had been terribly sick since the age of three, suffering horrendous headaches that often caused him to be miserable. The doctor diagnosed them as migraine headaches, which ran in our family on both sides. Nothing seemed to ease Caleb's pain, however. On Mother's Day we were at the doctor's office once again, and Caleb was given a shot of Demerol. Not even that powerful painkiller helped.

He was such a wonderful, brave little boy! He tried to live as normally as he could for those five years, which were characterized by such unrelenting pain. Then, just after he turned eight and soon after he was baptized, he started participating on a Little League team! He had been blessed with superior coordination, and we knew he would do well. He was so excited, and we as a family were really looking forward to his future in sports and watching and attending all his games.

At his third practice, Caleb held his arm up to catch a fly ball with his mitt; he missed, and the ball landed directly in his eye socket. He had a huge black-and-blue eye—but worse, was so embarrassed. Our hearts went out to him at that tender age.

Soon after, he began to be extremely sick most of each day. We had to carry pain medication, ice packs and a bucket for Caleb to vomit in everywhere we went. We were told once again by the doctor that his headaches were psychological.

Finally, I demanded a CAT scan. The scan revealed the reason for his coordination problems and his pain: a brain tumor fully engulfed one-fourth of his brain. We now faced an emergency: The brain tumor had to be removed before it killed him.

The night before he was to have surgery, the anesthesiologist told me Caleb would not live through surgery because of the size and location of the tumor and the pressure it was exerting on his brain. If Caleb somehow survived, he said, Caleb would be a vegetable. It was the worst moment of my life.

While Caleb was in surgery for ten hours the next day, we were surrounded by our dear ward families from two different places where we had lived. I fasted and prayed all day.

Finally, the doctors emerged from the operating room to give us the news. The doctor who had told me that Caleb would not live was the first one to reach me. He excitedly told us that Caleb was moving his arms and legs and even talking a little. Our prayers had been answered! Within two weeks Caleb was home.

While Caleb was in the hospital, I tried very hard to find another parent in a similar situation so I could understand what the future might hold for us. There is great comfort in being with another who understands a difficulty because he has also lived with one. But I was able to find no one.

A year later, two nurses put together a brain tumor support group; the huge conference room filled up for the very first meeting. After several years, I became the main facilitator. That support group—which I named BRAVE (Brain Tumor Resource and Vital Encouragement)—still continues, and has helped many families that have a child with a brain tumor.

Caleb is doing wonderfully; he put himself through college in four years and is applying for medical school.

One day I was shocked to realize that my patriarchal blessing had been fulfilled through Caleb's brain tumor. The section in the blessing that stated I would have the opportunity to help those less fortunate than myself had come true. I was facilitating a brain tumor support group, and since the group started in 1991, I have been sad to see many children leave this life. But I have also been given the gift to listen and comfort others who are "less fortunate" than myself.

I am grateful for this blessing every day of my life and

for the gifts my Father in Heaven has bestowed upon me
in so many ways! I feel blessed beyond words to share my
comfort and support with families who are enduring the
most devastating thing in their lives.

Valerie Baker

My Testimony Knew No Bounds

And it shall turn to you for a testimony.
Luke 21:13

A few years ago I had the opportunity to spend five months living and working in New Zealand. While serving as a student-affairs administrator at Bowling Green State University in Bowling Green, Ohio, I was invited to be part of an exchange at the University of Waikato in Hamilton, a bilingual institution where Maori is the second language.

Having never traveled outside of the continental United States, I anticipated the trip with a mixture of excitement and apprehension. Making the necessary arrangements in my home and for my pets for that length of time seemed overwhelming. I questioned whether it would be "worth it."

After doing some checking to find out the presence of the Church in the area, I was delighted to learn that there were two stakes with more than 5,000 members in the area, significantly more members than there were at that

time in the Toledo, Ohio, area. The members were predominantly Maori and Pakeha, and, like me, were in the
minority. Best of all, I found out that the first temple in the
South Pacific Rim, the New Zealand Temple, was located
in Hamilton. I had never lived within ten minutes of a
temple! With these exciting pieces of information, I knew
this was something I needed to do—a once-in-a-lifetime
opportunity.

The experience turned out to be not only an outstand-
ing professional and cultural opportunity, but a very significant spiritual time in my life.

As a visiting scholar, my work setting at the University
of Waikato was in student services, with a specific assignment as a counselor in the Counseling Center. Having
worked in higher education for more than thirty-seven
years, I was used to having regular interaction with young
adults at critical points in their lives—and my experience
was put to good use in New Zealand.

Early in the term, a young woman came in to talk to me
about her insecure feelings in adjusting to the university
community. As she was talking, she noticed that I was
using a planner. She immediately asked if I was LDS.
Before I could answer, she told me that she knew that
Americans who used those planners were LDS. Out of this
chance encounter, I developed a very special relationship
with this bright and energetic college freshman, an active
member of the Church who successfully completed her
first term at the university.

I attended the Chartwell Ward in Hamilton. I was
warmly welcomed, and within a short time received a calling as the Laurel advisor. What an amazing opportunity it
was for me to get to know those wonderful young women
and learn more about their culture.

Hamilton was privileged to have some very special visitors that May: President and Sister Gordon B. Hinckley,

two of their daughters, and Elder Henry B. Eyring came to Mystery Creek in Hamilton for a regional conference. Members attended one of two sessions, maximizing the opportunity for everyone to listen to the prophet.

It was the first time I had seen President Hinckley in person, and I was thrilled to be in the right place at the right time! President Hinckley was the first Church president to visit Hamilton in twenty-one years. He admonished us to attend the temple regularly, to make ourselves temple worthy and to take advantage of living close to a temple. He said, "If there are men who have not taken their wives to the temple, shame on them! Get temple ready!"

President Hinckley's words warmed my heart. I delighted in living so close to the New Zealand Temple, and I tried to attend a session at least once a week. Further, I used the temple as a place to work out any concerns or resolve any issues that might have arisen in my life as a result of visiting in a different culture. The process worked! My testimony of temple attendance knew no bounds. I even bargained with the Lord that if He would only see fit to build a temple in Ohio, I would attend at least once a month.

At the October General Conference, President Hinckley announced the building of two temples within reasonable driving distance of my home—the Columbus Ohio Temple and the Detroit Temple in Bloomfield Hills, Michigan. What an incredible blessing!

My time in New Zealand came to an end, but my journey was not quite over. A colleague from Bowling Green, a colleague from my exchange institution in New Zealand and I attended a conference in Brisbane, Australia, planned by the Australian and New Zealand Student Services Association. It was an exciting time to meet, share and exchange ideas with professionals from both of these countries. One of my Australian colleagues even dubbed me "the Kiwi Yank."

In order to return to the United States, I flew from Brisbane to Sydney. The flight to Sydney was a little more than an hour. About thirty minutes into the flight I knew my adventure was not over in a conventional way. A frightening episode caused me to reflect on my experiences of the past several months.

The plane was about thirty minutes out of Brisbane, and I was dozing. Suddenly, a horrific bang interrupted my reverie. One of the engines of the plane had blown as we were flying over the ocean. My first reaction was fear. But then I remembered something very important.

The Sunday before I left Bowling Green, Ohio, excitedly anticipating the five months that lay ahead of me, I had arranged to have my bishop and one of his counselors give me a blessing. As I reflected on the content of the blessing, my fear became calm. Among a list of wonderful things, I was told that I would return home safely. I knew that I had tried to keep my end of the bargain, and I knew the Lord would keep His word.

When I reflect on this time in my life and when I read my journal entries, I count my blessings. Hamilton, New Zealand, was a special place for me to be; I loved the temple, my colleagues, the students at the university and the members of the Church in a different culture—not to mention my excitement at a visit from the prophet. Indeed, my life had been remarkably enriched through this experience. I know for sure the effort was "worth it."

Barbara Keller

We Might as Well Dance

Happy is the man that findeth wisdom, and the man that getteth understanding.

Prov. 3:13

Too many people put off something that brings them joy just because they haven't thought about it, don't have it on their schedule, didn't know it was coming or are too rigid to depart from their routine.

I got to thinking one day about all those women on the *Titanic* who passed up dessert at dinner that fateful night in an effort to cut back. From then on, I've tried to be a little more flexible.

How many women out there will eat at home because their husband didn't suggest going out to dinner until after something had been thawed? Does the word "refrigeration" mean nothing to you?

How often have your kids dropped in to talk and sat in silence while you watched *Jeopardy* on television?

I cannot count the times I called my sister and said, "How about going to lunch in half an hour?" She would freeze up and stammer, "I can't. I have clothes on the line. My hair is dirty. I wish I had known yesterday; I had a late breakfast. It looks like rain." And my personal favorite: "It's Monday...." She died a few years ago. We never did have lunch together.

Because Americans cram so much into their lives, we tend to schedule our headaches. We live on a sparse diet of promises we make to ourselves for when all conditions are perfect! We'll go back and visit the grandparents when we get Stevie toilet-trained. We'll entertain when we replace the living-room carpet. We'll go on a second honeymoon when we get two more kids out of college.

Life has a way of accelerating as we get older. The days get shorter, and the list of promises to ourselves gets longer. One morning, we wake up, and all we have to show for our lives is a litany of "I'm going to," "I plan on," and "Someday, when things are settled down a bit."

When anyone calls my "seize-the-moment" friend, she is open to adventure and available for trips. She keeps an open mind on new ideas. Her enthusiasm for life is contagious. You talk with her for five minutes, and you're ready to trade your bad feet for a pair of Rollerblades and skip the elevator for a bungee cord.

My lips have not touched ice cream in ten years. I love ice cream. It's just that I might as well apply it directly to my stomach with a spatula and eliminate the digestive process. The other day, I stopped the car and bought a triple-decker. If my car had hit an iceberg on the way home, I would have died happy.

Now—go on and have a nice day. Do something you WANT to—not something from your should-do list.

If you were going to die soon and had only one phone call you could make, who would you call and what would you say? And why are you waiting?

Have you ever watched kids playing on a merry-go-round
or listened to the rain splattering against the ground?
Ever followed a butterfly's erratic flight
or gazed at the sun into the fading night?
Do you run through each day on the fly?
When you ask someone, "How are you?"
do you hear the reply?
When the day is done, do you lie in your bed
with the next hundred chores running through your
     head?
Ever told your child, "We'll do it tomorrow,"
and in your haste, not seen his sorrow?
Ever lost touch? Let a good friendship die?
Called just to say "Hi"?
When you worry and hurry through your day,
it is like an unopened gift—thrown away.

Life is not a race. Take it more slowly. Hear the music
before the song is over. Remember: "Life may not always
be the party we hoped for, but while we are here, we
might as well dance!"

Sue Ayres

Satisfaction

*And your hearts are not satisfied. And ye obey
not the truth, but have pleasure in unrighteousness.*
D&C 56:15

*As a rule, man's a fool.
When it's hot, he wants it cool.
When it's cool, he wants it hot.
Always wanting what it's not.
Never wanting what he's got.*

I need a computer. I can't keep up in school without a computer. Everybody's got a computer except me. If my parents would get me a computer, I'd never ask for another thing.

A cell phone. All my friends have cell phones. But they don't call me because I don't have a cell phone. I'd be happy if my parents would get me a cell phone.

A bike. I need a bike. Then I could come and go as I please. If I had a bike, I'd never ask for another thing.

This bike stuff is for babies. I need a car. How am I supposed to get from school to work without a car? I'd be happy if I had a car.

A girlfriend. What good's a car without a girlfriend?

A job. I can't afford a girlfriend without a job. It costs a fortune to date. If I could just find a job, I'd never ask for another thing.

Some time off. Between school, work and a girlfriend, I barely have time to sleep. A day off would make me happy.

College. I'm never going to make any money in this dead-end job. I need a degree, a skill, a profession. If I could go to college, I'd never ask for another thing.

Am I ever going to graduate?

A job. I've interviewed with every major company. If someone would just give me a chance. . . .

Work, work, work. That's all I ever do. I need to get a life. Find the right girl. Settle down. Then I'd be happy.

A baby. All we want is a baby, and we'd never ask for another thing.

Is the baby ever going to sleep through the night?

Is the baby ever going to walk?

Talk?

We're expecting another baby?!

Money. I need to make more money. I'm up for that promotion. That'd make me happy.

A house. With a yard for the kids. I'd never ask for

another thing if we could just get into a house.

A new car. I've been driving this heap since high school. A new car would make me happy.

Did you see the neighbor's new boat? Boy, I wish we had a boat. Think of the fun we'd have. I promise, a boat and I'll never ask for anything else.

Jet Skis.

Motorcycles.

Snowmobiles.

I'd be happy if we could just get out of debt.

Kids, kids, kids! That's all I ever do. If they were just a little older, a little more independent, a little more helpful. . . .

Teenagers! Who do they think they are? Never lifting a finger. Always taking off. I miss the good old days when they were all babies.

When are the kids coming home? Do they think college is a permanent vacation from parents? Call and tell 'em we want to see 'em this weekend. What do you mean, they're busy? I wasn't too busy to raise them! Once a month is all I ask.

Married? You're just a baby!

What do you mean, "Gramps"? I'm too young to become a grandfather. A boy? Oh, to hold my own son again.

When are the grandkids coming again? I know they were just here! When are they coming again?

When are the grandkids going home? I'm too old for all this fuss and bother.

We haven't seen the grandkids in ages. I know they're grown and gone, but we're their grandparents.

I'm so tired all the time. A boost of energy is what I need.

I ache all over. I'd be happy if this pain would just go away.

The heat.

The cold.

I'm so lonely. I never get out anymore. Nobody ever visits. . . .

Who are all these people? Don't they know I need my rest?

Oh, to live again.

Ah, to finally die.

As a rule, man's a fool.
When it's hot, he wants it cool.
When it's cool, he wants it hot.
Always wanting what it's not.
Never wanting what he's got.

Peg Fugal

READER/CUSTOMER CARE SURVEY

CEHG

We care about your opinions! Please take a moment to fill out our online Reader Survey at **http://survey.hcibooks.com.**
As a **"THANK YOU"** you will receive a **VALUABLE INSTANT COUPON** towards future book purchases as well as a **SPECIAL GIFT** available
only online! Or, you may mail this card back to us and we will send you a copy of our exciting catalog with your valuable coupon inside.

First Name		MI.		Last Name
Address				City
State	Zip		Email	

1. Gender
❑ Female ❑ Male

2. Age
❑ 8 or younger
❑ 9-12   ❑ 13-16
❑ 17-20 ❑ 21-30
❑ 31+

3. Did you receive this book as a gift?
❑ Yes   ❑ No

4. Annual Household Income
❑ under $25,000
❑ $25,000 - $34,999
❑ $35,000 - $49,999
❑ $50,000 - $74,999
❑ over $75,000

5. What are the ages of the children living in your house?
❑ 0 - 14   ❑ 15+

6. Marital Status
❑ Single
❑ Married
❑ Divorced
❑ Widowed

7. How did you find out about the book?
(please choose one)
❑ Recommendation
❑ Store Display
❑ Online
❑ Catalog/Mailing
❑ Interview/Review

8. Where do you usually buy books?
(please choose one)
❑ Bookstore
❑ Online
❑ Book Club/Mail Order
❑ Price Club (Sam's Club, Costco's, etc.)
❑ Retail Store (Target, Wal-Mart, etc.)

9. What subject do you enjoy reading about the most?
(please choose one)
❑ Parenting/Family
❑ Relationships
❑ Recovery/Addictions
❑ Health/Nutrition
❑ Christianity
❑ Spirituality/Inspiration
❑ Business Self-help
❑ Women's Issues
❑ Sports

10. What attracts you most to a book?
(please choose one)
❑ Title
❑ Cover Design
❑ Author
❑ Content

TAPE IN MIDDLE; DO NOT STAPLE

BUSINESS REPLY MAIL

FIRST-CLASS MAIL PERMIT NO 45 DEERFIELD BEACH, FL

POSTAGE WILL BE PAID BY ADDRESSEE

Chicken Soup for the Latter-day Saint Soul
3201 SW 15th Street
Deerfield Beach FL 33442-9875

FOLD HERE

Comments

Do you have your own Chicken Soup story
that you would like to send us?
Please submit at: **www.chickensoup.com**

"Brother Henderson—thinking outside
the box again, are we?"

4

HOLIDAYS

Rings and jewels are not gifts, but apologies for gifts. The only [true] gift is a portion of thyself.

Ralph Waldo Emerson

Good or True

But when the Comforter is come, whom I will send unto you from the Father, even the Spirit of truth, which proceedeth from the Father, he shall testify of me.

John 5:26

When I was a little girl, Easter was always an incredibly exciting day. But the year I was eight, Easter brought more than just jelly beans and a lacy dress.

The early-morning activities mirrored previous years as my family hunted for eggs, explored our Easter baskets, and then piled into the station wagon to travel to church. As we entered the chapel of our Protestant church, I thought mostly of the cookies that were sure to appear in the cultural hall following the service. I didn't expect the church service on this particular Sunday to vary greatly from what was offered on any other Sunday.

Squirming in my seat, I tried to understand the minister's sermon. He spoke about the atonement and the resurrection, words that weren't very meaningful to me at that time. I felt relieved when the congregation stood to sing "Christ the Lord Is Risen Today." I always enjoyed singing, and that day the people around me were singing the words with vigor.

All of a sudden, I looked over at my mother and realized that tears were rolling down her cheeks! I was very disturbed. In all of my eight years, I didn't remember ever seeing my mom cry. Worried, I interrupted her singing.

"Why are you crying, Mom?"

"I'm not really sure, honey," she replied. "I think I just feel happy about Jesus."

I was perplexed. I cried when I was sad, but she was crying because she was happy. I pondered her answer for a while longer, and I never forgot the incident.

Three years later, my family met two young elders. I liked the missionaries because they were funny and very nice to our family. One of them could spin anything on his finger, and another could play our piano and sing.

One summer day, we were sitting on our couch in the living room listening to the elders teach us. It seemed kind of strange that we were talking about religion so much, because my parents hardly ever mentioned the subject— so I tried to pay close attention to what the elders were teaching us.

On that particular day, Elder Hall started explaining about something he called the Spirit. He taught us that the Spirit made you feel happy inside and would tell you when something was good or true. He said that people feel the Spirit in different ways. "Sometimes you may feel peaceful," he explained. "Other times your insides will feel like they are going to burst. People often cry when they feel the Spirit testify to them."

Immediately my mystery was solved! I exclaimed, "Mom, that's why you were crying about Jesus on Easter. The Spirit was telling you to be happy because Jesus really lived!" I felt pleased to finally understand why my mother had cried years earlier.

On October 4, 1988, my family was baptized. When I received the gift of the Holy Ghost, I truly had a testimony of the ordinance. Now, when I attend sacrament service on Easter Sunday and sing the hymn, "Christ the Lord Is Risen Today," I feel a peace come over me as I remember my mother's tears—and I am grateful that she was able to feel the Spirit that Easter Sunday so long ago.

Heather Ford

(Originally published in the LDS Church News, *reprinted with permission.)*

My Thanksgiving Babies

That I may publish with the voice of thanks-giving, and tell of all thy wondrous works.

Ps. 26:7

I was on my knees scrubbing my kitchen floor the Tuesday before Thanksgiving, 1977; we were expecting two other families to eat Thanksgiving dinner with us, one of which was coming from out of town. My five-year-old daughter was at school and my dog was taking a nap on the couch, so I grabbed the opportunity to scrub the floor.

Suddenly, my husband walked through the front door. I was shocked—it was only two in the afternoon, and I asked him what he was doing home. He told me he had to pack his bags because he was going on a trip.

How could this be? I needed his help getting ready for the big day—and I expressed these feelings to him.

"I need to go to Chicago," he said, "and you need to come with me. They've got a little baby girl waiting there for us to pick up."

I told him it wasn't nice to tease me this way—but he

insisted it was true. I then became hysterical—which is defined as a fit of uncontrollable laughter or crying, and I was doing both at the same time. My husband had gotten the call at work just a short time earlier: An eight-week-old girl in Chicago was to be placed in our home, and we needed to come and get her the next day.

Laughing and crying and jumping up and down, I called my mom and dad with the good news. We then called Richard's mom and dad; I distinctly remember Richard's mom screaming with delight when she heard the great news. I then called a good friend and neighbor—and she came running over with a plate of cookies, anxious to hear the whole story.

We got out our suitcases and quickly began packing. All our baby clothes were packed away in boxes, so I quickly tore through them looking for diapers, outfits and blankets that would work. When Cori Jo got home from school at three and we told her we were going to Chicago to pick up her new sister, she was so excited—and she quickly packed her own suitcase, grabbing her pillow and several of her favorite toys to share with her new sister.

We loaded up the car and started our exciting journey. Even our dog, Benji, went with us. The day was cold, but there wasn't too much snow on the ground. We don't really remember too much about the seven-hour drive; when we pulled into Chicago around midnight it was dark and cold, and Cori Jo was sick. She had suffered a stomachache for the last part of the drive, and when we checked into our dreary motel, she started throwing up. She threw up all night. After getting up with her a couple of times, I finally put on my clothes, because it was too cold to be out of bed.

None of us slept well that night. In addition to Cori Jo being sick, we were all so excited about meeting our new baby.

We got up early the next morning and ate a hurried breakfast, then drove to the Social Services office, where we met our social worker. We talked for a while and filled out some papers. Finally, the time we had been waiting for arrived: We went down the hall to meet our new baby.

There she was—lying on a table, smiling at us. We were so excited! We held her, kissed her, cried and laughed. We named her Mindy. It was a wonderful moment for all of us. We changed her clothes, told our social worker thanks for the millionth time, and then headed home. When we opened the car door, even the dog was happy to see the new baby. It was a wonderful seven-hour ride home.

I can honestly say that was the best Thanksgiving we ever had—or ever will have. Our families and friends were all so excited for us. Cori Jo took Mindy to school for show-and-tell. She lifted her out of the car seat and carried her right into the room to show her classmates. She was always such a loving and caring sister.

As I look back on it now, I think of the two little baby girls we lost between Cori Jo and Mindy. When our bishop, Alan Anderson, suggested that we put our papers in for adoption after we lost our two little girls, I wasn't happy. I didn't want to adopt a baby. How silly that was of me! I am so happy we filled out the papers and went through the strict process of getting ready for adoption. It was all so worth it. Because of that adoption, we have had many experiences we might not otherwise have enjoyed.

Many years later, a young woman came to visit me. I had known her for a long time. She remembered how happy we all were when we came to church—how everyone there surrounded us and supported us. Our ward members knew all about our sad times, and they were now enjoying our good times. Later, that young woman became pregnant out of wedlock, and she decided to place her baby for adoption because after seeing us, she knew how happy it would make another family.

I am now a volunteer for LDS Family Services, where I work with birth mothers and do presentations about adoptions. At one point, I had a young woman stay at my house while she was waiting to place her baby. It gave me the opportunity to see the other side of the picture. What a sacrifice that young girl made! It was the right decision for the couple who received the baby and the right decision for the birth mother. Her Heavenly Father has blessed her; she is now getting into school, has a job, has moved back home with her parents, and has turned her life around for the better.

My daughter Cori Jo has not been able to have children. After eight years of marriage, she and her husband were able to adopt a darling little boy who we all love so very much. Mindy has a particularly strong love for him, because the two of them share a special bond—and I know she will be able to help him if he encounters some rough times.

I know Cori had some of the same thoughts about adoption that I originally did—and I know those thoughts evaporated the second she held that newborn baby in her arms. We have all had such a good time with him. He is truly a wonderful gift for our family. In fact, we spent his first Thanksgiving with them, and it was our best Thanksgiving since the one when we brought Mindy home.

And what about Mindy? She is a beautiful woman. She served a mission for the Church and is now finishing up her college degree so she can be a teacher. She is a talented pianist and has a beautiful singing voice. She is a wonderful daughter, sister, aunt and friend—and we all love her very much.

Susan Watts Coon

A Tale of Two Christmases

. . . Remember the words of the Lord Jesus, how He said, "It is more blessed to give than to receive."

Acts 20:35

I have many happy memories of Christmas when I was a child, but there are two in particular that stand out from the others. The first took place when I was in the sixth grade; the second a year later.

Dad would line up five kitchen chairs in the living room (one for each of us kids) after we had gone to bed on Christmas Eve. Out of coat hangers, he had made hooks that fit over the backs of each chair; on each, he hung the large red and green Christmas stockings my mother had made for each of us. Presents too big to fit into our stockings were placed on and under the chairs.

On this particular Christmas morning, Mom and Dad were sitting on the couch at one end of the living room watching us hastily tear into the packages. Excited yells of "Look what I got—look what I got!" added to the din we made as we played with each toy briefly before discarding it and ripping into another present.

I don't remember what gifts I received, but it wasn't the presents that made that Christmas memorable.

We had finished opening the last of the packages when my younger brother John and I happened to glance over at our parents, who were still sitting on the couch. Both of their faces were lit with beaming smiles.

"Mom and Dad," asked my brother, puzzled, "why are you smiling? You didn't get anything."

At the time, I didn't give much thought to my brother's question—or to my parents' actions. After all, I had gotten what I wanted. All was well with the world, and I expected that future Christmases—because of the presents I would receive—would bring me even greater feelings of joy.

The next holiday season began like all the others. My friends and I reminded each other on a daily basis of how much time remained until Christmas. Weeks turned into days, until finally, Christmas Eve arrived. It was the day before "the Big One."

I went to bed that night as excited as I had ever been. Thoughts of all the wealth I would soon inherit filled my head. It was rough, but somehow I managed to drift off to sleep.

Finally, Christmas morning arrived. Being the oldest, I felt that it was my solemn duty to lead the stampede to the presents—and so I did. The ripping of paper was punctuated with the usual excited squeals of happiness and the shouts of "Look what I got!" as my brothers and sisters noisily showed off each newly opened gift.

I was tearing the wrapping from my second present when I noticed that something was wrong. Pausing to take a quick inventory of my emotions, I realized that my feverish excitement of the night before was gone. *Well, no need to panic yet,* I thought. After all, the first present had been the usual can of Planters peanuts from my dad, so maybe the present I was now opening would restore my excitement back to its proper level. Encouraged by that thought, I finished opening the package. Inside was a plastic rocket. It could be partially filled with water, pressurized with the included plastic pump, then launched about 30 feet into the air. My younger brother John was practically drooling all over it with envy. And I . . . didn't even want it.

A third and final present proved to be equally unexciting, so, bored, I picked up my toys and carried them to the dining-room table.

Mom and Dad noticed my let-down look.

"Terry," my dad said above the laughter of the other children, "you missed a present. It's under your chair."

Unexcitedly, I opened a small, white, two-inch-square box. Inside was a Westclox brand pocket watch. I had never owned any watch before, and while I decided that this present was definitely the most practical one of an otherwise sorry lot, I was still very disappointed. The Spirit of Christmas, it seems, had left me.

Vanished.

Poof!

Gone.

I was trying to come to grips with this unexplained emptiness when suddenly I remembered my brother's question to my parents the previous Christmas when he had asked: "How come you're smiling? You didn't get anything."

Something happened inside me then. I looked over at my mother and father, who were sitting in their usual positions on the couch. The same beaming smile as before was on their faces. *Maybe*, I thought, *they knew something I didn't*, so I walked over to the couch and sat down beside them.

And I watched.

A different kind of Christmas began for me then. I found myself smiling broadly at the delight a brother or sister would display upon opening a present. I felt particularly pleased when a small gift I had bought for one of them was given more appreciation than it really deserved. I felt pride when one of them would come to me requesting my help in putting together a toy or a game.

That year, just like Dr. Seuss's Grinch, I found out that Christmas doesn't always come in a box. That year, Christmas—for me—came in the shining eyes and joyous smiles of my younger brothers and sisters. My one regret was that they couldn't see what I was seeing from my position on the couch.

They just didn't know how much fun they were missing!

Terry Tippets

Yuletide Windows of Heaven

Saying, Surely blessing I will bless thee, and multiplying I will multiply thee.

Heb. 6:14

Christmas of 1994 was going to be small. My husband had been in the hospital for more than a month, and I was a stay-at-home child-care provider in Prescott, Arizona, where we lived. But I was spending much of my time in Santa Barbara, California, sleeping next to my husband's hospital bed, while friends helped out with my regular daycare children.

I had purchased a few Christmas gifts for our two small daughters, but without my income we wouldn't have money for more. As Christmas approached, my husband was able to come home for the week, but we knew he would have to return to Santa Barbara right after Christmas.

I received a phone call from my bishop, who wanted to know what the ward could do to help with Christmas. I told him that we would be fine—that I had purchased a few things ahead of time. Soon after that I received a call from the Relief Society president asking what sizes my daughters wore and what we needed or wanted as a family. She told me that someone in the ward wanted to be our "Secret Santa." I felt funny accepting the idea, but she wouldn't take no for an answer.

I resumed watching my usual daycare children, and when payday came, I found out that some of the friends who had helped me out had asked the families to pay me instead of them. I called them to say thank you, but told them I would be sending the money to them. Each responded with, "We want you to have a merry Christmas. Please let us serve you."

On the Sunday before Christmas, we attended tithing settlement with our bishop. I hadn't been home all month, so I needed to pay all of our tithing for the month that day. I struggled with the idea that I could pay double next month and use this money for Christmas, but I felt I should be thankful for all the love we had been shown and pay my tithing then. I handed the bishop our tithing envelope. He put it down and, without opening it, handed me a check. He explained that several families in the ward wanted to make sure we had a merry Christmas.

I thanked him with tears in my eyes, and then I l ooked at the check. The amount of the check was 25 percent more than the tithing I had just paid! I felt so overwhelmed.

The blessings didn't stop there. On Christmas Eve, one of the elder's quorum counselors stopped by with a huge box of food. He said they had decided to use their small budget to purchase Christmas dinner with all the trimmings. Later, one of the sisters in the ward stopped by with some "leftover gifts" from the ward party; among them were several wrapped gifts for the girls. That night as we were getting ready for bed, the doorbell rang. I opened the door to find a huge box of wrapped gifts for the girls. The pile under the tree had grown so big!

As we were putting the gifts out, my eight-year-old daughter looked at me and asked, "Why does everyone feel sorry for us?" I looked at her, and all I could say was, "They don't feel sorry for us—they love us."

It ended up being the best Christmas I've ever had. I felt so blessed to be a part of such a wonderful and caring ward.

Lori Amavisca

A Christmas Family

To give light to them that sit in darkness and in the shadow of death, to guide our feet into the way of peace.

Luke 1:79

One Christmas as a single mom, I was left at home without my children for several days. I had family close by, and had spent time with them and with my aging parents. Still, I felt a nagging loneliness because my children were not there to share the joys of the day. It's a feeling I imagine is shared by all parents who have experienced this situation at Christmas.

I had decided late that evening to visit an old friend and her husband; I had not seen them for a while, and I knew they were having some health problems. I felt the visit would occupy my time and help fill the empty space.

I enjoyed a nice visit with them, and was feeling very glad that I had gone. As I was returning home, the fog had settled thickly on the roads and orchards, and it was difficult to see my way with the car headlights on. I turned the main headlights off, and with only my parking lights to alert other drivers to my presence, I drove very slowly along the quiet country lane. Eventually I was forced to stop—the fog was so thick that I couldn't see at all. I was feeling really boxed in, so I left the parking lights on and got out of my car. The thick white clouds floating near, through and around me created both an eerie and a beautiful sight.

Suddenly I saw a blur of movement near a light pole. I thought it was a deer walking up the road in front of a small group of homes. I moved toward the lamppost and, as I came closer, I saw a trail of deer—probably ten or more—that were walking slowly together. They seemed to be in pairs, and were winding slowly in a chain between the houses and yards. It was a magical experience on this lonely Christmas night as I watched and followed them through the neighborhood. It was as if they were Santa's reindeer, who had dropped off the old guy and were making their way home, exhausted at the end of a busy day.

I was filled with a sense of peace and well-being. All was not lost after all. I had seen firsthand the reality of a family unit, drifting through the fog and haze, making their footprints in the snow as they traveled through this sacred night of Christ's birth. I knew that the Lord was watching over me and understood my loss that day. He knew that I had needed that vision to ground me to the realities and possibilities of my life—and that He understood the difficult road I was taking in my journey to get home.

Diane Moss

Granting a Christmas Wish

. . . The Christmas spirit is the Christ spirit, that makes our hearts glow in brotherly love and friendship and prompts us to kind deeds of service.
                                          President David O. McKay

Every once in a while a toy comes along that takes the world by storm and forces parents into a frenzied holiday hunt to make their child's Christmas wishes come true.

For a few years it was Pokémon. Then it was Power Rangers, then Tickle Me Elmo. Before that, of course, we had the eighties—the generation that brought us Care Bears, Go-Bots and the Big Wheel. One toy, however, seems to stick out in many people's memories when they think of the eighties and a toy trend that surpassed all others: Cabbage Patch Kids.

The Phenomenon

Parents would stand in lines for hours at the shopping mall or Toys "R" Us after having successfully clawed, clubbed and clamored their way through the melee of desperate holiday shoppers also trying to get their hands on the high-demand dolls. But these were not ordinary dolls; these dolls were not merely purchased—they were adopted, and came with an official birth certificate, name and adoption papers. They even came with a birthday card for the "Kid's" first birthday!

In 1984, right around the height of Cabbage Patch mania, I was seven years old. I lived in American Falls, a small town outside of Pocatello, Idaho. Clearly, this doll craze really was enormous—even little American Falls and its population of 4,000 weren't left out of the loop.

I wanted a Cabbage Patch Kid more than anything. I would think about what I would name mine (officially changing the doll's name was an option with the adoption papers) and also about exactly what color hair and eyes I wanted mine to have. Several of my friends had them, and though I probably didn't fully understand the phenomenon, I did understand that these Kids were a hot commodity. I remember seeing spots on the news about the Christmas hunt to find them, and that only fueled my desire to have my own.

At the same time, I didn't get my hopes up. I knew that I probably wouldn't find one underneath the Christmas tree, at least not that year.

Most of my memories of the eighties were great. I would sing along to the theme song of "Punky Brewster" every week, and couldn't wear my favorite red stirrup pants often enough. Some people called me Olive Oyl (after Popeye's girl) because I was so skinny, but my scrawny frame didn't properly reflect my boundless energy. My seven-year-old imagination was definitely overactive, and I could keep myself entertained for hours. In many respects, it was a great time of life.

Learning to Adapt

Those memories still make me smile. Unfortunately, not all of my memories of the eighties were happy ones. During this time, my father suffered from lymphoma, a form of cancer. Though I don't remember that time perfectly, I do remember he became very sick as Christmas approached. I was very much a daddy's girl and remember the confusion and sadness I felt at watching him sit alone in his chair. I felt helpless, but decided that the best thing I could do to help my family was to make sure I was not causing any extra problems. I tried hard to be very good.

My father and mother owned a small, home-based carpet-cleaning business. My dad also worked for some time as a mail carrier. Though we lived comfortably, we were far from wealthy. Then the cancer came and the financial situation of the family became pretty scary. My dad could no longer work, and because of the time it took to care for him, my mother also couldn't work much. The doctor and pharmacy bills just kept growing, and I remember my mother explaining to us kids (I have two sisters and a brother who at the time were ages two, twelve and fourteen) that we probably weren't going to be able to have many Christmas presents that year. At that point, I knew my dream of adopting a Cabbage Patch Kid just wasn't going to happen. I didn't even ask.

The year before, my mother created a homemade Cabbage Patch doll for me that looked quite similar to the ones in the stores. I really did like it and appreciated the work she put into it. It had long, blonde yarn hair and beautiful painted-on eyes. I placed it on my bookshelf in its own special spot. I liked it very much, but I couldn't deny that I still wanted a store-bought Kid. I wanted to be able to "adopt" mine. I wanted the Xavier stamp on the doll's bottom. I wanted the same thing my friends had.

But even at that young age, I knew I shouldn't be greedy and never brought it up, though I'm quite sure my mother still knew how much I wanted one.

Santa's Secret Helpers

Then one night, probably around the beginning of December, we started to get visitors. The doorbell would ring, one of us would answer it, but no one would be there. Left on the porch were several wrapped packages. It was so exciting! The next evening, the same thing happened— and then again the night after that. Suddenly the feeling in our home was changing. Maybe we were just finally having some fun, or maybe it was the Christmas spirit starting to break through the sadness. Whatever it was, I remember it was fun and it felt good. As the days continued, more and more presents, treats and dinners continued to arrive.

Soon, our little living room was overrun with piles of presents. I remember snooping around them and discovering a My Little Pony with my name on it! I'd wanted one of those as well. I played with my best friend Jamie's ponies almost every day, and now I had one of my own. It was so fun to have my own little secret under the tree.

My dad was a little embarrassed about the tremendous number of presents filling the room, and started putting them in a corner of a bedroom instead of under the tree. Then that corner started spilling over! I had never seen so many gifts.

My Christmas Miracle

About a week before Christmas, the doorbell rang again one night. My mother answered the door and told my younger sister and me to come and look. There it was: my Cabbage Patch Kid! What an emotion of joy and excitement I felt at that moment. But this was even better! It was a Cabbage Patch Kid Preemie! This smaller version of the recent phenomenon was the latest and greatest creation from the doll makers, and I could hardly believe it was sitting right there on my porch.

I knew I was experiencing my own mini-miracle. These dolls were not exactly cheap and they were also not always easy to get, yet someone (I still have no idea who) knew the heart of a little girl and understood that although a new pair of shoes or something of that nature was probably a more practical gift, this funny-looking little doll could bring a child a piece of happiness and escape that she needed even more than new, sturdy shoes.

Whomever this thoughtful person was, he or she understood that emotional desires are sometimes just as important as physical needs. I certainly didn't need that doll in the same way that I needed food in my belly, but nonetheless, that doll made me feel a little bit more like a normal little girl. It gave me a bit of joy at a time when it was sometimes hard to be happy, and joy is something everyone needs—especially at Christmas.

The Real Gift

Years later, my mother told me that this whole month-long event for our family made her very upset at first. We were rarely able to figure out from whom the gifts were coming, and she simply wanted to be able to thank the people who were helping her family. Christmas cards holding money would come to the house, and no name would be signed to them. One day she went to the drug-store to pay a $300 bill, and she was told that it had already been paid. Though she was very grateful, the anonymous generosity was overwhelming and she was sick with the thought of not being able to even say thank you.

She told me that she opened her scriptures one night with tears in her eyes, not only because her husband was so sick but because she felt even more helpless at not being able to thank those who were helping her. Then she unintentionally came across 3 Nephi 13:2-4:

"Therefore, when ye shall do your alms do not sound a trumpet before you, as the hypocrites do in the synagogues and in the streets, that they may have glory of men. Verily I say unto you, they have their reward.

"But when thou doest alms let not thy left hand know what thy right hand doeth;

"That thine alms may be in secret; and thy Father who seeth in secret, himself shall reward thee openly."

She felt her prayer was answered that night in reading those few verses. She knew that the blessings her secret helpers would receive from Heavenly Father were far greater than any thanks she could give to them. After this experience, we stopped rushing to the door to try to catch our neighbors. Instead, we would wait for a few minutes to give them time to run away.

I've never forgotten the wonderful feeling surrounding that Christmas. I learned at a very young age what it was like to be the recipient of the true love of Christ and how important it is to give that love to others as well. My father passed away about a year later, and when I think of him, this special Christmas is one of the times that I cherish most.

I don't think of that time so much as the year my dad was so terribly sick, or even as the year I received one of the first Preemies to hit the shelves. I remember it most as the very special year when our family became part of a little miracle, when I felt a love so strong it was almost tangible, and when I learned what the phrase "the spirit of Christmas" really means.

Bridget Rees

(Originally published in LDS Living *magazine, November/December 2004; reprinted with permission.)*

Creating the Twelve Days of Christmas

*The greatest joy we can receive in life is giv-
ing—to bring into the life of someone else a little
joy and happiness.*

Elder L. Tom Perry

It's difficult to keep Christmas special when it has
become so commercial. When we were young, we never
saw a hint of Christmas until the day after Thanksgiving.
Years later, Christmas started making an appearance right
after Halloween. Now we see signs of Christmas as early
as Labor Day. So, in our young parenting years, we created the Twelve Days of Christmas to keep Christmas special the entire holiday season.

First of all, Christmas started for our four young sons
the day school ended for the holiday. That evening they
were allowed to open whatever gifts we might have
received from friends and neighbors.

The next night, they were allowed to open any gifts that
might have arrived from extended family.

The third night before Christmas, they were allowed to

open games to play with each other during the holidays.

The fourth night before Christmas, they were allowed to open books to read and/or crafts to do during quiet times throughout the holiday.

Christmas Eve, they always opened new pajamas, often made by Grandma.

Christmas morning, they came downstairs to their unwrapped Christmas toys from Santa, two each, which forced us not to overdo. (Unwrapped because who ever saw Santa in a sleigh full of wrapped presents? Santa flies around in a sleigh full of toys!)

The day after Christmas is when the fun started. Each person chose a day between Christmas and the New Year to present his or her personal gifts to each family member in an individually unique way.

A tradition that allowed me to shop the after-Christmas sales I preferred. I always presented my gifts wrapped in blankets.

A tradition that allowed Peg more time to prepare her gifts, making Christmas less hectic for her. She always presented her gifts in beautiful Christmas gift wrap with all the trimmings.

A tradition that allowed our young sons' homemade or less expensive gifts to shine on their own without competing with other store-bought gifts. One presented his gifts wrapped in newspaper. Another presented his gifts still in their store bags.

A tradition that allowed our sons to experience the true spirit of giving, because they received no gifts the day they presented their gifts. That alone is what made Christmas special for our family every year.

One Christmas one son discovered that his friend received only one gift for Christmas, which he opened on Christmas day. When the friend visited our house after Christmas and discovered mounds of still-unopened gifts, he was visibly confused, if not a bit envious. Noting his reaction, our son pulled one of his own gifts out from under the tree and handed it to his friend. It was a beautiful sweater our son had especially wanted for Christmas. When we asked later if we could replace it, he replied, "No."

One year another son found a little red wagon similar to the one his grandfather had given him when he was a baby. He spent weeks restoring it, completing the labor of love just before Christmas. He had planned to keep it for himself. But when a neighborhood child admired it, he gave it to the child for Christmas.

Our sons had learned the true spirit of giving.

Our Twelve Days of Christmas usually filled the time between school ending and school resuming, which made the holiday all the more fun-filled.

Having grown up with those traditions, our sons knew nothing else. When they grew older and starting visiting friends in their homes on Christmas day, they were surprised to learn that their friends had opened all their gifts that day. "How dumb," they said upon returning home, "what do they do the rest of the holiday?"

We have kept our Twelve Days of Christmas tradition alive even today with grown sons and daughters-in-law and grandbabies. Family members present their gifts on whatever day best works for them during the holiday. We allow the grandbabies to open one gift each time they visit during the holidays, which makes them want to visit every day, our favorite Christmas present from them!

Sherm and Peg Fugal

Reprinted by permission of Patrick Bagley ©2004.

5

MIRACLES

God also bearing them witness, both with signs and wonders, and with divers miracles, and gifts of the Holy Ghost . . .

Heb. 2:4

Angels in Disguise

Shortly after college graduation, I found myself in a financial bind. The "dream job" I envisioned wasn't materializing, and I had managed to accumulate a significant amount of debt waiting for it to happen.

It was the summer of 1990. I was living in a high-rise apartment in a not-so-nice neighborhood in Dayton, Ohio. I had just completed a six-month temporary assignment, and I was now among the ranks of the unemployed.

A dear friend, LeAnn, came to visit me for a week to help me get my mind off of my situation. We did our best to find free entertainment. One day we walked into the heart of the city. It was an extremely warm and humid day, so we stopped at a small restaurant to get a couple of sodas.

I had three dollars to my name. The sodas cost two dollars. As we were leaving the restaurant, an unkempt-looking homeless man approached us and asked us for change for bus fare. I told him I only had one dollar, and asked if that would be enough. He took my hand in both of his and gazed directly into my face. His eyes were the deepest blue I had ever seen, and they seemed to smile all on their own. He said, "God bless you, my child. The next time I see you, I'm going to give you two dollars." I smiled back, knowing the chances of ever seeing him again were next to nothing.

As we walked away from him, LeAnn began berating me for giving my last dollar to a homeless man. She reminded me that he might use it to buy alcohol or drugs. I told her that if he did, he did. It was his choice, and not for me to judge. LeAnn was not of my faith, so I shared with her my philosophy on giving to those in need. I told her about the lessons contained in King Benjamin's address in the Book of Mormon on this very topic. She listened, but she maintained that I had unwisely thrown my money away.

Two days later, LeAnn and I were walking along the river when we encountered a gentleman sitting quietly by himself. He motioned us over and wanted to chat. He seemed lonely. He told us all sorts of tales about Dayton and the changes that had taken place there over the years. When it came time for us to leave, he reached into his wallet. I refused profusely, but he insisted that we take the money from his hand.

It was exactly two dollars. He said, "I've really enjoyed spending time with you girls. Please go buy yourselves two sodas on me."

We thanked him and left in silence. After several minutes, LeAnn looked at me and said, "Those are the two dollars that homeless man promised to give you!"

I smiled and said, "I know." Neither of us could explain what had just happened, but both of us were certain that on both occasions—with each of these random strangers— we had been in the presence of angels in disguise.

Rochelle Johnson

Why Am I Here?

And the LORD sent an angel . . .

2 Chr. 32:21

I was canning peaches in the kitchen one day in 1973, and was very busy with the project. All of a sudden, I went downstairs. I was halfway down the stairs before I realized what I was doing. I had no reason to go downstairs, and remember vividly my thoughts as I did so.

Why am I here? I silently asked. *I am busy upstairs, and I have no need to be here.*

When I reached the bottom step, I stood quietly, still wondering, *"Why am I here?"*

We had just purchased a new chest-style freezer, and we had not yet put anything in it. The old one was still there, complete with the contents—which we planned to move into the new one later. We had left the new one sitting there with the lid up, and we had not even plugged it into the wall socket.

As I scanned the room, I noticed the lid was down on the new freezer.

That's strange, I thought. *Why is that lid down?*

I walked over and lifted the lid. What I saw made my knees buckle, and I had to hold on to the side of the freezer in order to remain standing. Inside the freezer sat our son, Neil. His knees were tucked up under his chin, and he had the biggest grin on his face.

I was so startled I could hardly speak. Finally I managed, "What are you doing in here?"

"I was just waiting for you to come and get me. I was playing hide and seek."

Later that day I regained my composure along with my ability to breathe. That took a long time—because I knew that had I not gone down the stairs when I did, Neil would have died.

Why did I go downstairs? I heard no voice, no warning. I was literally pushed down the stairs. I know today that it was the power of the Holy Ghost that took me where I needed to be.

Almost thirty years later, I still start to shake when I think about it.

President James E. Faust has said, "If worthy, we are entitled to receive revelations for ourselves, parents for their children and members of the Church in their callings." I will always be grateful that at the time I was worthy of that personal revelation.

Lester Ann Jensen

This One Red Rose

. . . The peace of God, which passeth all understanding.

Philippians 4:7

September 25, 1976: The day for Eagle Flight had finally arrived! This special scouting event was the culmination of months of planning, and it would be the highlight of my husband Keith's career. He worked professionally for the Cache Valley Council of the Boy Scouts of America—which meant he was paid a salary for doing what he loved most: working with boys and their scout leaders.

Keith and Leron Johnsen, a volunteer scouter, planned to honor those boys who had attained their Eagle rank that year. An experienced helicopter pilot, Leron offered to take each boy and his father on a helicopter ride over the south end of the valley. This would be followed by a hearty meal, prepared by Leron's wife and children.

We overslept that beautiful autumn morning. Keith quickly gulped down some granola, and then we had family prayer with our three preschoolers. He promised to be home by early afternoon, because he wanted to attend a funeral for a fellow scouter's daughter who had been killed in a car accident. Keith kissed each of us good-bye and dashed out the door. He hopped into the Jeep, waved and was gone.

I spent the day tending the children, shopping for groceries, canning vegetables and bottling grape juice. We depended on our garden produce and bottled fruit for our winter food supply. The day went by quickly.

By late afternoon, Keith still had not returned from Eagle Flight. I wondered if perhaps he had gone straight to the funeral. I was becoming worried, so I phoned Leron's family to see if they might know what could be delaying Keith. They were concerned, too, because Leron was not home, either—but they had heard nothing. They said that Leron's plan was to fly the helicopter from Eagle Flight to Tremonton, where he had left his car.

Shortly after 5 P.M., the doorbell rang. Through the open screen door, I saw our stake president, Garth Lee, dressed in his gardening overalls. Mike Stauffer, a county sheriff and friend in the ward, stood next to President Lee in his uniform. I noticed Mike's official car parked in front of my house. A feeling of panic seized my heart as I noticed that their faces were etched in pain.

I invited them in and forced myself to ask the dread-filled questions: "What happened? Where is Keith?" They guided me to the sofa and made me sit down. They cried as they tried to tell me the awful news: "Keith was killed today in a helicopter accident. We don't know very many details, except that he and Leron are both dead. We're so very, very sorry. . . ."

I sat there, stunned and speechless. My mind whirled; my heart broke. We cried together. Yet, almost immediately, a sense of peace surrounded me. I marveled at the feeling of comfort and calmness.

After Mike left, President Lee walked with me through the backyard to Keith's parents' home. Instinctively, I took his hand in mine, feeling like a little child clinging to a father's hand for courage. As we entered their home, I sensed that they already knew, somehow, what had happened. In fact, my four-year-old daughter, Ann, later related, "When that man asked Grandpa to come down off the roof so he could talk to us, someone said to me in my head, 'Ann, your daddy has died.'"

President Lee told us what he knew of the accident: An eyewitness, a man from Brigham City, had been on Lookout Peak across from Mantua Lake. He heard an explosion, and as he glanced up, he saw a puff of smoke. He watched in horror as the helicopter spiraled downward to the ground. He immediately notified the sheriff and directed rescuers to the crash site, which was in a secluded and wooded area.

The report said that Keith and Leron had both died instantly. The other passenger, Bryce White, had survived. Bryce later related that they had heard a loud noise. Leron shouted, "Hang on, we've got trouble!" Then Bryce's seat belt had somehow come loose. He remembered falling from the helicopter before it crashed, but then lost consciousness.

After telling the news to Keith's family, President Lee left. I walked back to my house with my sister-in-law, Lois. Suddenly she stopped and exclaimed, "Look!" I looked east to where she was pointing. A beautiful rainbow arched perfectly over the mountains. I then glanced west, where a few clouds hovered in the brilliant sunset.

Why a rainbow? I wondered.

Lois spoke reverently, "It's a kind of promise, isn't it? When my brother died, there was a rainbow like this on the day of his funeral."

I was in awe of its beauty, and marveled at the peace I

felt. Though I had just lost my eternal companion in death, I was not afraid. Truly the Comforter had enveloped me in "the peace of God, which passeth all understanding" (Philippians 4:7). I felt that this particular rainbow was a personal witness of God's love for me.

Family and friends strengthened and sustained me through those first hours and days. Keith's father, brothers and uncles gave me a blessing. My parents and sister arrived the next day from out of state. Ward members came with tears and services.

After the children were settled into bed that first night, I began to reminisce about our brief time on Earth together: We had met exactly six years before, to the very weekend. Keith's cousin, Louise, introduced us at church on the first day of fall quarter at Utah State University. I was starting my senior year, and Keith was a newly returned missionary. Our romance began with a mutual feeling of familiarity that we had known one another in our pre-mortal existence. Within two months, Keith had asked me to marry him.

On my next birthday, Keith formalized our engagement with a diamond ring and a single, long-stemmed red rose. We were later married for time and eternity in the Oakland Temple.

Upon the birth of our first daughter, Ann, on Thanksgiving Day, 1971, Keith gave me a beautiful red rose. When Amy was born eighteen months later, another red rose appeared in my hospital room. Our son, Andrew, was born the next year. I again received from Keith a single red rose as a witness of his love.

I was brought back to reality by the phone ringing. A friend called to tell me that the accident was being reported on the late-night news. How unreal it seemed to hear about my husband's accident and death on the television.

After watching the news, I began to write in my journal, because I couldn't sleep. Into the night, my feelings and thoughts flowed onto paper. My head was struggling to comprehend what my heart did not wish to accept: I was a twenty-seven-year-old widow, with three tiny children to rear alone.

The next morning, the front page of Sunday's newspaper covered the accident. Though I wanted to deny that my husband was dead, I could not. I had heard about it on TV, had read about it in the newspaper. It had really happened. There was nothing I could do to bring my husband back to life.

From Saturday to Tuesday, I moved through the blur of phoning family and friends, making funeral arrangements, providing a life sketch for the obituary, choosing a burial plot in the Hyrum cemetery, ordering flowers for the casket. This was my first experience dealing so closely with the death of a loved one. The numbing shock of grief cushioned me.

Then miracles began: One young friend, Lisa Summers, asked if she could sing a song, "Look Up to Him," for the funeral. Kelly Liljenquist, a Boy Scout in the ward, offered to play taps on his trumpet for the burial. All twelve of Keith's summer-camp staff agreed to be pallbearers and honorary pallbearers. The details seemed to fall into place as if Keith himself were planning his funeral.

The Boy Scouts in the ward washed all the family's cars before the funeral. They mowed and trimmed the lawn. Then they set up tables and chairs in the shady backyard in preparation for the after-funeral dinner for family members and close friends.

The funeral itself became a testimonial tribute to a young man who had served others selflessly, giving his time and energy to his family, to the gospel and to his fellow men. The chapel, classrooms and basement of the old

Hyrum 1st Ward building were overflowing with people who came to honor Keith.

That evening after the funeral, the doorbell rang. A new member of the ward, Penny, stood at the front door. Rather hesitantly, she said, "Even though I don't know you very well, I wanted to do something for you. After the burial, I went to the cemetery and rearranged the flowers on the grave."

She then handed me a flower she had plucked from an arrangement. "I don't know what it means," she said, "but your husband wanted me to bring you this one red rose."

Valaree Brough

Angels of the Road

For it is written, He shall give his angels charge over thee, to keep thee.

Luke 4:10

I was recently divorced and determined to begin a new life in a new place—so when I got accepted into the graduate English program at George Mason University in Virginia, I rented out my house in Orem, Utah, packed my Volkswagen with linens and clothes and dishes, and headed east with my daughter. Jen was seventeen and wanted to finish her senior year in Utah, so after she helped me drive to Virginia, she planned to fly back to live with her older sister. My two youngest children would then fly out to live with me. On our journey across country, Jen and I weren't alone. Our home teacher, his wife and their five children were traveling along with us in their car on what for them would be a business trip and family vacation.

We were just west of Chicago, not far from Naperville where my sister lived, when I felt a strange bumping under my car. I pulled off onto the shoulder of the road and stared at my tires. The back retread had split apart. My flimsy jack was somewhere under all my stuff. My friends helped me half unload, we tried the jack and realized it wasn't going to work. Cars and trucks whizzed past us. Suddenly a truck pulled up behind us and a short, muscular man got out. Within minutes he placed his hydraulic jack under my car and changed my tire. Jen and I were soon waving good-bye to this angel of the road— and to our friends, who headed off toward Kalamazoo on business as we headed for Naperville to stay overnight with my sister and brother-in-law.

He wasn't the only angel of the road we encountered on that trip—or since then. The next morning my brother-in-law insisted on buying four new tires for my Volkswagen—and slipped me an envelope stuffed with ten twenty-dollar bills. When we got lost and found ourselves in a rough neighborhood in Ohio, two dark-haired angels stopped to help—and led us to our motel.

Once on a rainy night in northern Virginia when the clutch in my car went out and I was stranded on the Beltway, a stranger stopped to give me a ride to a telephone. When I glanced at the magazine in the front seat of his car, I saw the *Ensign.* "What ward are you in?" I asked, smiling. Instantly, though we were strangers, we knew each other—members of the kingdom who were striving to be saints.

"Our bishop just cautioned us not to stop for strangers on the road," he told me, "but for some reason I just decided I'd do it this time."

Because so many human angels had helped me, I was always on the lookout for payback opportunities. A few years later as my daughter and I were heading out of the Vienna metro station late one afternoon, we saw a man standing under the bridge. He was well-dressed and appeared to be in his late sixties or early seventies. He didn't look like a vagrant, but we live in a dangerous world where appearances can be deceiving. But in those few crucial moments after I first saw him, I felt impressed enough to offer him a ride.

Within minutes after he got in the car, he told me that his car was in the shop, that he was an hour away from his home in Front Royal and that he was a retired Presbyterian minister who was hoping someone would give him a lift. He said if I could at least take him to Manassas, he would see if he could catch another ride there—and he protested when I told him I wanted to drive him all the way.

"I need to pay back some human angels who helped me when I was stranded," I explained as I headed for west 66.

He smiled and settled back for the ride. He told me two other times he had been picked up at the metro station as he was hoping for a ride—both times by members of the Church of Jesus Christ of Latter-day Saints.

I hadn't done anything so wonderful after all—I was just another in a long line of angels of the road! As the apostle Paul said, "Be not forgetful to entertain strangers: for thereby some have entertained angels unawares" (Hebrews 13:2).

Ann Best

He Carried Us Up the Mountain

And neither at any time hath any wrought miracles until after their faith; wherefore they first believed in the Son of God.

Ether 12:18

We were the last of the entourage, Kari Ludwig and I, charged with getting two very reluctant young women up Fairview Canyon to camp. Because of both our schedules and theirs, we had to leave a day later than everyone else—and, on top of that, we had to leave much later in the afternoon than I had planned. One of the girls was my own: Jessica had stubbornly resisted going to camp and had acquiesced only when I assured her that I would be there with my own car—and that she could let me know at any time if she absolutely had to go home. The other young woman was a stubborn, rebellious, but beautiful girl who lived through the back field from us—the little sister of Jessica's best friend. Shortly before six, we finally tucked the last of our supplies into the trunk, said a heartfelt prayer for safety and guidance, and started on the two-hour drive to Camp MIA Shalom.

The camp, nestled at the top of Fairview Canyon in central Utah, is sheltered by towering pines, fringed by delicate aspens and dotted with wildflowers. Groups of tents are clustered along the hilly terrain that spills from the main pavilion. A shimmering lake, fed by babbling streams that cascade through the trees, divides the camp into two main sections. Tall grasses stand sentinel at the shores, waving gently in the breeze that keeps the camp cool during even those hours when the sun is at its highest point in the cloudless sky. To get there takes an hour over well-traveled paved roads to the town of Fairview, then an ascent over winding, gradually narrowing mountain roads. Located almost at the top of the canyon, the turnoff is a rocky unpaved section of roadway that hairpins through the pines until it reaches camp.

We made the first hour of the trip without incident—Kari and I laughing and visiting in the front seat, Jessica and Amber hunched angrily in the back, heads buried in their pillows. Every once in a while one of them would interject something into our conversation, usually a defiant expletive about being forced to go to camp. We did our best to keep the spirit in the car light and happy, and even elicited a chuckle or two.

We stopped in Fairview at a convenience store where I filled the car with gas. Kari treated everyone to a round of ice cream treats, I bought a bag of red licorice, and we started up the road that would lead us to the top of the canyon. It was unseasonably hot for the second week in June, and I ran the air conditioner as we started up and around the curves that had been engineered into the rocky mountainside. About one-fourth of the way up the canyon, the car began to stall; after a few sputtering lurches, it stopped completely.

Kari and I looked at each other. The air outside was

heavy with heat and oppressively silent; the only sound that broke the stillness was the occasional chirp of a cricket. The sun skirted near the edge of the horizon, and we knew it would soon be dark. We knew, too, that the road was traveled only twice a week: once by the caravans going up to camp, and again five days later when they came back down. Despair flooded my heart. Should we try to walk back to Fairview? And what about those at camp who were waiting for us—two of the leaders—to arrive? What would we do with the girls, who at their best refused to cooperate with even the simplest requests? It was clear to us that the adversary didn't want Jessica and Amber to partake of the spiritual feast that awaited them at camp. . . .

After a few minutes of quietly controlled conversation, we decided on the obvious solution: We would petition Heavenly Father in great faith and humility to help us get to camp. We knew we had no other options. The girls bristled and shrugged off the suggestion with snickers, but we invited them to participate. With bowed heads and pleading hearts, first I and then Kari asked Heavenly Father for help. We spelled out to Him our vulnerable situation and confirmed that He was our only source of rescue.

No one in the car spoke as we concluded with the final "Amen." The four of us sat, heads still bowed, drinking deeply of a sweet and assuring Spirit that brought comfort and peace. Within a minute or two, we heard the lazy drone of an engine; as we looked up, we saw two men in a green pickup truck grind to a halt in front of our disabled car. Both ambled out of the truck and approached us, smiling. They were covered with dirt and grease; their sweat-stained shirts were worn, and their Levi's were torn and patched. "You ladies need some help?" one of them asked, ducking his head in the window.

The girls stayed in the car while Kari and I popped the hood and stood helplessly by while the two inspected the tangle of hoses and metal. After some grunts and groans, the two exchanged knowing looks and then explained our dilemma: The car was in serious trouble. In no way was it safe—or even possible—to climb the rest of the way up the mountain. Our best bet, they said, was to try to coast down the road we had just traveled, back to the hamlet of Fairview, where we could possibly find a mechanic who could work on it in the morning. The taller of the two rubbed his chin thoughtfully. "You want us to follow you down the mountain, just to make sure you make it?" he asked. Against all logic, I shook my head. "No, we'll be fine," I said, "but thanks so much for the offer." They shrugged with wonder and clamored back into the truck. Within less than a minute, they were out of sight, and the cover of dusk was creeping up the mountain to where we sat, disabled at the edge of the road.

"We can do this," I told the girls. Kari nodded. "Heavenly Father will help us. We're expected at camp, and that's where we're going." The girls were incredulous.

"What?" Jessica cried. "You heard them! We can't make it! We'll get stuck in the dark!" The angry tears stung her cheeks; Amber stared sullenly out the window.

"Yes, we will make it," I said softly. "Heavenly Father will help." Outside the car, as the sun rapidly disappeared below the distant horizon, Kari and I dropped to our knees in the grasses at the side of the road and offered a desperate prayer. Settled back in the front seat, I started the ignition and eased back onto the road. The car hummed quietly and drove smoothly, with no sign of engine trouble.

Within a minute or two, I glanced into the rearview mirror and saw with relief that another car was behind us. "Look!" I said to the girls. "There's a car behind us! We'll be just fine. If anything happens, they can help us." The girls turned around and rested their heads on the back of the seat, gazing at the car that kept a close distance behind our own. As we ascended higher and higher up the mountain without incident, I monitored it closely as well. Its pair of bright headlights stayed in perfect sync with us as we rounded curves and negotiated sharp turns. "I wonder if they're going up to camp?" I asked Kari. "There's really nothing else up here, unless they're going over the mountain to Scofield."

By the time we reached the turnoff to camp, the darkness was inky black, broken only by the beams of our headlights and theirs. Approaching the turnoff, I slowed perceptively in order to make the turn onto the rocky, unpaved road—and I watched in the rearview mirror to see if the other car would follow or would ease around to our right and continue down the road. I blinked with astonishment to see the headlights vanish.

I punched the brakes and slammed to a stop. The girls bolted upright. Kari looked at me with surprise. "The car," I stammered, "it's gone." All four of us turned around and intently gazed through the blackness. Nothing. There was no car, no headlights, no familiar sounds of engaged engines or tires crunching through the gravel. We were alone, there at the little dirt road less than a mile from camp.

The car that Heavenly Father had sent to escort us safely to camp had done its job. The headlights that penetrated the darkness—His light, carrying us up the mountain—were no longer needed. We had arrived at our destination, safe and sound.

As we rolled into the grassy parking area, girls and leaders ran toward us, shouting their questions simultaneously. What had taken us so long? Where had we been? We were so worried about you! Imagine my unbounded joy when, from the backseat, a small but deliberate voice related the first miracle she had ever witnessed:

"Our car stopped working. Sister Frandsen and Sister Ludwig prayed. Heavenly Father carried us up the mountain to camp."

He did, indeed. Delivered safely from His arms, we brought with us the spirit of faith in and gratitude for a loving Father who watches over even the smallest sparrow.

Kathy Frandsen

A Little Tiny Miracle

And said, Verily I say unto you, Except ye be converted, and become as little children, ye shall not enter into the kingdom of Heaven.

Matt. 18:3

It was a little thing. Insignificant to most. But significant to me. A brand new convert. With the faith of a child. We were so very poor. Students living in an old basement apartment. With a new baby. Living off what my husband could earn on weekends. And what I could make working part-time at a department store.

It was time to bless our baby. I had saved and saved until I had amassed the $11 necessary to purchase the beautiful two-piece white knit outfit I had seen at the department store where I worked, the outfit in which I wanted to bless my baby.

It was a lovely day. Many of our family members were there in our university ward, filled with single students who so loved our baby. As nervous as he was, my husband pronounced a lovely blessing on our first precious son. He bore his testimony, I bore mine, many family members did the same, as did ward friends. The meeting ran long, but no one seemed to notice.

I wanted to put the blessing outfit away, to save it for our son to bless his first son in. But we were poor. And it was the baby's only nice outfit, only church outfit. So, I continued to dress the baby in it every Sunday until he had nearly outgrown it.

As luck would have it, it was that very Sunday that the baby's bottle dripped orange juice on the white knit outfit. I washed the outfit in hot water, which set the stain. (I never made that mistake again.)

I was crestfallen. I could not fix it and I could not afford to replace it. There was no need to save it. But, with the faith of a child that so many new converts have, I prayed anyway, "Heavenly Father, this outfit is very important to me and my baby and our history. I wanted to save it and now I have ruined it. Please help me know what to do."

I put the outfit in the dresser drawer and waited for inspiration.

The next time I pulled the outfit out of the drawer, the stain was gone.

Had my husband fixed it? Not likely.

Had I fixed it and forgotten? I would not have forgotten.

Heavenly Father heard the little tiny prayer of a new convert, a new mother, and performed a little tiny miracle in answer to my childlike prayer of faith.

I have never forgotten it.

It was the beginning of a lifetime of little tiny miracles that have kept my childlike faith alive and well and working.

Peg Fugal

An Angel in My Car

For he shall give his angels charge over thee, to keep thee in all thy ways.

Ps. 91:11

It was early in the afternoon on a rainy November day as I left the restaurant in Park City, where I worked with my younger sister Debbie. She didn't have a car, and had gotten a ride with our father to work. It would be about a half-hour drive to take her from work to my father's house.

Something just didn't feel right as I eased my little green Volkswagen Beetle out of the parking lot and onto the road; I felt like something bad was going to happen, like there was going to be an accident. I silently prayed that there wouldn't be an accident—and that there was another reason for my feelings. I kept my feelings to myself, and talked and laughed with my sister about the day at work. I figured there was no reason to worry her.

Nearly a third of the way home I could no longer keep the nagging feeling that there was going to be an accident to myself and told my sister.

"Oh, I sure hope not!" she gasped. There—I had said it, and now she was worried—exactly what I had wanted to avoid. Now I was no longer praying that we wouldn't be in an accident, but that if an accident were to happen, it wouldn't take place while my sister was in the car with me.

We reached my father's home safely, and I reasoned with myself that my fearfulness had been unnecessary, possibly a result of being tired after a long day of work. I stayed and visited with my sister for a while before heading back in the direction from which I had just come. It would be an hour-long drive to my apartment in Heber City. As soon as I left the country road and merged on to the freeway, I had the feelings again—only this time the apprehension was stronger than before. I began to silently pray again that I would not be in an accident and that my feelings would vanish.

I don't know if you believe in angels, but I do. As I neared Heber City, I felt as if someone was sitting on the seat beside me. "Slow down," I could hear someone say, "you are going too fast." I lightly tapped on the brakes, and my car slowed down for a while. But as I started going downhill, I was soon speeding again—and the warning came once more. And I slowed down again.

The rain had finally let up, but the roads were still quite wet, and there were puddles of water here and there. Suddenly and without warning, my small car started to hydroplane on the wet road.

"Please, no!" I screamed. "Heavenly Father, don't let me hit anyone!" I had lost control of the car. As my Volkswagen spun around, I thought I could hear a laugh as a voice said, "Here we go—we're going to flip over." I thought of my dad and all he had gone through when my mom had died a few years earlier. "Please don't let me die—my dad has gone through enough," I pleaded as the car hit the dirt on the side of the road.

My little green Volkswagen flipped backwards and flew through the air. With a deafening crash, it landed upright in a swamp on the side of the road. I found myself on all fours, bouncing on the back seat. I don't know how I got back there, but I slowly opened the door and crawled from the car. I wasn't hurt except for a small cut on the back of my shoulder. The officer that came to the scene later told me that I was very lucky to be alive: Most accidents like mine don't end so well.

I don't know if you believe in angels, but I do. There was one riding beside me the day I wrecked my green Volkswagen Bug.

Heidi Butters

The Shepherd of Apache Junction

Thus God has provided a means that man, through faith, might work mighty miracles; therefore he becometh a great benefit to his fellow beings.

Mosiah 8:18

Our daughter Kimi had struggled with activity in the Church during the year since her marriage to a nonmember—but after a spiritual experience during the open house of the St. Paul Minnesota Temple, she had promised herself and her Heavenly Father that she would try to get to sacrament meeting every week if possible. It was a difficult goal to attain: Her husband resisted her religion. Added to that was her typical weekend work schedule—the Renaissance Faires she worked at usually only operate on Saturdays and Sundays. Regardless, many small miracles occurred as she tried to keep that promise. The following was one of the more memorable.

Several years ago, Kimi and her husband followed their Renaissance Faire circuit to Apache Junction, Arizona, for the Arizona Renaissance Festival. One Saturday evening shortly after they arrived in Apache Junction (near Mesa), we received a phone call. Kimi was in tears: she had tried all day, without success, to find a ward to attend the next day. She had been on a pay phone for hours, calling ward numbers in the phone directory, but getting only answering machines and hall phones. She had even called the Mesa Temple, hoping to narrow her search for a ward close to the Renaissance Faire site, but the switchboard was closed.

Kimi was near hysterics, and I tried to think of a way to calm her down and get her the information she needed. I had been to Mesa, and I remembered there was a Wal-Mart not far from the Faire site. I told Kimi to call the Wal-Mart and ask if any Mormons worked there; I told her to ask that employee to tell her the location of the meeting-house closest to her, as she wasn't familiar with the addresses in the phone book.

After we hung up my husband, youngest daughter and I had a quick family prayer, asking that Kimi get the information she needed. I prayed that she would find a "shepherd who was in need of a little sheep to care for and befriend." We had barely finished the prayer when Kimi called back and said, "Mom, you're brilliant." The person at Wal-Mart who answered the phone said that the only Mormon employee she knew wasn't working that night—but if Kimi would read her the addresses in the phone book, she'd tell her which one was closest to Wal-Mart. Together they found a building close to the store that she would be able to find. Kimi felt calm and was sure she could get to church.

I didn't hear from her until later that week when she called to say that a friend from the Faire had offer her a ride to Mesa that Sunday, and that they had had no problem finding the building. She said the people in the ward were very friendly, and one young brother had even offered to drive her back to the Faire after the meeting—quite a sacrifice, since it was at least fifteen miles away.

Kimi said they stopped at the man's house on the way to the Faire site to pick up his wife and child, who had stayed home from church that day because the child was ill. They all enjoyed the ride out to the site, and Kimi offered them complimentary tickets to the Faire for the next Saturday in appreciation of their kindness to her.

I told Kimi I was so grateful for the ward, and especially for the young man who had taken her back to the Faire site. I told her I had prayed that the Lord would send her a "shepherd who was in need of a little sheep to care for and befriend." After a long pause, Kimi quietly said, "Oh, Mom, the last name of the brother who took me home was Shepherd!"

I couldn't believe how intricately the Lord had answered that prayer! It's obvious that He loves each one of us so much when He goes to that kind of trouble to let us know that He has heard our pleas for help. Our experience helped me to know that the Lord hears and answers my prayers—no matter how insignificant my problems may appear—and gave Kimi a sure witness that He loves her!

Chrystine Reynolds

A Choir of Angels

And being thus overcome with the Spirit, he was carried away in a vision, even that he saw the Heavens open, and he thought he saw God sitting upon his throne, surrounded with numberless concourses of angels in the attitude of singing and praising their God.

1 Ne. 1:8

When my wife and I met, the Provo Temple was being built. We attended both the open house and the dedication. We did temple work there. It was our temple for more than twenty years.

Then the Church announced that a second temple was to be built in Utah Valley—the Mt. Timpanogos Temple in American Fork. Assuming it was for stakes north of the Provo-Orem area where we lived, we were both surprised and delighted to learn that our Orem stake would be in the new temple district.

My wife and I both worked at the open house. My wife

was in the first greeting tent and nearly froze to death. I was comfy and cozy inside.

We also attended the open house with our sons. We went again when my wife's LDS brother visited from New York.

We knew tickets for the dedication were scarce. One day when the stake president (who was also our neighbor) dropped by, my wife kiddingly asked, "Did you get us tickets for the temple dedication yet?"

"No," he answered hesitantly. "Was I supposed to?"

"Yes," she replied, still kidding.

A few days later he returned with two tickets to the dedication. Tickets that seated us in the celestial room. We were shocked. "You're kidding, right?" I asked.

"No," he said, "were you?"

I clutched the coveted tickets and thanked him profusely.

With too much traffic and too little parking, we reached the celestial room a few minutes late. Not disrespectfully so. In fact, luckily so.

Due to over-attendance, the only seats left were the ones reserved up front for the families of general authorities. Those are the seats to which my wife and I were led. Many rows in front of our beloved stake president who had so generously provided us with the tickets. He kiddingly glared at us. We innocently smiled back.

Never in my life have I sat so close to a general authority, let alone a prophet. It was a thrilling experience.

As luck would have it, our stake choir was the one performing during that particular dedication session. It was a small choir by necessity; there was so very little room left after everyone was seated. There could not have been more than two dozen voices, many of whom we knew and smiled at, not daring to wave.

One of the general authorities spoke of a branch in

Brazil where members had to travel for a week to reach their temple. (We had to travel five minutes to reach ours.) Our second son, Josh, was serving a mission in Brazil at the time. The day was growing more special by the moment.

Then the choir rose to perform their first number. I do not recall the name of the piece. I just remember it was one of my favorites.

Then something happened that we will never forget.

That choir of two dozen voices suddenly sounded like a hundred voices.

I looked at my wife.

She looked at me.

We both eyed the choir.

We checked out the sound equipment.

There was none.

How did they amplify two dozen voices to sound like a hundred? we wondered.

Then it dawned on us.

We were in the presence of angels.

Angels adding their voices to our humble stake choir in celebration of a new house of the Lord.

My wife and I looked at each other, awestruck.

Though we could not see angels, we most certainly heard them, and they were glorious beyond description.

Most of the rest of the day was a blur, so overwhelmed were we by our deeply spiritual experience. So much so that we dared not speak a word of it to anyone.

Then it started coming out.

Members of the choir sharing the same experience. Singing with angels.

Other guests in the celestial room. Hearing the same angels we heard.

Then we knew.

We had been blessed with a rare gift from God that we treasure to this day.

Though I worked as an ordinance worker in the Mt. Timpanogos Temple for more than five years and enjoyed many wonderful experiences during that time, the thing I remember most is the choir of angels I heard during its dedication, and I thank God that he allowed me such a miraculous glimpse into the Heavens.

Sherm Fugal

Reprinted by permission of Patrick Bagley ©2004.

6

MISSIONARY WORK

*A*nd this gospel of the kingdom shall be
preached in all the world for a witness unto
all nations; and then shall the end come.

Matt. 24:14

They Gave Away Their Beds

He shall enter into peace: they shall rest in their beds, each one walking in his uprightness.

Isa. 57:2

While serving in the New Zealand Auckland Mission, I often sang Hymn 219, "Because I Have Been Given Much," in district meetings. With the frequency of the meetings and the limited number of songs everyone knew in English, I soon wearied of repeatedly singing this same hymn.

While serving in Ellerslie, a suburb of Auckland, Sister Scofield and I lived in a little flat without heat that was furnished with one table and two chairs—that was all. We had no beds—only piles of blankets and a pillow each. We joked with each other that we were like the legendary Matthew Cowley, who had also slept on floors as a missionary in New Zealand. But as the days in my new area became weeks, and as summer turned to fall, the temperatures decreased, as did our joking.

Several weeks after I transferred to Ellerslie, we had a dinner appointment at the home of the Fafitas, a member family. The other missionaries in our ward—Sisters

Cameron and Larson—were with us as well, and Sister Fafita visited with us all as we ate the huge roast dinner she had prepared for us. As we were talking, Sister Fafita asked us if we needed more blankets. We thanked her, but told her we had enough. She persisted, asking if we needed anything else, and that, whatever it was, they would get it for us. The other pair of missionaries mentioned that they could use some drinking glasses and a portable heater. Sister Fafita said, "No problem," and started making a list. Then she told me to write down what we needed. I looked at my companion, hesitated a moment, and then wrote "beds."

Sister Fafita looked at the list. "Beds?! You mean you don't have beds?"

"No, we don't," I said. "We've been sleeping on the floor."

"Sisters," she said, "you should have told me about this before! We will get you some beds right away."

The very next night she called to say that both she and her husband were coming over. They arrived in their little red pickup truck and proceeded to unload various pieces of disassembled beds. Brother Fafita put them together quickly. When we looked into our room and saw twin beds with lace coverlets and big fluffy pillows, it was one of the most beautiful sights we had ever seen. That night we were so grateful (and warm) as we thought of the generosity of the Fafita family.

It was not until our next district meeting that Sister Scofield and I learned how generous the Fafitas really were. Sister Larson said, "Don't tell them that I told you, but the beds they gave you were their beds. They didn't want the missionaries to be without beds." That day, when we sang Hymn 219 in our meeting, I sang the words—"I shall divide my gifts from thee/With ev'ry brother that I see/Who has the need of help from me"— loud and energetically, my heart full of joy.

Larisa Schumann

Missionary upon the Waters

Arise, go unto Nineveh, that great city, and preach unto it the preaching that I bid thee.

Jonah 3:2

I had served in the U.S. Navy for ten years, during which time women were placed on combatant naval vessels. It was my time to go to sea, and my heart was filled with anxiety and uncertainty; my sweet, supportive husband bid me farewell on the pier as I waved good-bye with my sea bag in tow. I knew we were going to deploy and support the other ships at sea, but did not know what might lie ahead.

The Sunday before I left, I had been called to be a stake missionary. I couldn't imagine at the time why my stake president would extend me a calling knowing that I could be gone for at least six months, but the reason became very apparent a few months into the cruise.

I worked in a department where I was the only woman, and it was a testing ground. I could tell right away that the men in the department were not at all pleased with the decision to bring women onboard. I had a tough road ahead of me. I came into the work center hearing foul language and horrible music demeaning women. How could I possibly make it through this?

Along with articles of clothing and pictures of my sweet husband, I also brought with me my scriptures, my Gospel Essentials manuals and uplifting Church tapes, my favorite of which was by Michael McLean. On the tape was a song titled "You're Not Alone." I felt so very alone in a world considered to be a man's world! I couldn't have felt more alone. I listened to that tape every day and wept silently in my rack (what some might call a bed). It was a place of solitude where I could go to pray for strength.

I had been receiving numerous care packages and mail from members of my ward and my husband. A sailor in my department wondered why I got so much mail. He rarely got a letter from anyone, and he was as amazed as I was at the quantity of packages. I knew I had a huge support group back home and an extended family in my ward that cared about my well-being. I was truly blessed. This man asked me where it was all coming from, and I explained to him that it was from my friends at church. After that, he noticed that when it was slow on our watch, I would read from my Gospel Essentials manual.

One day he asked me what I was reading, and it happened to be a lesson on prayer. He said he had never prayed for anything in his life. I shared with him parts of the lesson, and he became very interested in its message. I talked to him about the power of prayer, especially in a situation like we were in. We were the first fleet in support of Desert Storm— a situation that called for many prayers! I explained to him the things we should pray for in our lives and the things that we should not. I could tell from his face that he felt something. We both were relieved of our watch, and we headed down to our racks to get some sleep before the next watch.

When we met back at our watch eight hours later, he handed me a letter and a small package. He said he would prefer that I keep it to myself, so I did. I began to read the letter in a spare office—and, to my amazement, it was a testimony of the power of prayer. He had prayed for the first time in his life and had received a testimony from the Holy Spirit about the power of prayer in our lives. My heart was so full! How could I have made such a big difference in someone's life, especially out here in the middle of the ocean? I finally realized that I was a missionary sent by God to do His work, and that I was willing to share the joy and happiness I had been blessed with if it would guide another back to Him. Along with the letter was a small plain box. I opened it and saw a small Hummel figurine of a shepherd boy standing next to a lost sheep, praying. My tears flowed faster than I could wipe them away. I felt the Savior's love for my sailor friend and for me.

We continued to learn lessons from the manual, and we talked increasingly more about the Church. He decided that when we returned to Norfolk, Virginia, we would contact the missionaries and he would start the discussions.

We got home seven months later; he asked me to contact the missionaries, and he started the discussions. Within two months, my friend was ready for baptism. One of the elders baptized him in the font where I had been baptized in Chesapeake, Virginia. He was the happiest person I had ever seen—and I knew his joy, because I had known the same joy the day I was baptized some six years earlier.

I introduced my newly baptized friend to a returned missionary I knew, and before you knew it they were engaged to be married. My friend received his orders to Germany, and the two of them were sealed in the Frankfurt Temple for time and all eternity. To this day I still think about my friend, although he now lives in another country. I think about his joy in finding the Lord and the blessings that have come his way. I know that I was chosen to be a missionary for this one person, and that no matter where we are or under what circumstances we find ourselves, we can all testify of the love our Savior has for us and bring another one of his sheep back to the fold.

I now find myself supporting my husband as he fulfills his duty to our country and to his brothers and sisters onboard an aircraft carrier at sea. I know that he will have the opportunity to bless the life of a fellow sailor and bring joy to that person's life just as I did, because he is willing to share the joy and blessings he has enjoyed in his life. Knowing and loving the Savior gives us the strength to share it with another. It takes a lot of faith to take on the world, but we can do it one person at a time.

I will always remember, as the song says, "You're not alone—even though right now you're on your own." He is always there to guide us and hold us near. I will always remember, too, that nothing is impossible with the Savior's love—nothing.

Esmeralda Carter

Every Corner of the Vineyard

I own an advertising agency and produce commercials for a living. I was filming some television commercials in an LDS home recently and noticed a world map hanging on the kitchen wall. It was mounted on foam core and framed, without glass covering it, and it was studded with multicolored pins. There was a color key in the upper-right-hand corner:

- The red pin marked the location of that family's missionary.
- The orange pins indicated where the parents had served.
- The yellow pins marked where the missionary's friends had served or were serving.
- The green pins indicated where uncles and cousins had served or were serving.
- The blue pins marked where grandparents had served or were serving.
- The purple pins indicated where the family had lived around the world.
- The white pins marked all the places the family had visited around the world.
- The black pins marked all the Church historical sites.

There were fifteen people in my crew that day, and every one of us spent time studying that map and commenting on it while quizzing the mother for more details.

I have loved geography and studying maps my whole life. In fact, I keep an atlas on my bedside table, which I reference often. But my atlas was old and outdated—it showed Russia still controlling all of Eastern Europe, which is no longer the case. Country boundaries and names have changed all over the world in the past couple of decades, and I needed a new atlas.

My son is an advertising executive with *National Geographic Adventure* magazine. When he asked what I wanted for Christmas, I told him I wanted the new *National Geographic World Atlas,* which came with a big, beautiful world map. I had the map framed and hung on the gameroom wall downstairs where we gather as a family to play. After studying the pin-studded map mentioned above, I decided to do the same sort of thing with our world map. Because it has glass over it, I decided to use colored adhesive paper dots.

In studying my family's map (as well as the one mentioned above), it suddenly occurred to me the incredible worldwide reach of just one active, missionary-focused LDS family. Multiply that influence by 12 million members worldwide, and it's easy to see that we as a Church family are literally laboring in every corner of the proverbial vineyard, while Daniel's prophesied stone rolls forth filling the whole Earth.

Peg Fugal

Swept Clean by Strong Winds

And if it so be that the church is built upon my gospel then will the Father show forth his own works in it.

3 Ne. 27:10

The dream was so real it awakened me. Trying not to disturb my sleeping missionary companion, I slipped from my futon (Japanese-style bedroll) and groped through the predawn shadows for my journal—I wanted to record the dream before it was reduced to hazy impressions.

"You have been swept clean by strong winds," said the man in my dream as he studied my face intently. Then he smiled and stepped off the platform where I had stood, trembling. Who was he? Where had I been standing and why? What did the words mean, exactly? His brief, poetic assurance was branded on my heart as surely as if by fire.

My mission in Japan was nearly over. I would be leaving the Tokyo South Mission in a matter of days and, like most missionaries close to the end of their missions, I had been reviewing my accomplishments with a critical eye.

Had I done everything I could to be a successful missionary? A good part of the time I had, notwithstanding my imperfections. The last month or two had been particularly challenging, though. The heat had been terrible, and my companion remained the victim of a debilitating virus. I had become disheartened and felt the need to evaluate my efforts in a more positive way, acknowledging the good I had accomplished with its concomitant personal growth.

Street contacting in the bitter February chill, for example, had resulted in the baptism of Shizuoka Ward's newest Young Adult representative. Abiding by our mission president's "total dedication plan," we had been blessed with the opportunity to meet and teach other stalwart members-to-be. Learning to live harmoniously with a variety of personalities had taught me greater patience and love. Bearing frequent testimony to thirsty souls had brought me closer to Heavenly Father. And suffering a "dry spell" in the baptism department had cultivated a greater dependence on Him. Indeed, I had had a part in changing lives for the better, including my own.

The words rang again in my ears, "Swept clean by strong winds." Yes, I was sure that the Spirit had communicated something important to me.

The comfort I received from the dream carried me through the remaining days of my mission with vigor and grace. Familiar sights, sounds and smells planted themselves firmly in my memory. Seaweed-covered rice balls never tasted better; the crowded, rattling trains were actually fun to ride; and, of course, the smiles and handshakes from my Japanese friends were sweeter than ever.

Sadly, though, it appeared that I had had my last glimpse of Mount Fuji weeks earlier, before the summer haze settled in, obliterating my view. Only a few miles from the mountain for half of my mission, I had come to delight in her beauty and strength and, in fact, had penned these lines in her honor: Lofty summit/Pristine mountain/Rising noble in the midst of mediocrity/ Morning monarch/Evening guardian/Symbol of my own sky—reaching possibility.

Grateful that I had been permitted to enjoy the inspiration of Fuji for so much of my mission, I determined to waste no time regretting that I would not see her again.

My renewed efforts and prayers of faith were rewarded by my Father in Heaven. New members brought their friends to us to learn how they, too, could find such joy. Contacts who had received the introductory lessons months earlier called, requesting that they be able to hear the remaining discussions. The proprietor of a noodle shop asked for help designing an advertising campaign to attract English-speaking foreigners and enthusiastically accepted the Joseph Smith story in the process. During the last week of my mission, six people were baptized. Packing my suitcases, I realized that the frustration and heartache of earlier weeks had evaporated, giving way to a feeling of profound peace and satisfaction.

My morning departure was a blur of bags and farewells. Too rushed for breakfast, my companion and I bolted from the apartment to the van that would take us to the train station. Once outside, I felt a peculiar exhilaration, quite distinct from the natural anticipation of seeing home and loved ones. The breeze! Yes, it was the breeze we had missed for so long in the sultry summer heat. Brilliant sky replaced the dense gray mist that had shrouded the area since the previous May. Wind-whipped waves pounded the coast with a vigor that replaced the stagnant air with a fresh sea mist.

My friends and I were exultant. Then, instinctively, I lifted my eyes—and there she was in all her splendor. Not a single cloud floated between Fuji and me to obstruct her clear, straight, imposing form. As my suitcases were being loaded onto the van, I stood alone for a moment, gazing upon one of God's most magnificent creations, from which I had received the inspiration to "fight the good fight."

Interrupting my reverie, a young Japanese sister ran toward me, eyes wide with disbelief and pleasure. "Shimai, shimai! (Sister, sister!)," she cried, as she grasped my arm and gestured animatedly toward the mountain. "Fuji-san!"

She continued breathlessly, "You can see Mount Fuji so well today, Shimai, because the air has been swept clean by strong winds!"

Susan Eliason

(Originally published in the Ensign, October 1983; reprinted with permission.)

Those Guys on Bikes

Behold, and lo, I will take care of your flocks, and will raise up elders and send unto them.

D&C 88:72

As a child I was always curious about the men on the bikes. I would see them all the time in Vallejo, California, in the early fifties—and I would always ask my dad, "Who are those men on the bikes?" He always told me they were Mormons.

On one occasion, as we drove to visit my great-aunt, I remember seeing a beautiful lighted building on the side of the Oakland hills. When I asked my dad what it was, he told me it was the Mormon temple. I remember gazing out my window, transfixed, until I could no longer see it; I felt it had pulled me in.

Many years later, after I was married, two of those bike riders came to my home and gave me some literature about the Church. I felt compelled to ask them in, but I didn't. As they left, I remember feeling profound sorrow. To this day, I don't know why I didn't listen to the Spirit and call them back! The situation bothered me for years.

Several years later, a patient I met at work had two children who attended BYU.

"Just what is this church about?" I asked.

He asked if I wanted a Book of Mormon, and I said yes. I expected him to bring the book to me—so when the missionaries appeared at work instead, I had to tell them not to return or I would lose my job.

As time went by, I began doing family research for my in-laws at one of the LDS genealogy libraries. I was surprised that they never tried to tell me about the Church. Eventually, my husband and I divorced after twenty-three years of marriage. My life seemed to be in ruins, and my girls followed my example by reacting like I did. I cried out to God to help me, convinced that I couldn't do it alone any longer.

One day as we drove home, my daughter Tami told me the cutest guys were just at the house to see me. They were following up on a book that had been given to me years ago. At that time I lived in the mountains of rural California, with dirt roads branching off old logging trails and no street signs. The missionaries had managed to find an old log sign that a logger had made for me with my first name on it—and, following up on an old list of copies of the Book of Mormon that had been distributed, he had found us. Eventually, my daughters and I all joined the Church.

As a result of our conversion, my older daughter Tracy's roommate joined the Church as well. She ended up marrying the son of the man who gave me the Book of Mormon. There were many other conversions through us, representing unique and wonderful blessings.

My daughter Tami and I were so excited to live where we could be close to a temple, so we held a pin, closed our eyes and stabbed it into a map to pick the spot where we would live. The pin was stuck in Tooele. We laughed, and pronounced it "Too-Lee." A year later Tami married a man from Tooele!

Thirteen years later, I was at last able to move to Utah. I bought a beautiful home against the mountains—in Tooele, of course, just three blocks from Tami and her family. So here I am at last, exactly where I want to be, thanks to the help of those guys on the bikes who never gave up on me.

Jody Hastey

I Always Wanted a Brother

Wherefore, the Almighty God gave his Only Begotten Son, as it is written in those scriptures which have been given of him.

D&C 20:21

Her name was Jillian.

When I was eighteen, I packed up my car and moved to New York. A family on Long Island was looking for a young LDS girl to be the nanny for their two young children, and I had the opportunity to care for their two beautiful girls; Jillian was six and Emily was a few months old when I arrived. I jumped at the chance for the job and couldn't have been more excited to experience New York for myself. Being born and raised in a very small town in northern Utah, moving to New York City was like going to a whole new world.

I was blonde-haired and blue-eyed, and it was easy to pick out my west-coast country accent. I couldn't really hide my background or the way I was raised. The family I would be living with and working for was Jewish. I didn't know anything about their beliefs before I moved in with them, but after living with them and growing closer to them, I wanted to learn more about their beliefs.

I was able to experience the Jewish holidays with them, and they used the opportunity to enlighten me about Jewish customs and traditions. In return, I was able to introduce many things to them as well. I was always introduced to their family members and friends as "their Mormon" rather than as their nanny.

My first Christmas with them was quite an experience for all of us. Members of the Jewish religion don't believe Jesus Christ is the Savior—so, naturally, they don't celebrate Christmas. That was a concept I had never even imagined! Jillian was extremely curious about almost everything I did. One of my friends sent me a Christmas calendar with candy on each of the days counting down to Christmas day. Being a normal six-year-old, Jillian wanted some of the candy and asked endless questions about why Santa comes and why I celebrate Christmas. I found it difficult to explain to her at first, but her questions made me think in-depth about the true meaning of Christmas.

Jillian knocked on my door every Sunday morning as I was getting ready for church. She was always dressed in her best dress, and innocently begged to come with me. Her parents usually had plans that prevented her from coming, but one Sunday, her parents let her join me.

Since many members of our singles ward were LDS nannies living on Long Island, you'd expect to see a few children with their nannies. But it was actually quite rare to see a child in our ward. Jillian held my hand tightly as we found a seat next to my friend Harlow and the rest of the guys. Jillian had a crush on Harlow, and told everyone that he was her boyfriend—so she sat quietly between Harlow and me as we waited for fast and testimony meeting to begin.

Jillian was very well behaved for her age, so the first part of the meeting went well. Every few minutes she asked questions about what was happening. Why do you sing those songs so much? Why do those boys hand out bread and water? Are they for snacks because everyone is hungry? Why is everyone so quiet, and why do we have to whisper? Harlow and I just kept laughing to ourselves as I tried my best to explain to her.

Jillian listened carefully as each person went up to the podium to share his or her testimony. After one particular testimony, the room was very quiet as we sat and waited for the next person to go up. Jillian leaned over to me. "Who is Jesus Christ, Britnee?" she asked loudly.

I was shocked. I looked up at Harlow, who had the same expression on his face. I heard a few people around us snicker. I didn't really know what to say. Then she asked me again, very loudly, "Britnee, who is Jesus Christ they keep talking about?"

Who is Jesus Christ?

A million thoughts ran through my head! I was a life-long member of the Church. I was taught who Jesus was practically before I could walk. Every Sunday I learned about Jesus and Heavenly Father in Primary. There was no doubt in my mind that Jesus is my brother and that he gave His life for me. I know it. I have faith in it. But here was an innocent young girl who had no idea about the man named Jesus that everyone was talking about.

Harlow leaned down, whispered in her ear and explained who Jesus is. He explained that Jesus is God's son and our brother—that He died for us, and we love Him very much because he did that for us.

Jillian smiled, looked at me, and asked, "When are you going to go up there and talk about Jesus?"

She made a good point. I was overwhelmed with the innocence of this little girl. The next thing I knew, I found myself standing in front of my ward, with a smiling little girl standing behind me, holding my hand. I bore my testimony of my love for our Savior, my gratitude for my knowledge of the gospel and my upbringing in the Church. I was touched by the Spirit and shed a few tears as I explained to the rest of the congregation what Jillian had said to me before I got up to bear my testimony. Many eyes were wet with tears as we sat down. All the young men who were sitting on the row with us got up, one by one—they, too, were touched by Jillian and wanted to express their love for our Savior.

That six-year-old girl really opened my eyes. She strengthened my testimony of Christ without even knowing it. She made me sit back and really ask myself, "Who is Jesus Christ?" It might be a question we don't think about often—but we should. We should know who He is and get to know Him through the record of His life and His teachings.

When we got home from church that day, Jillian eagerly ran to her parents to talk about everything that happened at church. Her mother laughed a little when she told about this man, Jesus Christ, who died for her; it didn't upset her parents, because they realized she was simply learning new things.

I don't know if I made a difference by reaching out to this wonderful Jewish family. I stood for what I believed in and shared the gospel with them by example. I know Jillian will always carry those memories with her. And, who knows? Maybe one day when she's grown, two young men in suits and ties may knock on her door with a message about a man named Jesus Christ.

She'll remember. She'll remember her "Mormon nanny," Britnee. She'll remember the missionaries that came to her house to have dinner with her. And she'll remember that Jesus is someone we love very much.

Jillian came to church with me a few other times. She became very well-known, and everyone loved the warm spirit she brought with her. I'll never forget something she said to me a few weeks after that fast and testimony meeting. She came up to me and motioned for me to kneel down so she could whisper in my ear. She threw her arms around my neck and gave me a huge hug.

"Remember when I learned about Jesus at your church?" she asked.

"Of course I do, sweetie! Why?"

"Well, Britnee, I always wanted a brother, and now I have one. . . ."

Britnee Gilbert

Wrong Number

For as many as are led by the Spirit of God, they are the sons of God.

Rom. 8:14

Knowing they'd soon be transferred, the missionaries in our ward set a goal to reach as many inactive members as possible during their last weeks in Bonner County, Idaho. One older couple interested them, because the wife— Sister B.—had served a mission and held callings in the Church for years, with a special talent for genealogy. But her husband, who wasn't a member, gradually pulled her away. She'd been inactive for years, and Brother B. refused to let the missionaries visit their home.

One evening the missionaries were scheduled to join a ward family for dinner. As usual, Elder S. called ahead to let the cook know they were coming. When a woman answered the phone, he said, "This is Elder S., and we'll be at your house in fifteen minutes."

Suddenly the elder realized he'd dialed Sister B.'s home by mistake; her name was listed in the ward directory next to that of the family he meant to call. As he opened his mouth to apologize, Sister B. said, "I'm so glad you called! I've been talking to my husband all day about the Church, and he just agreed to let you visit. Can you come over right now, before he changes his mind?"

The missionaries missed dinner that night, but they held a special meeting with Brother B. A few Sundays later he attended his first sacrament meeting and enjoyed a wonderful Primary program. Wearing a huge smile, Sister B. went right to work in the family history library. Within a few weeks, Brother B. was baptized by the elder who dialed a "wrong number" at the right time.

Sammie Justesen

There's a Lady in Our Midst

Dare to be a Mormon,
Dare to stand alone,
Dare to have a purpose strong,
Dare to make it known.

Richard L. Evans

While growing up in the mission field, I always carried the above saying on a small card in my wallet. It reminded me that often I stood alone in my actions and choices, for I was a Mormon girl and proud of it.

Because my father was a lieutenant colonel in the U.S. Air Force, we moved often, and I soon realized that it didn't take long for my friends to become aware of my high standards. But my first introduction to the students in the high school I would be attending outside of Washington, D.C., was more humorous than religious.

I attended an after-school activity so I could get acquainted. When the students asked me where I was from, I replied, "A little bit of everywhere," since we had moved frequently around the eastern part of the United

States. Somehow the topic of religion came up, and I said I was a Mormon. Immediately one of the boys asked, "How many wives does your father have?" I was surprised. This was the late 1950s, and I couldn't believe that the only thing this new friend knew about the Mormons had to do with the long outdated practice of polygamy.

Instead of trying to explain that this practice had been done away with many years earlier, I decided to joke back with, "Oh, my dad has a wife in every closet in our house."

The boy got a funny look on his face, and I hoped I hadn't embarrassed him—but I also hoped he realized his question was as silly to me as my answer was to him.

It didn't take long for these same classmates to become aware of what Mormons did believe. Soon I found myself answering questions about our standards: No, we don't drink beer and we don't smoke—but yes, I can wear lipstick and I can dance. I realized I was being watched, and sometimes watched out for. My friends knew the standards I lived by and they expected me to live up to them—at all times.

One semester I took a backstage drama class where we learned about and helped with the behind-the-scenes activities during our school plays. After a lunch break one day, I walked into the classroom and heard several people laughing. Suddenly one of my male friends said, "Quiet! There's a lady in our midst." Looking around, I saw several boys and girls nervously giggling. I realized I had been paid both a compliment and a mark of respect—a respect that had not been shown to the other girls in the room, who were embarrassed that they had been laughing at the off-color jokes. I felt both pleased and challenged, for I knew my friends not only admired me for my Mormon standards, but they also expected me to live up to them as I "dare[d] to make it known."

Nancy Reynard Gunn

The Family Fast

While serving as a missionary in Italy, I was fortunate enough to receive regular letters from a loving and supportive family. However, in the days before e-mail, letters typically took about two weeks to reach me. My mother, who was my most faithful correspondent, always kept me abreast of the main events in my family during my absence—but sometimes it felt like the "news" was more like ancient history by the time it got to me!

One afternoon as I opened Mom's letter, I read something quite different from her typical cheery updates. I learned to my horror that an unspeakable tragedy had happened in my family. As I read on, my initial shock turned to grief, and I wished with all my heart that I could do something—anything at all—to help my young cousin. Although I had a firm conviction that my mission was truly the work of the Lord, and I knew that as His messenger I had urgent work to do, for that moment I longed to be home with my family, both lending and drawing strength and comfort. I kept reading, and discovered that my extended family had held a fast for my cousin. But the date of the fast had been nearly two weeks earlier, and once again, news had reached me too late. Even that small gesture had been denied me, and I felt completely powerless, adrift in painful and distressing thoughts.

Still stunned and grieving, I found myself picking up my missionary calendar without really knowing why. Before long, an idea struck me, and I picked up Mom's letter again, searching for the date of the family fast. With a warm rush of gratitude, I realized that I actually had been fasting that day—and, in fact, I had even started my fast at an unusual time that compensated for the eight-hour time difference between Italy and my Idaho home. Naturally, I didn't know at the time that anything was wrong in my family. I had simply felt a desire to demonstrate my devotion to the Lord and to seek His blessings in my labors. Nevertheless, I realized that this remarkable "coincidence" was in fact an extraordinary blessing. Although I was not consciously aware of doing anything that might help my family, I had actually participated in this family fast. My voice had been heard.

This realization brought a flood of tears, springing from an odd mixture of sorrow, love and thankfulness. I felt a powerful sense of the Savior's love for my cousin and for me. In that moment I knew that in spite of the horrible events that had so deeply scarred my family, the Lord was indeed mindful of us. I knew that although my missionary service did not spare me, or my family, from the trials of mortality, I had no need to fear. And although my pain was insignificant compared to that of my cousin, my Heavenly Father was just as aware of my needs as He was of hers. Unquestionably, God's hand is extended over all of His children.

Lisa Freeman

A Double Portion of the Spirit

But when the Comforter is come, whom I will send unto you from the Father, even the Spirit of truth, which proceedeth from the Father, he shall testify of me . . .

John 15:26

As a Spanish-speaking missionary in the Texas Houston Mission, one of my areas was in a part-English, part-Spanish ward. Occasionally, I had the opportunity (and challenge) to translate during church meetings. I discovered that, although difficult, it was very rewarding. Once I translated during a testimony meeting and was amazed at how the Spirit worked through me to convey the truthfulness of the speakers' testimonies. It was in this area that we missionaries learned with certainty the truth that the Spirit is the same in every language.

One of the members in the area, whom I will call Sister Johnson, accompanied us one day as we went to visit an investigator, whom I will call Maria. Maria was a sweet mother who loved our message, but who had never been able to attend church because her husband would not allow it. We were not sure how successful the visit with Sister Johnson would be, since she did not know Spanish and Maria did not know English, but we introduced them to each other and then asked Maria if she had any questions for Sister Johnson.

Maria paused for a moment, as though worried about the language barrier, but then suddenly started asking questions while we translated. What transpired next was incredible. The questions she asked were ones she had asked us before—and Sister Johnson didn't say much that we had not already told Maria—but because we had never been married and Sister Johnson had already raised a family, the answers had much more significance coming from her.

When Sister Johnson bore her testimony of how even one person living the gospel in a family can bless the entire household, the Spirit bore powerful witness of the truthfulness of her words. Then as we translated, our voices bearing her testimony anew, the Spirit bore witness just as powerfully a second time, without ever having departed—thereby doubling in strength. I found myself believing Sister Johnson more than I believed my own testimony, because she had lived that which she testified. With the strength of the Spirit of truth borne of experience, there was no room for doubt.

Sister Johnson and Maria thoroughly enjoyed meeting each other and became quite good friends, despite their language differences. Even when they could not understand each other's words, they could both understand their sentiments and could feel the Spirit when they spoke. Sister Johnson's testimony helped Maria immensely. Ever since that day, instead of being frustrated at her husband's close-mindedness, she developed a strong and sure faith that her devotion to the teachings of the restored gospel would bless her family—and a bright hope that someday her husband would let her attend the church she loved. That one visit with Sister Johnson helped Maria more than we ever could have done alone as young sister missionaries. The language "barrier" became a blessing in this case: It required every testimony to be borne twice, naturally invoking a double portion of the Spirit.

SummerDale Beckstrand

Three Generations Later

. . . Remember how merciful the Lord hath been unto the children of men, from the creation of Adam even down until the time that ye shall receive these things, and ponder it in your hearts.

Moro. 10:3

My maternal grandmother, grandfather and their two oldest children joined the Church through missionary efforts in south central Alabama in the 1920s. They were never active.

My mother was baptized by the missionaries in the Conecuh River in Red Level, Alabama, when she was sixteen years old. She was never active.

To me, one of the signs of the true church is that they never lose track of their members.

When my mother married my father and moved to Vermont, the LDS missionaries found and visited her there.

When our family moved from one dairy farm to another in western New York, the missionaries found and visited us.

I remember coming home from elementary school one day and finding the missionaries in the backyard talking to Mother. My first impression was: They're so tall!

The missionaries visited regularly. One time they followed us children into the haymow and, still wearing their suits, swung from the fat rope that was draped over the rafters and dropped into the sweet-smelling hay below, much to our delight. Naturally, we accepted their invitation to go to church with them, while Mother stayed home and made dinner for them.

During one visit they gave me a blue paperback Book of Mormon to read. It was way over my young head, but I was most intrigued by the Arnold Frieberg pictures.

Because my only exposure to religion were visits from the Mormon missionaries, when my fourth-grade teacher asked my religion (which is illegal today), I answered, "Mormon," much to her shock.

Relating the incident to my family at the dinner table that evening, my father slapped the table, arose from his chair and declared, "You are not a Mormon." (No wonder my mother was inactive.)

Shortly thereafter, we began attending the Methodist church, in which my father had been raised. I liked the big, gray, gothic-looking cathedral and joined the choir. When the choir director ran off with the Sunday-school president, both leaving behind devastated spouses and children, my father declared, "If that's what religion does to people, then we don't need religion."

He changed his mind when his five children became teenagers. The United Church of Christ had the best youth program in the county, so we started attending that church. My two older brothers and I were baptized and confirmed, and we served youth work missions in Puerto Rico, painting church buildings and clearing a church stadium. When the minister started flirting with the young women, we left that church too.

When I was a sophomore in high school, my mother was hit by a car while chasing her pet mallard ducks out of the road during a rainstorm. She lay in a coma for weeks while we prepared for her impending death.

One day, the LDS missionaries showed up at her hospital room door. I just happened to be there with my father. One missionary addressed my father: "Your wife is a Mormon; we heard about her accident; we'd like to give her a priesthood blessing."

My father who had heretofore hated Mormons was desperate. His wife was dying, leaving him to raise five teenagers alone. We had tried and failed at two other churches. And here were the Mormons again. "Go ahead," he consented.

I watched as the missionaries anointed and blessed Mother. She immediately awoke from her coma, made a full recovery and finished raising her children. She is seventy-seven years old at this writing.

Intrigued by the miracle I had witnessed, I began investigating the Church. I had a school music teacher, a former minister, who was shocked to learn I was investigating the Church and went to great lengths to convince me otherwise. Confused, I lost interest in the Church and left for prep school shortly thereafter.

While I was away, my younger sister investigated and joined the Church, and had four missionaries, twice the usual number, waiting to teach me when I returned.

Like so many investigators, I made appointments that I broke, or ran and hid whenever the missionaries arrived. They soon grew wise to my tricks.

One day when I was sewing at the machine that sat next to the stairs, up which I normally escaped when the missionaries visited, the missionaries came in and sat on the stairs, blocking my escape route, and began teaching me.

They told me the Joseph Smith story, which, surprisingly, made a great deal of sense to me. Of course, the ancient Church of Christ had dwindled with the death of the Apostles. Of course, all churches since have been the work of man. Of course, Heavenly Father and Jesus would return one day and call a prophet to restore the Church.

They told me about the Book of Mormon, which, also surprisingly, made a great deal of sense to me. Of course, God would preserve his scriptures, church and people by sending a prophet and his family into the wilderness just before his covenant people were destroyed. Of course, he would lead them to a promised land saved for the purpose of preserving the gospel and Church. Of course, those were the people Columbus found when he discovered America.

I had been visiting different churches with various friends since I was a little girl, and I had never learned anything so simple, so logical, so beautiful or so promising. I joined the Church. My sister and I were the first active members in three generations.

I attended Brigham Young University where I met and married a returned missionary whose family had settled Pleasant Grove, Utah, as converts to the Church from Denmark. We raised four sons in the gospel, who all served missions. (Our oldest son was one of the first missionaries in Eastern Europe.) Two of our sons are married and raising children in the gospel. Two of my four siblings joined the Church, married Church members and raised children in the gospel. After my father died, my mother became active, and we children took her to the temple, where we did the temple work for most of our dead relatives.

I often look back at the number of years and generations and missionaries it took before my family grasped the restored gospel and Church, and I marvel that God and the Church and the missionaries never gave up on us. I hesitate to think where I would be, where my family would be, without the gospel to guide and direct us, and marvel again that the Lord offered us that blessing. To thank Him, I never hesitate to share the restored gospel with less active fellow Mormons and non-Mormons (often to the embarrassment of my family). And, I have never lost the wide-eyed wonder I felt when I first learned of Joseph Smith and the Book of Mormon.

Oh that the whole world could know what we know, have what we have, and join in this marvelous work and wonder.

Peg Fugal

A Witness of the Truth

*And now, behold, you have received a witness;
for if I have told you things which no man
knoweth have you not received a witness?*

D&C 6:24

While I was serving as a missionary in São Paulo, Brazil,
our mission president instructed us to use the Book of
Mormon in all of our contacts. We broke up the monotony
of the nearly constant rejection of our message by finding
new and creative ways to introduce this most powerful
book of scripture. I will never forget the way in which I
learned that the Lord Himself provides a witness of the
veracity of this book.

While on a split in my area, my companion and I ran
into a man on the street. As was our custom, we stopped
him and began to tell him who we were. We asked him
about his feelings toward God and religion, and he admitted that he had been praying for the truth. This seemed
like our opening, so we began explaining about the Book
of Mormon and Joseph Smith.

He stopped us after a minute and told us he could never accept the Book of Mormon. We tried to discover his concerns, but after numerous vague responses to our probes, my companion bore testimony of the Book of Mormon and said to the man, "If you received a witness from God that the Book of Mormon is true, would you accept it then?"

The man explained that he was Catholic and that, even if he received this divine witness, he would not join our church. We bore our testimonies again and told him the address of the meetinghouse if he ever wanted to visit. Then we went on our way.

A few days later, while we were walking down a different street in our area, this same man came running toward us. He said that he'd been looking for us all over the area for the last two days. He told us he had a dream in which he was under much condemnation for refusing the Book of Mormon. I thought that our prayers had been answered, and asked the man when we could come and teach him and his family the gospel. He let me know in no uncertain terms that he wasn't interested in a visit from us, but that he just needed a copy of the Book of Mormon. When our efforts to convince him otherwise failed, we gave him one of our spare copies, and he left.

As we continued down the street, I explained to my companion how I had met this man while I had been on splits. We discussed the strange way in which he had acted, and we decided to pray that he would receive a witness of the truth of the Book of Mormon and that he would have the courage to act on that witness. Not knowing where the man lived, we left it at that.

A few days later, we were working on another street when we found this same man sitting in a car in front of a house. We approached him somewhat tentatively and found him reading the Book of Mormon. He was excited to see us and told us that he hadn't been able to put it down since he started. He'd spent every spare second of the last few days reading, and he was nearly two-thirds of the way through.

Not only was he interested in hearing our message, but he wanted us to make an appointment and return when his entire family could be there. We returned the next day and taught an incredible first discussion; the man bore testimony to his family that Joseph Smith was indeed a prophet and that the Book of Mormon is true. We were able to schedule the rest of the discussions and a baptismal date on that very first appointment.

I was transferred before this special family could be baptized, but I will never forget the incredible way that the Lord himself confirmed the witness of His humble servants concerning this most powerful book of scripture.

Kimberlee Garrett

Proud to Be an American

And more blessed are you because you are called of me to preach my gospel—

D&C 34:5

My companion and I were walking up the sidewalk in San Remo, Italy—a city on the Italian Riviera—during the winter of 1982-1983. A woman about seventy years old planted herself right in front us and said, "I need to tell you something." She spoke in perfect, unaccented English—something that didn't happen very often in our area.

"Okay," I said, a bit uncertainly.

"I'm an American citizen," she explained. "My late husband was a merchant marine, and when he retired he decided that he wanted to retire here in San Remo. He'd fallen in love with it over the years he made calls here.

"I see so many young American kids come through here," she continued, "and all my Italian friends see them, too. Those kids are scruffy—long hair, unshaven, unkempt, holes in their jeans, backpacks. All my friends here think that's what American kids are all about.

"When I see you young men walking down the street—clean-cut, well-dressed and respectful—you make me proud to be an American. I grab my Italian friends and point you out to them every time I see you, and I say, 'That's what American kids are really like.' Thank you."

We smiled for the rest of the day!

Rich Rogers

Little Red Brick House

If ye fulfil the royal law according to the scripture, Thou shalt love thy neighbour as thyself, ye do well.

James 2:8

We had been renting a house in Oklahoma City for a couple of years when my husband decided it was time for us to buy. I was reluctant to purchase anything because his job required frequent moves. However, I went out with a Realtor one day, and as we drove through the Sky Ranch subdivision, one little red brick house seemed to catch my attention. We walked through the house, and for some reason—unknown to me at the time—I knew it was the house I wanted. I brought my husband back to see it, and because I seemed so sure of this house, he agreed.

The Allen family next door had seven children. I watched as they all piled together in the van to go to church each Sunday. I watched as they all worked in the garden together. The children came to our house to play, and I was very pleased with the example they were setting for our children. Our children played at their house and came home to tell me of all the fun things they did as a family; they even told me about all the barrels of food they stored in their garage. Their children invited ours to church, and one of our daughters went a few times. Mrs. Allen often called to say, "I'm going to the dairy. Can I pick up a gallon of milk for you?" She had to be one of the busiest women I knew, and her taking the time to think of me meant more than she'll ever know. I didn't know what made this family so special, but whatever they had, I wanted it!

One day on my way home, I stopped to visit with her as she cleaned vegetables at the side of her house.

"I heard Donny Osmond got married today," I laughed. "I guess our girls' hearts are broken."

"You know, Donny Osmond belongs to the same church we do," she said.

"Really?" I asked. "I thought Donny Osmond was a Mormon."

"Well, the real name of our church is The Church of Jesus Christ of Latter-day Saints. We are members of the Church here."

"Oh." I wasn't quite sure what to say. I mumbled something about my father being a minister and never having all the answers to my questions.

"You know, we have the missionaries at our house all the time," she said. "Maybe they could answer your questions. It's worth a try."

"Okay."

"What about one day next week? Would Tuesday work for you?"

Before I knew it, I had agreed to meet with the missionaries.

On the appointed day, my daughter and I went to the Allen home to meet with the missionaries. I didn't go with any expectations. When I left home at sixteen, I declared that I'd never go back to church—but as my children were born, I realized we needed to be involved in a church. Every time we moved, I would try a church in the area, but each time I left there feeling empty.

I don't remember what the missionary discussion was about that day in 1978, but when it ended, I remember that they asked me to offer the prayer. I was nervous about it, but I agreed. As I started to pray, I remember my body being filled with an energy I'd never felt before. Tears came to my eyes, and I knew that I had found something good.

As we walked back to our house, I asked my daughter what she thought. She said she liked it. I said, "I think what they are teaching us is true." She was only eleven years old, but she agreed that we needed to learn more.

We continued with the discussions and I knew I wanted to be baptized. It wasn't until they said they would need my husband's permission that I knew I was stuck! I hadn't even told him I was taking these discussions. I thought I could just get baptized and go to church, but this was an important decision that involved my entire family, and I was told I'd need to talk to him about it.

I prayed about it and went to him with my request.

"Joey and I want to be baptized."

"You've already been baptized," he reminded me.

"Joey hasn't. Besides, I wasn't baptized in the right church."

"Are you talking about those Mormons?"

"Yes."

"No. I don't want to be married to a Mormon."

The conversation had gone about as I expected. He refused. I decided to leave it alone for a few days and try again. The results were the same. No.

I went back to the mission leader and told him about the situation. The missionaries and all those who had been involved in teaching us agreed to fast that Wednesday, praying that my husband's heart would be softened and he would allow us to be baptized. I started my fast on Tuesday night and exercised every bit of faith I had that the Lord would answer my prayers.

The next day, a coworker invited me to lunch. I told her I was fasting, but I would go and visit with her while she ate. Once inside the restaurant, I looked around and saw that the ward mission leader was having lunch with some friends. I walked over to the table and asked him about it. "Isn't today the day we're fasting?" I asked.

"I started my fast yesterday at noon, and am breaking it with this meal."

"Oh," I responded. I wasn't sure what to say, but his explanation was good enough for me. I believed what he said and continued with my fast.

Four days later, as I got up on Sunday morning to get ready for church, our youngest daughter said, "Daddy, why don't you let Mommy and Joey get baptized?" At that point he said, "I don't care if they get baptized. I'm just tired of hearing about it."

I rushed to the bishop's office to tell him that we had approval for baptism. Somewhat apprehensive, he asked me to tell him exactly what my husband had said. I could tell by the look on his face that he wanted something more positive! That day after church, he greeted my husband in our front yard. "I'm sure glad to hear that you've agreed to allow Joyce and Joey to get baptized." My husband didn't object, so he set the wheels in motion, and that Friday, he took both of us into the waters of baptism.

I believe the Lord led me to that little brick house that day. The Allen family next door was prepared to talk to others about the gospel, and when the appropriate time came, Sister Allen offered me the opportunity to talk to the missionaries. They had taught their children correct principles that made it easy for my daughter to accept. Our hearts had been touched, and we were being prepared to hear the message. I am so thankful for a woman who had the courage to extend an invitation to someone who was probably not a logical candidate for baptism. I am thankful for a daughter who heard the truth and accepted it. I am grateful for a loving Heavenly Father who heard my prayers, knew the sincerity of my heart and made it possible for me to change my life.

Joyce Pierce

Thank You, Mommy; I Love You

Behold, I will send you Elijah the prophet before the coming of the great and dreadful day of the LORD: And he shall turn the heart of the fathers to the children, and the heart of the children to their fathers, lest I come and smite the earth with a curse.

Mal. 4:5–6

I was widowed in July 1993 when I lost both my husband and our twelve-year-old son in a drowning accident. By the time I met the missionaries, I was at a point in my life where I didn't care what happened to me. I simply wanted to know whether I would ever see my child again. When the missionaries assured me I would, I joined the Church.

Shortly after my own baptism, I was able to have my son baptized by proxy. I sat all alone at the edge of the baptismal font in the basement of the Toronto, Canada, Temple. My youngest son was doing the baptism for both my son Christopher and my husband.

As the officiator said Christopher's name, I felt a pair of arms wrap around my neck and hug me tight. I was startled, because I was the only one sitting there. As I turned to see who it was, I saw the image of my son; he whispered, "Thank you, Mommy. I love you!" I immediately started to cry; he wiped away my tears and waved good-bye.

I was so startled that I couldn't speak. I watched as he faded away and was joined by my husband and many angels. From that day on I never worried whether I'd ever see him again; I knew I would. And I know that in the meantime, he's in a good place.

I moved to Arizona for a fresh start; I have one more semester of college, and when I graduate in May 2005 I will have four associate degrees. I just turned fifty in November—and who would have thought that after quitting school at sixteen I would have been able to return to college? I would have never been able to achieve that goal if the heavy burden of worrying about my son had not been removed from my shoulders.

Meli Cardullo

Something to Discover

And, behold, it is your duty to unite with the true church, and give your language to exhortation continually, that you may receive the reward of the laborer. Amen.

D&C 23:7

I was born in Argentina in 1970 in a middle-class family and had two younger sisters, Cynthia and Veronica. We grew up in a very conservative society, where the Catholic Church was the dominant religion. We went to church every Sunday in a small town where my dad grew up; it's a beautiful town that has a lake at its center surrounded by old buildings, museums and a large clock, which is the main attraction. The Catholic church where I attended Mass was one of the old buildings across from the clock.

We initially attended church every Sunday as a family, but in 1985 things changed. The economic situation in Argentina started to decay, leaving many without employment. Things were very difficult for middle-class families, and extremely difficult for the lower-class families. As a result, my father decided to go to the United States to seek work and find a better future for his daughters.

My mother had to start working full-time jobs—which included working on Sundays—so she had to stop going to church with us. Still, she sent us every Sunday, and made sure that we participated in Christian organizations. My sisters and I prayed for her and for our father, asking that we could someday be together again and attend church together as we once had.

It was difficult to see my mother working so hard and to see my father sending us money from a foreign country to try to help us keep up.

When I was nineteen, I started to attend the university. I couldn't go full time because of the cost of transportation, and I had to copy most of the books and notes. I saved money by going to campus only to take tests and do all my hospital practices.

One day I was on my way to a hospital for practices. I used to wait for a church to open its doors very early in the morning, because I always liked to pray before I started my day working or studying. That day as I was waiting, I had the special feeling that I wasn't alone—and that there was something else about Heavenly Father and Jesus Christ that I had to discover. After that day, I had that special feeling with me all the time.

I earned my degree as a physical therapist in April 1994, at the age of twenty-three. In 1995 my father invited me to come to the United States. He was living in New York; I liked it and wanted to stay with him, but things changed. A friend of mine from Argentina was living in Salt Lake City at the time, and she invited me to stay with her for a week.

While I was in Salt Lake visiting, her nephew worked with three young men who had been missionaries for the

Church of Jesus Christ of Latter-day Saints. Two of them
had served in Argentina as full-time missionaries. My
friend invited them over, we had maté (a very popular
drink in Argentina), and we talked and listened to music.
We had a great time.

Later that week, Sergio—one of the former missionaries
I met at my friend's house—called to invite me to an
activity they were having with the single adults of the
Church at Temple Square. It was the first time I had heard
of Temple Square. I was astonished by the beautiful sight
and the magnificent view of the Salt Lake Temple. I felt so
humble—then, in a flash, I remembered that special feeling I had experienced in Argentina while praying in the
church that morning.

Everything was so clear, so pure; I felt so tranquil and
knew that everything was going to be all right. It was as if
Jesus grabbed my hand and helped me to do whatever I
needed to do at that time. I filled out a form for the missionaries who were serving in a Spanish branch, because I
could not speak English when I came. By the time they
finished teaching me I decided to get baptized.

When I called my mother, she supported me; she was
happy for me, and told me that if I wanted to be baptized,
she was with me. The next day, she saw the missionaries
riding their bikes; she stopped them and told them, "My
daughter is getting baptized as a member of your church,
and I need to know more about it." They went home with
her and started to read the Book of Mormon; my mother
had had the book for a while, but had never paid much
attention to it. Within two weeks, my two sisters got baptized, and my mother decided to get baptized in the
United States.

In the meantime, Sergio and I started dating; we married
in August 1996. My father left everything in New York,
and my mother and two sisters left everything behind in

Argentina. They all came to Utah for our wedding, and our family was reunited for the first time in ten years.

Sergio baptized my mother. Six months later, my father also joined the Church.

Being a member of the Church of Jesus Christ of Latter-day Saints has been a great blessing in my life. I can feel the Savior's love stronger every day, and I know He is with me—and has been part of my life—always.

Silvana Norat

The Longest Day of My Mission

Then saith Jesus unto him, Get thee hence, Satan: for it is written, Thou shalt worship the Lord thy God, and him only shalt thou serve.

Matt. 4:10

We all know that Satan, desiring the misery of the entire human family, works especially hard to keep people from making the sacred covenant of baptism. In the week before a scheduled baptism, numerous obstacles usually come at the new convert from all sources; they generally include such things as feelings of doubt or opposition from friends and family. Those sources had had no effect on one man I taught during my mission, however, and the desperation of the adversary as he sought for ways to prevent the baptism resulted in what felt like the longest day of my mission.

A few days before the scheduled baptism, we went to visit the man, whom I will call Carlos. We were surprised to find that he had not yet come home, and we decided to wait. A few minutes later he arrived, leaning on a friend who helped him hop up the stairs. He had sprained his ankle playing soccer! He was in obvious pain, so we offered to reschedule our meeting—but he insisted on visiting with us right then, assuring us that he would not let his injury get in the way of his baptism.

Since that didn't work, the adversary tried another plan of attack. After a miscommunication prevented Carlos from getting a ride to a church activity, he became very worried about depending on someone else for transportation to church that Sunday—and to his own baptism Sunday night. So he resolved that he would walk all the way to the meetinghouse both times, on his sprained ankle! We told him not to do so, and promised that we would ensure his safe arrival. We gave him multiple plans and scenarios to account for any unforeseen complication.

Later we received a call from the ward mission leader, whom Carlos had asked to baptize him. The ward mission leader—I'll call him Brother Gonzalez—had dislocated his right shoulder. We tried to imagine the pain of lowering someone into the water with a dislocated shoulder, but the ward mission leader assured us that he was determined to perform the baptism anyway.

All his efforts had failed—so Satan switched his plan of attack to us, the missionaries. After our morning studies on the day of the baptism, we prayed and headed out to our car so we could go out and preach the gospel.

Our car was not there.

At first we thought it had been stolen; it was a nice car that the mission office staff had loaned us while our usual car was in for repairs, and we were in a poor area. We later discovered that the car had actually been towed, because the parking sticker for our apartment parking lot was obviously on our other car. At any rate, we were stuck in the apartment while we waited for return phone calls.

Naturally, all the other missionaries, namely our district

and zone leaders were already out proselytizing. All of the office missionaries, the mission president and his assistants—that is, anyone who had a cell phone—were at church meetings. (Fortunately, our own ward started later in the day.) As we frantically waited, we spent a good deal of time calling ward members in search of someone who could not only take us to our meeting, but who would also be willing to lead a new investigator, whom I'll call Rosa, to the meetinghouse for her first time. She had been trying to come to meetings for the previous three weeks, but every time something had prevented her from going.

The members who agreed to help us were late, so we arrived at Rosa's home exactly as our meetings began. To add to our stress, she greeted us with the news that she did not think she had enough gas to get to the meeting and back. We checked her gauge, assured her that she would be fine, and promised that members of the ward would follow her home to make sure she arrived safely. Then we helped her and her four boys (all under the age of six) into her car and headed to church, ashamed that we were bringing her so late and worried about her ability to feel the Spirit in the face of all these obstacles. Fortunately, she somehow enjoyed it—despite our tardy arrival and her restless boys, who were unaccustomed to sitting still so long. We were so preoccupied with her that we scarcely had time to check on Carlos and to make sure he was still ready for his baptism that night.

After church, we headed back to the parking lot and discovered that the members had apparently forgotten their promise to follow Rosa home—and they had already left. Miraculously, we quickly found others willing to follow her, and they even had a spare gallon of gas just in case she did not make it. The Lord also works hard on baptism days.

Once Rosa was safely on her way, we called the elder

who would be bringing us our car. He told us to call back ten minutes later, so we rushed off to the ward correlation meeting, which had already started without us. We frantically reviewed the details for Carlos's baptism, making sure all was in order, then called again about our car. The elder was on his way, but needed directions we could not provide—and the map was in our missing car! We tried to direct him the best we could, then promised to call again a few minutes later.

Meanwhile, we still needed to make a master program for the baptism—something we couldn't do before Sunday, because there had been the possibility that another person would also get baptized that night. The other person postponed due to a family crisis (which could make for an entire story in itself), which left us precious little time to compose the program on a computer that was already in use by someone else.

We called the elder again—by this time he was completely lost, but fortunately was near streets whose names we recognized. We stayed on the phone with him and were finally able to guide him to us. At last we had a car again!

Our five o'clock appointment cancelled on us—which, though otherwise unfortunate, gave us time to make the baptism program. Getting it to Brother Gonzalez involved intense study of the map, one U-turn and a lot of stress, but we finally arrived, leaving him only forty minutes before the service started to make all the copies.

We returned to the meetinghouse at six-thirty, the exact time we had told Carlos to meet us there. He had not yet arrived. Suddenly it occurred to us that Carlos thought Brother Gonzalez was going to take him to the meetinghouse—but Brother Gonzalez thought someone else was providing the transportation. We panicked and tried to find a phone. A few minutes later, Carlos arrived. Brother

Gonzalez arrived in time with the programs and a much-improved shoulder.

At last, we were able to hold the baptismal service. We witnessed Carlos hobble into the waters of baptism and make the sacred covenant with the Lord, oblivious to the stress that had exasperated his missionary friends that day.

Satan may throw a thousand obstacles in our path, but if we are on the Lord's side, we will come out victorious—as did Carlos.

SummerDale Beckstrand

A Light unto José

For they were set to be a light unto the world, and to be the saviors of men. . . .

D&C 103:9

When I had been a missionary for about a year, my companion and I wanted to show a recent convert part of "How Rare a Possession," a video that had been released a short time earlier. We had no place to show the movie, so we decided to take Maria to the home of the member family where we lived.

We had just put the video in the VCR when the phone rang. I answered, and the male voice at the other end introduced himself: "Hola, me llamo José . . . (Hello, my name is José.) May I speak with Elder Craig, please?"

"Elder Craig is no longer here. Sister missionaries now live here. Is there something I can help you with?"

I then heard the extraordinary tale of how the Lord's hand touched a young man and his family.

About a year earlier, José had met two elders who had been tracting in his neighborhood. The elders taught several discussions—and while José and his wife were interested in the teachings, there was no apparent progress toward a commitment on their part. The Book of Mormon remained unopened, the search for truth was halted. This young family stopped receiving the missionaries, but their hunger for truth persisted.

Another set of evangelists eventually approached the couple, and they began a year of fairly intensive Bible study. That study left them still searching for the peace the Lord promised to those who follow His teachings.

Approximately one year after the initial visit from the missionaries, a young salesman knocked on José's door. The two men talked, and José expressed his surprise at his visitor's mastery of the Spanish language. The salesman told José that he'd been a Spanish-speaking LDS missionary.

The discussion then turned to the experience José and his wife had trying to find the true church. The young salesman testified to José that he would never find the true church by studying the Bible alone—that he needed to study the Book of Mormon and ask God if what he read was the truth.

I spoke with José on a Tuesday afternoon. He told me, "Hermana, I met this young man Saturday—three days ago. I started reading the Book of Mormon right away. I am only at the end of Mosiah, but I know it is the word of God. I came to church on Sunday, and I was looking for Elder Craig to ask him to baptize me, but I didn't see him. That's why I called the phone number he had left me a year ago. I want to be baptized."

It didn't take me long to get in touch with Elder Craig—he was due to end his mission two or three weeks later. Elder Craig was allowed to come back to our ward, where he baptized José the following week. He was confirmed a member of the Church and given the gift of the Holy

Ghost. José was then ordained a priest, and he baptized his wife.

We tried to find the young salesman to let him know how he blessed José and his family, but nobody seemed to know anything about him. He was truly a light unto that family—a savior of men.

Nadja Pettitt

The One-Armed Man in the Plaza

Their first Saturday in a new area, Elder Castro and Elder Ramirez went to the plaza in search of a map of the area. As they entered the plaza, they heard a one-armed man calling out to them; he asked that they go with him and teach his sister and other relatives the gospel. He was already a member of the Church, but his family members were not.

The discussions went well, the family was baptized and they became active members of their local congregations. Oddly, though, the elders never again saw the man with one arm who had asked them to teach his family.

Six months later, Elder Castro was transferred to another area. When he arrived at district conference, he saw the one-armed man. He approached the man and asked, "Do you remember me?"

"No."

"Remember the day in Rio Grande when you showed a couple of missionaries where your family lived?"

"Oh, yes," the man smiled. "What happened?"

"Your entire family got baptized—your mother, your father, your sister, your brother and all their children."

In tears, the man called his wife to tell her the good news, which they had not known. Then he shared the following story, explaining why he had been in Rio Grande that day:

> *My brother and I had been sharing a bank account. A couple of weeks before I met the missionaries, I arrived home one day to find that my wife was very sick. We took her to the doctor, and after several tests, they said she needed surgery. They told me they needed a lot of money for the surgery by the next week, when the surgery was scheduled. It was urgent, and couldn't wait.*
>
> *I didn't have any money, so I went to Rio Grande to look for my brother. I was having trouble finding him, so I decided to relax and take my child to the plaza. While there, I saw the missionaries, and took them to my family's home. Several hours later, I found my brother, got the money I needed from the bank, and went back home—a six-hour distance from Rio Grande.*
>
> *The next week, when my wife arrived at the hospital for the surgery, the doctor did another test. Much to his amazement, my wife no longer needed the surgery. She was fine.*

God works in mysterious ways, and that one-armed man was in the right place at the right time to help the missionaries bring the gospel to his family. We need to remember the counsel of President Gordon B. Hinckley: It's great when members of the Church not only pray for the missionaries, but pray to know how to help the missionaries in their ward. I know that as we do so, we will help others obtain the blessing of the gospel in their lives, and we will be blessed as well.

Lehi Yanez

Huehuetenango

The keys of the kingdom of God are committed unto man on the earth, and from thence shall the gospel roll forth unto the ends of the earth, as the stone which is cut out of the mountain without hands shall roll forth, until it has filled the whole earth.

D&C 65:2

I spent the last two months of my mission in Huehuetenango (way-way-ta-non-go), Guatemala, with Elder Evans, with whom I had entered the mission field almost two years before.

It was a beautiful little town in the mountains near the Mexican border. There were about five hundred members of the Church there, but only a couple dozen of them were active.

Elder Evans and I worked hard, had fun and enjoyed great success in Huehuetenango, baptizing and confirming eighteen new members of the Church. Naturally, we hoped all of our converts would remain active in the Church, but we knew better. The mission average was that one in twenty converts remained active after baptism.

I was released from my mission, toured the Book of Mormon ruins in Mexico, returned home to Utah and moved on with my life.

Twenty-four years later, I was reading the *LDS Church News* when I noticed that a second stake had been created in Huehuetenango. I read the news item again and again, and I could not believe it. I still can't.

I would never have imagined such growth in such a small town with so few active Church members.

We all know Daniel's prophecy about the stone being cut out of the mountain and rolling forth until it filled the whole earth. I have seen that prophecy come true in a little mountain village in Guatemala called Huehuetenango.

Sherm Fugal

The Baby Whisperer

Joseph Smith, the Prophet and Seer of the Lord, has done more, save Jesus only, for the salvation of men in this world, than any other man that ever lived in it.

D&C 135:3

As I sat in the waiting area of the temple, I overheard a mother talking to her daughter.

"Are you still doing it?" the mother asked.

"I try, Mum—I do—but sometimes it gets so busy that I'm not sure who I have done and who I haven't. Sometimes before I leave, I have to rush around and tell them all just to be sure."

The mother seemed satisfied—but I was curious.

After accepting my apologies for eavesdropping on their conversation, they shared their story with me. The daughter was a midwife, and her mother had challenged her to tell all her newborns that Joseph Smith was a prophet of God. That was simple enough.

For the rest of the day, I pondered her words. Why not

tell the newborns that Jesus is the Christ? Or that each of them is a child of God? Or even that the Church of Jesus Christ of Latter-day Saints is true? There were any number of deep and meaningful first thoughts you could share with a newly arrived spirit.

Then I realized the answer: If Joseph Smith is a prophet of God, then all the other statements are true, too—because those are the things he taught.

Years later, I also became a midwife. The memory of that day in the temple came back to me, and I became another baby whisperer. As each new spirit arrived, I would snuggle him or her close and whisper, "Joseph Smith is a prophet of God" before handing the precious bundle over to its mother.

There have been times when I have doubted the appropriateness of my actions, especially when delivering babies to parents who were not Christian, or who espoused no religion. But I believe that since I have this knowledge, I have a duty to share it. After all, it may be this child's only chance to hear the truth.

There have been times, too, when my actions have created treasured memories. Sometimes a pair of newborn eyes gleams back at me with a knowing glow, and I've "heard" a child say, "Yes, I know that."

I will never forget when a woman expecting triplets called me into her room; she complained that she didn't feel well, and I suspected she was going into premature labor.

Thirty minutes later, with a full delivery team assembled, I received Baby Number One into my outstretched arms. "Joseph Smith is a prophet of God," I whispered quickly as I rushed the baby to the waiting resuscitation team across the corridor, returning quickly for another.

With Baby Number Three, a girl, safely clutched to my sterile-gowned chest, I mumbled my belief again and delivered a second child to the team. Now I only had to tell Baby Number Two—but which baby was number two?

With all the babies safely delivered, my colleagues relaxed and stood back—but I still had an important quest. "Which one is Number Two?" I asked. Directed to the second son, I took him from his heated crib and softly floated my words across his downy head.

When time allows, I often expand on my message. I welcome the babies to a beautiful world, tell them they are special spirits and always admonish them to look after their mother. This time, Baby Number Two got the full message.

As I swaddled him back into his warm crib, a new doctor came up behind me. "Is it true?" he asked in a very quiet voice.

Oops! I'd been sprung! With a twinkle in my eye and a gleam born of pure joy, I answered, "Of course it's true. Would I tell a lie?"

"I guess not," he smiled, and then drifted off to check on the new mother.

Alone with my newly arrived "children of God," I finally had time to thank God for all of His gifts—and especially for allowing me to be part of this miracle called birth.

Patricia McKenna-Leu

7

OVERCOMING OBSTACLES

*For it must needs be, that there is an
opposition in all things. If not so . . .
righteousness could not be brought to pass,
neither wickedness, neither holiness nor
misery, neither good nor bad . . .*

2 Ne. 2:11

I'll Let Him Go

When Jesus heard it, he marvelled, and said to them that followed, Verily I say unto you, I have not found so great faith, no, not in Israel.

Matt. 8:10

I'll never forget that September morning in 1981 when I received an urgent call from my wife: Our thirteen-month-old son, Michael, had just been diagnosed with cancer. It was an anguished drive from my office to our home in Provo, then with Sharon to a meeting with our pediatrician, where he explained the unbelievable details.

Michael had a tumor the size of a grapefruit growing inside his abdomen, which had taken over his right kidney and which involved several other vital organs, including his liver, adrenal gland and aorta. It had a name I couldn't pronounce: neuroblastoma. At that time, no child with that type of cancer had ever lived to adulthood.

How could this be? Our precious, perfect little boy had not even been sick—he'd been a little fussy, but not sick. Sharon had taken him to see the doctor thinking he may have had an ear infection, but as Dr. Freestone poked and prodded he felt the tumor, tucked up under Michael's rib cage where it didn't show. He knew immediately what it was, but didn't tell us until the next day when hospital tests confirmed his diagnosis.

We became immediate friends with the pediatric cancer staff at Primary Children's Medical Center in Salt Lake City, where Michael was referred for treatment. We were told that with current treatment protocols they might prolong his life as long as two years, but probably less. There could be some surgery, but not until radiation and chemotherapy had reduced the size of the tumor. It would mean some extended hospital stays, numerous trips to Primary for chemotherapy and a series of sixteen daily visits to the radiology center, where he had to have general anesthesia each day so he could hold still for radiation treatment.

Our lives became a blur of grief, tears and comfort from loving family and friends; meals brought in by the Relief Society; and, through it all, a few rays of hope from priesthood blessings.

During one home evening while Michael was in the hospital, I remember giving our three older children a lesson about death and Heaven, explaining to them that Michael would probably go there soon, but that he would be happy and would be able to live again with Jesus and Heavenly Father. For their young minds it was an easy concept to grasp. They seemed happy for him.

Early in the treatment program the doctors asked if they could try something new—a set of drugs that were still considered experimental. Nobody knew if they would help for sure, but there was some scientific indication that they might. After all, Michael wasn't going to live very long, so what harm could it do? After fasting and prayer we decided to let them try.

After a few months, the doctors said the tumor was small enough to consider removing it with surgery. Did we want to put Michael through that? This type of cancer was considered to be particularly aggressive, and surgery might actually cause it to spread. Did we want to risk that, or did we just want to let him live his final months without the trauma of additional hospital stays?

We decided on surgery. Sharon stayed that week with friends in "Shot Lake," as Michael had begun calling it, spending sixteen to eighteen hours a day in Michael's hospital room at Primary. I went up for the weekend so she could have some time with the children at home. The recovery from surgery wasn't going very well. The doctors had been able to remove the tumor along with Michael's right kidney, but he wasn't recovering as he should. They said he could get along just fine with only his one remaining kidney, but as the week progressed he became increasingly ill. Nobody could adequately explain why he wasn't getting better.

That Sunday afternoon I spent in his room looking at this helpless, unconscious eighteen-month-old baby hooked up to several monitoring devices, I was in the depth of despair. I had partially prepared myself for his death, but I hadn't really let go yet. I knew that his death was inevitable and could come at any time. I also knew in my mind that Heaven was a better place than Earth life. I knew, too, that Heavenly Father, in his infinite wisdom, had a plan for Michael that might not include the rest of us at this time. But I was still selfish enough to want him to stay—for me, for us.

All alone in that hospital room, I began to pray aloud. The Spirit filled my heart and for the first time I told Heavenly Father that I would accept His will in this matter. A flood of relief came into my soul as I realized that I had just come to terms with Michael's deteriorating condition. I said aloud, "Heavenly Father, Michael is your son also, and if you need him now, I'll let him go." Much more was said, most of it positive, as I felt my heart begin to heal. I finished praying, and with tears streaming down my cheeks I reached over, kissed Michael's tiny, sleeping face, and said good-bye. He didn't stir. I expected the end to come at any time, but had finally found a tenuous peace. I could accept it. I would accept it. And I would go on living, with a sure knowledge that at least one member of my family would achieve Eternal Life.

That same evening Michael awakened. It began with a weak cry. I called the nurse. She was genuinely grateful for some sign of consciousness. The next day he was actually better. He began to recover and was released from the hospital later that week.

Why did he come so close to death only to be given more time? I could only believe it was for me. I had to learn some hard lessons. I had to be humbled. I had to give my will over to God's will. It was hard. I fought it. But I had a feeling in my heart that said something like, "My son, this ordeal wasn't for Michael, but for you—you are precious to me also. You had to learn."

Miraculously, Michael got better. There was more surgery, more months filled with painful chemotherapy treatments. But two years came and went, and he was growing and seeming to be healthier than ever. He beat the odds, and he would become the first child ever to live through this type of cancer.

At age eighteen, after graduating from high school, Michael was diagnosed with cancer in his remaining kidney. It was removed. He had dialysis treatments three times each week for seven months. He became weak and lethargic before our only other son was approved to donate one of his kidneys. The transplant took place at LDS Hospital in Salt Lake.

A few months later Michael was allowed to apply for a mission. His doctor, a splendid man not of our faith, said, "You tell them you can't leave the United States and for them to send you someplace near a good hospital for follow-up treatment." He didn't understand that you don't "tell them" anything, but that the Lord is in charge. When his call arrived to Cleveland, Ohio, Michael asked the doctor if there was a good hospital nearby. He exclaimed, "Are you kidding? The Cleveland Clinic is the finest cancer hospital in the Midwest. You're getting the best!"

Michael served an honorable mission and is married to his eternal sweetheart, Erin. They're a precious couple, looking forward to adopting children to create a family of their own.

One of our precious granddaughters, Riley, was born with a cancerous tumor. Although I grieved, as any grandparent would, I breezed through the trauma of it knowing that Heavenly Father is in charge—and happy to let Him have His will. Riley's doing fine now.

And me? I couldn't be happier. The faith I developed through Michael's cancer ordeal is even stronger. I've passed it to my children, and can't wait until my grandchildren are old enough to understand what my heart yearns to teach them, too.

Stan Miller

This Is Not of the Lord

Lest Satan should get an advantage of us: for we are not ignorant of his devices.

2 Cor. 2:11

I joined the Church of Jesus Christ of Latter-day Saints when I was twenty-three. I had just started believing in God on my own terms again a few months before that, ending a seven-year spiritual drought during which I didn't believe in anything—especially myself. I had quit my job and was looking for direction in my life. I moved into the downtown YWCA and met a woman there who was investigating the Church. At that time, I wanted nothing to do with the Church for various reasons. However, about a year later, I could no longer deny my feelings and the truth, and I was baptized.

In the years before I joined the Church, I had struggled with depression but had always managed to overcome it. However, for the first five or so years that I belonged to the Church, the struggles became intense. I would be feeling happy, and things would be going smoothly. Then something would happen and I would start to spiral downward. During the last three of those years, it would be six months up, then six months down. I struggled against the darkness that threatened to overwhelm me so often. But there was always a faint glimmer of light, and that was all that kept me going sometimes.

The last time it happened, I lost my ability to feel any emotion at all. The experience really frightened me, and I prayed to Heavenly Father that I could find the answer to the puzzle. One of the reasons I spiraled downward is that I didn't understand why the Lord would give me something so heavy to carry when He knew I was incapable of it. I had heard lots of times that the Lord didn't give you more than you were capable of, but I was beginning to truly doubt that.

I remember that I somehow made it to church meetings, wanting to be there but not knowing how I was going to carry on if I didn't get some kind of answer. I was sitting in the chapel on Academy Road and was just so overwhelmed by feelings of worthlessness and not living up to what the Lord expected of me that I left the meeting and sat in the foyer. Tears overwhelmed me. I felt so lost and helpless!

Before I realized what had happened, someone sat down beside me and asked me what was wrong. I found myself pouring my heart out, explaining all the struggles I had gone through. I reiterated not understanding why the Lord would ask me to carry this heavy burden. The person then said something that changed my life. It was a simple statement: "This is not of the Lord."

What? Not of the Lord? How could it be? But, as his statement began to make its way into my mind, it started to make more and more sense to me.

My life literally turned around from that moment and hour and day. I knew what the source was, and that knowledge gave me what I needed to fight it.

I know now that what comes from the Lord gives light and inspiration. It uplifts. Anything that drags us to that place where I was comes from the powers of darkness. I have had a few bouts with that same discouragement over the years, but I no longer feel helpless—and those periods don't last long, because I know how I can conquer them.

I don't remember who talked to me that day—possibly it was an angel—but I have always been eternally grateful for the answer to my prayer. I testify that depression can be overcome, and knowing the source really can empower us in that process.

Cheryl Panisiak

Ultimately, It Is the Spirit That Heals

. . . They had been wrought upon by the Spirit of God, and had been healed . . .

3 Ne. 7:22

According to an *Oprah* show on abuse, one in every two women will be abused at some point in her lifetime, a sign of the degenerate times we live in and a warning to women and the mothers of daughters everywhere.

Unfortunately, most LDS women who have been abused neither report nor address it, wrongfully assuming the damage will go away as they more fully live the gospel, which is utter nonsense. Recovering from abuse requires professional help, which fortunately the Church offers.

I was sexually molested by my brother on a regular basis for six years between the ages of ten and sixteen. I buried the horrible experience deep within my soul until my late thirties. When my sister suffered a breakdown that was founded in the abuse she suffered at the hands of the same person, I checked myself into therapy, fearing the same breakdown.

I hated it. I dreaded it. I skipped many a session that I had to pay for anyway. I could not bring myself to say the words that described what happened to me, so the therapist had me write them down. I typed eleven single-spaced pages.

I angrily answered his questions, begrudgingly read the articles and books he assigned and hesitantly put to work the new behavior he taught me. And, in time, I began to heal.

But I was still mad. Mad that God had allowed this to happen to me. Mad that I had not been born into a family who would love rather than hurt me.

One day when I was driving to the city, I began railing at God in the privacy of my car. With tears streaming down my face, I screamed, "Why, why did you let this happen to me?"

Then I heard a voice.

I thought someone was in the car with me. I looked around, but there was no one.

Then I heard the voice a second time. "Don't you remember?" it asked.

"Remember what?" I whispered.

Then I had an epiphany, my own personal vision.

I saw myself in a room with my two Heavenly parents. They were explaining to me, "We're sending you into a tough situation: a mother who does not want another baby, a father who does not want a daughter and a brother who will abuse you."

I do not know how I continued to drive while I was having this experience, but I did. Perhaps it never really happened. Perhaps it happened in a split second. I do not know.

"But," they continued, "when you are older, the missionaries will find you and teach you the gospel. And later, you will marry a returned missionary in the temple with whom you will raise four sons who will become to you the brothers you never had."

That is exactly what happened in my earthly life.

I looked at my Heavenly parents and announced with all the confidence I possess today, "I can do that."

And that is the inimitable spirit with which I was born, with which I have faced and survived every challenge God has sent my way in this life, including abuse.

When the vision closed, my anger was gone, and I felt peace for the first time since my pre-abuse childhood. And I learned the most important lesson of my mortal experience: that even with our best efforts, ultimately, it is the Spirit that heals.

Patricia Diane

He Healed Me

O LORD my God, I cried unto thee, and thou hast healed me.

Ps. 30:2

After a decade or more of troubling symptoms, I was finally diagnosed with systemic lupus erythematosus during my late thirties. Lupus is an autoimmune disorder. The immune system, which normally mobilizes to attack foreign invaders—such as bacteria or viruses—mistakes the body itself as the "enemy." As a result, the immune system goes to work to aggressively destroy various body tissues and organs, such as the kidneys, heart or lungs. For reasons not completely understood by medical researchers, the disease manifests itself differently in each person; diagnosis is made with a blood test. Symptoms can be treated, and the eventual last-resort treatment is to suppress the immune system completely with medication. At that point, of course, the body is left defenseless against something as simple as the common cold. Lupus is eventually fatal.

In my case, the lupus caused severe pain in my joints, muscles and tendons, and affected my energy level. More serious than that, however, was the fact that my immune system was progressively attacking—and destroying—my lungs. In addition to my lupus specialist, I was being treated by one of the Intermountain West's noted authorities in pulmonary medicine, who monitored the progressive destruction of my lungs. He tried various treatments to keep my lungs working as well as possible. I was experiencing two or three episodes of lupoid pneumonia each year, each of which kept me confined to bed for six to eight weeks. Though lupoid pneumonia (like viral pneumonia) does not respond to antibiotics, I was treated with high doses of erythromycin to prevent secondary infections; the coughing was so severe that I almost always developed pleurisy, a condition in which the lining of the lung separates from the lung itself. Pleurisy causes a knife-like stabbing pain with each breath and almost unbearable ripping pains during coughing. Each recovery was a blessed relief, but left my lungs weaker, more deeply scarred and more susceptible to further infections. My lungs became so sensitive that I couldn't stay in the room if any kind of chemical cleaner was being used.

My condition finally deteriorated to a point that my team of doctors felt they had exhausted everything they could do for me, so they referred me to a lupus specialist in Salt Lake City for further evaluation and treatment. I brought all my blood work and X-rays with me to my first appointment, during which the doctor did a basic examination. He decided to order all new tests so he could know exactly where I was in the course of the disease. I walked across the complex to a lab, where I had extensive blood work and urinalysis done and had detailed X-rays of my lungs and hands. (Because the bones of the fingers are the most delicate in the body, they show the damage the earliest.)

Throughout this period, I had started working on my family history, and was doing as much research and temple work as my health allowed. As the only member of the Church on my father's side of the family, I felt a tremendous responsibility to bring the saving ordinances to as many of my ancestors on that side as possible—and I knew that I was the only person in that lineage who was doing the research. I felt I was racing the clock, and prayed continuously that I would be able to complete the necessary research before the lupus claimed me.

One Saturday morning I was driving to Salt Lake to the Family History Library, and I was praying as I drove. During my prayer, it suddenly occurred to me that I was not using the Savior's gift of the atonement as I could. I remembered Alma 7:11, in which we are told, "And he shall go forth, suffering pains and afflictions and temptations of every kind; and this that the word might be fulfilled which saith he will take upon him the pains and the sicknesses of his people." I knew that those "pains" and "sicknesses" included lupus.

Elder Neal A. Maxwell had explained, "Jesus' perfect empathy was ensured when, along with His atonement for our sins, He took upon Himself our sicknesses, sorrows, griefs, and infirmities and came to know these 'according to the flesh' (Alma 7:11–12). He did this in order that he might be filled with perfect, personal mercy and empathy and thereby know how to succor us in our infirmities. He thus fully comprehends human suffering." Jesus knew my suffering, and he had felt every pain and frustration I was now feeling. I knew that with every fiber of my being.

I began to weep uncontrollably and pulled off the freeway. My prayer at that point was simple: "Heavenly Father, my lupus is so difficult. It has made it so I can't do many of the things I'd like to. If it continues as it is, it will take my life. Father, I have so much to do. I want to find my ancestors and do their work, but I need to be strong and healthy. My ancestors are depending on me. I would not wish my lupus on anyone—but I know the Savior already took it in the garden of Gethsemane, and I need Him to take it again." I felt an overwhelming sense of peace as I eased back onto the freeway; somehow, I sensed that all would be well and that I would be able to finish the research I so desperately wanted to do.

In the following weeks, I began to feel stronger and healthier than I had in years. My energy increased and the pain in my joints and muscles eased. Approximately two weeks after my pleading prayer on the side of the freeway, I received a letter from the lupus specialist I had visited in Salt Lake. After analyzing the laboratory tests, he wrote that "there is no sign of systemic lupus. You will not need a follow-up visit."

I had been healed of a fatal disease for which there is no cure. The Savior, in His indescribable love for me, had suffered lupus as part of His atonement, and He had willingly taken it again, leaving me healthy and strong. Through prayer and the inspiration of the Spirit, I know the ability for the Savior to take my lupus had always been there; it was up to me to realize that possibility, to humble myself sufficiently and to exercise enough faith to enable the miracle. The Savior had already done His part; He was waiting for me to do mine.

As so eloquently stated by Elder W. Craig Zwick of the Seventy, "It is the wounded Christ who leads us through our moments of difficulty. It is He who bears us up when we need more air to breathe or direction to follow or even more courage to continue. If we will keep the commandments of God and walk hand in hand with Him in His paths, we will go forward with faith and never feel alone. Trust in His promise of eternal life, and allow peace and hope to distill upon you. When we connect with the Author of Peace and with His perfect and redeeming love, then we can come to know the reality of the Lord's promise: 'I the Lord thy God will hold thy right hand, saying . . . , Fear not; I will help thee'" (Isaiah 41:13).

I had needed more air to breathe, and my Savior bore me up and took me by the hand. I owe to him every breath I take, and I recognize Him as my literal Savior—not only in an eternal sense, but also in the healing of my mortal body.

Kathy Frandsen

Two and a Half Miracles

... They had been taught by their mothers, that if they did not doubt, God would deliver them.

Alma 56:47

"Can you do it?" My Relief Society president leaned over her kitchen table and gripped my hand tightly. "It would be a great service, and Alexa absolutely needs it."

I knew that. I probably knew it better than anyone. My mind flashed back to the first time Alexa and I had met. Sitting on my couch and clasping her husband's hand, she wore the same tense look and fake smile I had on my face—the one we'd both gotten from crying too much and then trying to pretend that we hadn't. She and her husband stayed with us for hours as we talked and tried, again, to hold back the tears. At the end, she stood to hug me and our large, round bellies bumped together. It made us laugh, despite everything. It was a gift only we could give each other.

Our bond was immediate, if a little unusual. She was carrying identical twin boys, recently diagnosed with twin-to-twin transfusion syndrome (TTTS). My husband, Jason, and I had recently learned that the daughter I was carrying had Turner's syndrome. Their babies had a 40 percent chance of survival; our baby had only a 10 percent chance, at best. The doctors had told both of us to prepare ourselves for the death of our babies.

Over the next month, Alexa and I ate lunch (and lost it), walked, shopped and prayed together. Over the next thirty days we shared in their elation as Alexa received a priesthood blessing, and the TTTS entirely disappeared by her next doctor's checkup. "It's a miracle," her doctor had said. "In all my years of practice, I've never seen this happen before. You are very blessed." Alexa squeezed my hand and whispered, "It will happen for you, too. I know it. Today we will have three miracles." I squeezed her hand back, and for the first time since I'd heard the words Turner's syndrome, I had real hope. She had her miracle; surely I would have mine, too.

But my daughter's tenure on this Earth was to be a short one, and after one final farewell kick, she stopped moving. I knew she was gone, but I still wanted to hope. I waited until the next day to have my fear confirmed by ultrasound. My doctor scheduled an induction for the next morning; finally, I would hold my little girl for the first and last time.

That was September 11, 2001. My daughter's birth was postponed by the crashing of two jets into the Twin Towers. The entire country mourned—and I cried for every mother who, just like me, had lost her baby that day.

The birth. The few hours with Faith Carina. The funeral. The visitors. It all went by in a haze of breathless sorrow. I wasn't sure if I could live, but every morning I woke up and stared at the ceiling and made the decision to breathe. Just one more time. I wasn't sure if I could do it. What the Relief Society president was now asking me to do seemed an insurmountable task, the final straw that would break my aching heart.

Alexa was on complete and total bed rest, her twins in jeopardy one more time. I was still on maternity leave from my job as a teacher. It made perfect sense for me to take care of her, right? I swallowed, my eyes filling with tears as I looked at the earnest face of Sister Johnson. I knew she wouldn't be asking if she didn't think I could do it—but to ask a woman who had just lost a baby to care for a pregnant woman who may or may not lose her babies, too, seemed almost unreal.

What if the babies died? Would it be my fault? What if the babies lived? Suddenly I could sympathize with the woman at the beginning of the story of Wise King Solomon—the one no one ever talks about except in terms of evil. All of a sudden I knew why that nameless woman had taken another woman's baby—it was because she couldn't bear the horror of waking up with empty arms.

"I can't even imagine how hard this must be for you, sweetie," Sister Johnson said, stroking my cold hand. "And please say no if you think it is too much. It's just that your name kept returning to my mind as I prayed about this."

Divine inspiration. Well, what could I say to that? "I can do it," I whispered. But I didn't believe myself.

The first day I showed up on her doorstep was awkward. We stared at each other, remembering the last time we spoke—which, of course, was at my daughter's funeral.

"How are you?"

"Oh, fine—and you?"

"Oh, fine."

We were both lying. I could see the fear in her eyes. I was what she was afraid of becoming. She could see the fear in my eyes, too. She represented everything I wanted—to still be pregnant, still be fighting for my baby.

She let me in and lay down on the couch on her left side,

just like she was supposed to. I did her dishes, cooked her meals, brought her endless bottles of water. We watched TV, each other and the large wooden clock. At last her husband came home from work and I was free to go—go home to my husband and the little memory box tied shut with a green ribbon, too small to contain every earthly thing of a real human being.

Thankfully it got better. We were friends once, and we were once again friends. Giggling over gigantic protein shakes, we watched the babies kick and squirm and grow, both of us more proud than we could express of their obvious health. I folded laundry as we talked about our mothers. I drove her to her doctor's appointments as we compared high school boyfriends. For a month, I held her hair as she threw up, caught her when she fainted and fed her Tums every few minutes.

Then one day, it happened: I woke up, excited to go to Alexa's. I realized that while my baby didn't need me anymore, I was still needed. I remembered, with some surprise, that Alexa was living, her babies were living and yes, I was still living, too. The days began to fly. I tried out new recipes to fatten her up (which she promptly threw up), we made crafts (which we hung up in the babies' room), and we talked and talked and talked. Finally we talked about Faith. She listened and asked questions. I smiled as I shared my precious few memories.

And then the one day I was not with her—not by my own choice, but because my husband needed his wife back for a day—the twins were born by emergency C-section, eight weeks early. As soon as I heard the news, I panicked. At barely two pounds each, surely they were too tiny to survive! What if I didn't see them before they died? What if I never got to see a living baby? I cried and begged my husband to drive me to the hospital.

"Our babies might die!" I wailed.

"It's going to be all right," he consoled me, his face white. I am sure he was wondering how he would fix me if this broke me.

By the time I made it to the NICU, to the teeny little incubators that housed their miniscule bodies, I was sure of it. They were dead. I braced myself for what I would see, afraid to look and afraid not to.

"You can hold them if you want." Alexa was standing by my side, hunched uncomfortably over her stapled wound. "Only immediate family is allowed, but I told them you're my sister." She smiled painfully at me. "You are the only person besides Carl and I that are on the list."

It was a privilege, an honor. I knew it. And yet I was afraid. She took out one (which one?), wrapped up tight like a burrito, and placed the whole tiny package in my arms, snaking the wires that were monitoring every sign of life around the chair. Then she stepped back and closed the curtain, leaving the two of us alone. He didn't stir, didn't open his eyes or coo. He was far too young. But he was alive. I could see it pulsing in his translucent skin, vibrating in his sealed eyelids, grasped tightly in his curled fists. "Hold onto it," I whispered, "for every minute is precious." I cried with relief. I realized I got my miracle after all.

I stand on Alexa's doorstep once again. It is a year later, to the very day. The twins' first birthday. They sit, wide-eyed and serious, watching the revelry around them. They cannot know, of course, what a momentous day this is for all of us, how hard so many people—not least of all, their mother—worked to get them to this party. I set my new-born son, Samuel, down in front of them.

"Hi boys. This is Sam. Sam, these are the boys. Be good friends with them, because they helped save my life." The twins smile at Sam as if they recognize him. Divine inspiration. What can you say to that?

Charlotte Andersen

Good Fruit

That the trial of your faith, being much more precious than of gold that perisheth, though it be tried with fire, might be found unto praise and honour and glory at the appearing of Jesus Christ.

1 Pet. 1:7

I was twenty-one years old, standing over my mother and trying desperately to get a response from her. My father had died four years earlier—and even though my parents had separated, I still felt the pain of losing him. Now, with tears streaming down my face, I knew I had just lost my mother as well.

I was so angry with the Lord! Silently, I screamed, *I have lived righteously! My mother was a good woman who brought me to a knowledge of the gospel. Why are you doing this to me? And why are you doing it again?"*

I was heartbroken. I was lonely. And I had just lost my best friend. I can't begin to explain the anger that I felt. In response, I turned my back on the Lord and refused to have anything to do with the Church. I no longer wanted the Holy Ghost as a companion. I figured that I was hurting, so I was going to make my Heavenly Father hurt, too.

A year later, I got a summer job in a local electronics factory between years at college. My boss was a cheerful young man who was well-liked and respected—by others, that is. Of course, I disliked him, because he was so happy. Since I was unhappy, I always tended to surround myself with unhappy people. Eventually, though, we became friends—and he even got me to smile a few times.

Then it happened: He asked me out on a date. I refused, of course—who was I to deserve to feel happy again? From then on, I went totally out of my way to avoid him. But something was happening inside, and I know now that my Heavenly Father was behind it.

At that time, though, I sure didn't recognize His influence. "I don't like him!" I would scream to Heavenly Father. "He's not my type!" But then it happened: Like a bolt out of the blue, I realized that I was in love with him. That scared me: I didn't want to be in love, but in the end the Lord always wins, and I realized I couldn't fight it anymore.

One evening, after a long friendship, he told me that he loved me—and I told him I felt the same way. I knew then that I had to face who I actually was and what I had wanted since I had been a young woman: I wanted to be sealed in the temple for time and all eternity to my eternal companion.

Was he the one?

I finally told him I was a member of the Church of Jesus Christ of Latter-day Saints. I was expecting the usual remarks—in England, Mormons are known as the strange people who won't drink coffee or tea. Instead, he expressed a desire to know more. I then explained that I was still very angry at Heavenly Father, and that I wanted nothing to do with the Church. Still, he wanted to know more.

He asked for the missionaries, and he began taking the discussions. After the final discussion, he was baptized. I couldn't believe it! I was so angry! I didn't want to go back to Church, but I felt I needed to support him, so I slowly became active again.

That was five years ago. We are happily married with two beautiful children, Brandon and Megan. I am so happy that they were both born in the covenant: My husband and I were sealed in the Preston England Temple. I love my family dearly, and I recognize each of them as a blessing from our Heavenly Father.

My husband now serves in the bishopric, and I can honestly say I am happier than I have ever been. I know the Lord works in mysterious ways; I often reflect on the scripture that promises us that even though our trials may be difficult now, they will eventually yield good fruit. My experience is one that helps me remember that whenever I am confronted with trials, I need to turn toward—not away from—my Father in Heaven.

Pamela Coyle

An Ordinary Woman

Who can find a virtuous woman? for her price is far above rubies.

Prov. 31:10

Joan and I were an unlikely pair. She married her high school sweetheart right after high school; I went to college and married my college sweetheart halfway through. She was a homemaker; I am a businesswoman. She did handicrafts; I write. She did not like to entertain; I love to entertain. She had barely ventured outside Utah; I had traveled the world. I loved teaching and speaking; she hated it. She had lived in the same old house for forty years; I moved every ten years. Her husband had the same job for forty years; my husband and I are entrepreneurs. But for some reason, Joan and I clicked the first time we met, and we stayed in touch, no matter where I ventured.

When Bob called and asked, rather angrily, if I had been getting Joan's messages, I knew something was terribly wrong.

Joan and I had been friends for more than twenty-seven

years. We were neighbors for twelve years. Our husbands served in a bishopric together for five years. I had worked with her daughters in Young Women. My husband, Sherm, had worked with her sons in scouting. We'd been fellow Beanie Baby collectors, so much so that I dedicated my bestselling *My Beanie Baby Binder* to her. We never had a family event when Remunds weren't at the top of our guest list, even before family, because, to us, they were family.

Joan and I talked on the phone at least once a week, went to lunch together at least once a month, remembered each other's birthdays and exchanged Christmas gifts. We kept each other posted on our favorite soap opera, neighborhood gossip, family news, the latest Beanie finds, and we read books together. I would never intentionally fail to return her calls.

Bob handed the phone to Joan and she meekly told me that she had a spot of cancer in her lung.

Joan was the type of person who never drew attention to herself, quite the opposite of me, who demanded everyone's attention always. Bob wanted her to tell me about the cancer; she did not want to tell me, or anyone. She did not want to draw attention to herself.

I hate to recall this for fear the very thought somehow affected the end result, but my first thought was, *Joan's going to die.*

Joan had had a persistent cough for some time. When she finally sought medical advice, it was the worst possible news—cancer. And so unfair. Joan had never smoked. *Only people who smoke get and die of lung cancer,* I thought. It was not only unfair, but also illogical.

Joan bravely underwent chemotherapy for six months; after each session, she was violently ill for days. Then she would be well for a few days, which is when we would get together, before the process started all over again.

Bob took time off work to attend every treatment with her. I offered to take his place a time or two, but he wouldn't hear of it. He and Joan had been together since high school. He was not about to leave her side. Fortunately, he had hours of sick leave built up at work.

Joan lost her hair and replaced it with a wig that was so identical to her real hair that I could hardly tell. It made me grateful for the kind and sensitive people who take care of such things for cancer patients. Joan once said, "It's so much easier than doing my real hair that I may shave my head and wear a wig for the rest of my life." I laughed, and then wondered how we could laugh in the face of something as deadly as cancer.

Once chemo ended, radiation began. Another six months. This time Joan didn't get quite as ill, but she was tired all the time and less interested in getting together. We vowed to do better once the radiation ended.

In August 2003, Bob and Joan and Sherm and I went to dinner at Chef's Table to celebrate. The chemo and radiation were over and Joan was cancer-free. We were triumphant and celebrating at the best restaurant in town, our treat. Our friend, owner and chef Kent Andersen, was so happy for us that he hovered over us all evening, wanting to make sure everything was perfect for Joan. It was a delightful evening.

On the first Sunday in September, Joan stood in fast and testimony meeting and announced to her fellow ward members, who had tended her so kindly, that she was cancer-free.

The first of October, I called Joan to tell her that we were headed to New York City to meet our new grandson. Our oldest son, Jayson, and his wife, Cori, had been unable to have children and Joan had mourned with me over the years as they tried and failed and finally decided to adopt. In fact, her oldest daughter, Teressa, who had seven children, had had a surprise pregnancy and I had teased her the whole pregnancy that we would take the baby for Jayson. "Tell Teressa her baby is safe," I said, and Joan and I laughed and laughed. Joan did not tell me that she was not feeling well. She did not want to spoil my joy. And she never drew attention to herself.

Whenever I left town I always called Joan and said, "If I die enroute, remember I loved you most of all." I concluded our conversation with that line and we both chuckled, as we always did.

When we returned from NYC, I immediately called Joan to tell her all about our new grandson. But she did not call me back, which was most unusual for her. She was even better about returning my calls than I was about returning hers.

A few days later, Joan's youngest daughter, Amy, called. "I guess you don't know what's going on," said Amy.

"What do you mean?" I asked.

"Joan's in the hospital in Hawaii."

I had forgotten the whole Remund family had been planning a trip to Hawaii for a year. It was so like Joan not to mention that she was leaving on a trip when I called to tell her that I was leaving on a trip, not wanting to diminish my news, not wanting to draw attention to herself.

"What's wrong?" I asked.

"They're not sure," she replied.

"Is the cancer back?" I asked.

"They don't think so," said Amy. "They think it's pneumonia; she's having a hard time breathing."

"Keep me posted," I said.

"They're going to fly her home Sunday."

"I'll call Monday."

When I called Monday, Teressa answered. "Is Joan there?" I asked.

"No," Teressa answered.

"Is she still in Hawaii?"

"No," Teressa answered more slowly.

"Still enroute?" I asked more anxiously.

"No," Teressa answered.

"At Utah Valley Hospital?" I asked, growing more frantic.

"No, she's gone," Teressa said.

"Gone where?" I almost screamed.

"She passed away yesterday."

I was dumbstruck.

Then I started crying.

I had not expected that. I had expected to visit her. I had expected her to get well. I had expected her to meet my new grandson. I had expected to grow old with her. I had not expected to go on without her.

The next few days were a blur. I was so depressed that I could hardly focus. Though I had lost family and friends before, I had never lost a best friend, a girlfriend. It was a whole new experience for me.

I napped a lot. And dreamt of Joan. I awoke crying her name once, and was slapped in the face with the reality that she is no longer here. I kept thinking of things I needed to tell her, only to realize that I could not. I spent a lot of time talking to Teressa. And calling Bob. Who did not return my calls.

As Joan's oldest, dearest friend, who is also a writer and a speaker, I fully expected to be asked to speak at her funeral, and was not, which hurt me deeply. I wanted to do something. I wanted the whole world to know the Joan I knew. To know how it felt to lose her. I sent a beautiful floral arrangement. It sat on the guest-book table. That was something.

The line at the pre-funeral viewing was long. Bob and the kids worked the line. When Bob reached us, he said, "Come in for the family prayer," which made me feel better. Like family.

When it was finally my turn to approach the casket, I burst into tears and openly wept for several minutes. A lady I did not know watched me, then touched my arm and said, "Bless you." *For what,* I wondered. For missing Joan and not being ashamed to show it? Bless me to survive without her? I needed that blessing.

Joan did not look like Joan. The final illness had left her looking different. She was arrayed in her beautiful temple clothes, wearing her wedding rings and a beautiful silver heart on a chain that I had never seen before.

The funeral was perfect. So many flowers. Such lovely talks and music. I was mentioned twice, which made me feel better.

I went to the funeral thinking I was Joan's best friend. I left the funeral learning that everyone thought they were Joan's best friend, and that was her gift. It humbled me, and I vowed to be a better person, a better friend.

I cried throughout the funeral. Then my cell phone rang in my purse during the closing prayer. I sat on it. While we were walking to the car, my husband, Sherm, said, "Maybe it was Joan calling to tell you to stop crying," which made me laugh and cry all the harder. Oh, that that were possible . . .

We followed the funeral cortege to the cemetery. We were invited to the family lunch at the ward building. Then we left. I had never felt so alone in my life.

Sherm took me to the mall and bought me the same silver heart necklace Joan had been wearing. I wear it nearly every day in remembrance of her.

When we returned home, my three-year-old granddaughter, Halle, called. "I'm sorry your friend Joan died." Whenever I wear my silver necklace, she toys with it and says, "This is for 'membering your friend Joan, right?"

"Right."

Then the holidays came. Thanksgiving. With no Thanksgiving card or note or pumpkin cookies or visit from Joan. Then Christmas. With no Christmas card or note from Joan. No hand-made gift in a gift bag handmade by

Joan. No visit from Joan. No pecan log from Joan. I hung the "Twelve Days of Christmas" cross-stitch Joan had worked on for two years before giving it to me and stood in front of it and cried and cried. I called and called Bob to talk, to ask questions. He never took or returned my calls.

After the holidays, I finally reached Bob and invited him to dinner. He came with my Christmas present from Joan, which made me cry. He had gathered and bound all her recipes and gave them to me. He had copied her funeral program on audiocassette and gave that to me. He had copied her life sketch on CD and we watched it together. He hooked up his digital camera to our TV and showed us his last pictures of Joan, surrounded by her family in Hawaii. Then he told us the story. The story I had been wanting to hear for the past three months.

Joan was pronounced cancer-free in August. Then she started getting sick again. The doctors determined it was the side effects of chemo and radiation. Instead, it was the cancer. Joan had never been cancer-free.

While vacationing in Hawaii, she started having a difficult time breathing. She was hospitalized. She grew worse. She wanted to go home. She would have to be sedated in order to make the trip. And that trip would have to be made on a medical jet with a medical crew, at a cost of $40,000, which Joan did not want to spend, but spent anyway.

The flight went well. When she landed at the Provo airport, an ambulance and crew were waiting to take her to Utah Valley Hospital. She never awoke. She slipped away Sunday afternoon, surrounded by her family.

That was seventeen months ago at this writing. Bob has sold the house he and Joan shared for forty years and built a new home on family property he is developing in Midway. Something he always wanted to do, something Joan never wanted to do. His oldest son, Lynn, built a house next door. The other three children have lots there, too. Bob is busy with kids and grandkids and his development and seems happy but also very much alone.

I had a dream about Joan recently. I visited her in Heaven. She was a greeter at a temple there. Though she was happy to see me, she was busy and referred me to someone else to give me a tour of Heaven. Because I grew up on a farm, I was shown a farm. It was just like the farms here, only perfect. Perfect fences, perfect fields, perfect buildings, happy families working together. Because I work in advertising, I was shown a printing press. It was just like the presses here, only perfect. Clean and organized, perfect printing, happy workers. I was so surprised and so pleased. So pleased to see Joanie happy and busy. So surprised to learn that life goes on as usual in the next life. Only better.

As different as Joan and I were on the outside, we were very much alike on the inside. We loved and served the Lord and our families and our neighbors. The same things that irritated her irritated me; the same things that made her laugh made me laugh. We confided things in each other no one else ever knew. We were like sisters, with none of the negative history.

On the surface, Joan appeared to be an ordinary woman, yet she was one of the most extraordinary women I have ever known. She loved with all her heart, something I have yet to master. She gave her all, something I do, too. But Joan always gave expecting nothing in return, something I am still trying to learn. While I have spent my life on a treadmill to the next achievement, the next accolade, the next acquisition, Joan quietly, meekly walked the path of life, stopping wherever and whenever she was needed for as long as she was needed.

It is that example in my life that I will miss, and emulate 'til we meet again.

Peg Fugal

I Will Pray Every Birthday

And as they looked to behold they cast their eyes towards Heaven, and they saw the Heavens open, and they saw angels descending out of Heaven as it were in the midst of fire; and they came down and encircled those little ones about, and they were encircled about with fire; and the angels did minister unto them.

3 Ne. 17:24

My life was going fairly smoothly—and I was at home taking care of my family, as my husband and I had agreed, while postponing my career as an English teacher. At the time, William was three and Kevin was seven months old. I felt through the Spirit that it was time to welcome another baby into our home, as I had felt with our previous two children; what a privilege to receive these sweet spirits!

Steven was born on March 18, 1994—and when I returned home with my baby boy, I brought with me a chronic disease that would alter my entire life. Because of my genetic code, I had developed a type of arthritis—even though there had been no indication of it earlier, and despite the absence of any medical explanation. The doctors thought for seven years that I had rheumatoid arthritis; finally, with the help of more precise medical examinations, an accurate diagnosis was made three years ago.

Since Steven was born, I have had various symptoms. I have had no use of my legs at all during some periods. Other times I have been unable to use my hands or move my spine. Countless times, my severely damaged knees needed to be drained. I ended up having knee surgery in both knees, had to undergo physiotherapy during the year it took to recover from the surgeries, and I had to quit teaching, which I had resumed.

I suffered two periods of depression due to my low self-esteem. My husband was a handsome professional ballet dancer at the time, and I reached a point of thinking that I was not worthy of the family that Heavenly Father had given me. I always reached out to Heaven through my prayers, and I always had long conversations with my Savior, Jesus Christ, but it was always through my husband and children that the Lord helped me the most.

The love of my husband never failed; whenever I wasn't able to do something, he filled in for me and walked the second mile. My children never complained when I was unable to cook and they had to eat cereal or simple snacks and sandwiches. When tears were rolling down my cheeks, they were always there to say kind words of loving comfort. It was hard when I couldn't move to serve the ones I love, but life eventually taught me that I don't necessarily have to move to serve. Instead, I need to "move" my heart and put it to work with sincere love.

I have learned that such love goes both ways. In 2001 on my son Kevin's birthday, he blew out the candles on his birthday cake and made a wish, as is the tradition in our family. As he blew out the candles, I felt through the Spirit that his wish concerned me. He smiled at me with such a look of love, and I knew he was pleading with the Lord that I would get well. He has been making the same wish ever since then. One time he whispered, "Mom, I prayed to Heavenly Father just now to ask Him to cure you—and I will ask the same thing on all my birthdays for the rest of my life until He does it." I felt such a strong presence of the Holy Spirit, testifying to me of the power of love and of the holiness of that simple act.

Since then I have started a new treatment at a local hospital, and I'm getting better than I have been. I testify that I'm getting better in great part due to the faith of my son—and, above all, as a result of the miracle of the Savior's love.

Alexandra Domingues

Collective Faith and a Priesthood Blessing

The power and authority of the higher, or Melchizedek Priesthood, is to hold the keys of all the spiritual blessings of the church . . .

D&C 107:18

I squinted at the gray screen, trying to make out the tiny arms and legs as the doctor expertly pointed to each appendage. I was only eight weeks' pregnant, so determining the baby's gender was out of the question, but I was thrilled to see the tiny heart pounding out a snappy rendition of "Jingle Bells." *How appropriate,* I thought. It was Christmas Eve, and I could think of no better present than seeing the gift of life on my doctor's computer screen.

As my husband and I hurried from the doctor's office, the cold clear air sent us quickly to the car. We had a little last-minute shopping to do, so we headed into the heavy traffic of downtown Salt Lake City. We drove several blocks to the nearest strip mall. We wanted to get home to the kids so that we could spend the afternoon together. Kira was thirteen and certainly capable of babysitting her five siblings, but still, we didn't like to be away too long.

We made our way through the store, looking for something to fill the blanks on our shopping list. Before we had time to find anything suitable, my cellular phone rang. I pulled it from my pocket and punched the button. "Hi," I began. I knew it was the kids, because no one else had that number.

Eleven-year-old Neal was hysterical. "Calm down," I nearly shouted. "What's wrong?"

I heard Kira grab the phone. She was sobbing, "I'm so sorry, Mom . . . Kiy was in the tub . . . she turned blue . . . she wasn't breathing. . . ." I was suddenly hysterical. What was she telling me? My sweet, blonde, fifteen-month-old girl was *where*? My hands were shaking so badly I nearly dropped the phone. Suddenly, the soothing voice of one of South Jordan's finest came on the phone.

"Ma'am? Listen to me." I tried to calm down. How could I be calm when they were telling me I'd just lost my baby? "Are you alone?"

"No," I managed to choke out. "My husband is with me."

"We want the two of you to drive carefully to Primary Children's Hospital. Where are you?"

"We're downtown," I managed. "We could be there in just a few minutes."

"Settle down and drive slowly. We're bringing your baby in on Life Flight. You'll get there before we do."

That trip to the hospital was the longest one I have ever taken. I screamed, I cried, I tore my hair. Why did we leave her home? When we finally arrived, I was a basket case. Kiylee was not at the hospital yet, and no one knew anything about her condition. It was about thirty minutes before we finally heard the helicopter. Moments later, we were allowed in the emergency room. Kiy was bloated and covered with wires and tubes. She was ice cold, but she was breathing. Yes, she was still breathing.

She was transferred quickly to the pediatric intensive-care unit and was attached to all kinds of monitors. The doctors sat down with us and told us to be realistic. They didn't think she would die at this point as long as they could warm her up carefully. The first twenty-four hours were critical, but if she made it through, we still had the possibility of brain damage or even physical damage. I didn't care. I hugged her as carefully as I could, kissed her and sobbed her name. She was still alive, and I could think of no better gift than to see the gift of life on the PICU's monitors.

We sat with her most of the night. We couldn't touch her because it would modify her temperature. I'd never felt so helpless in my life. My grandmother came to stay with our other children. They all agreed that Christmas would wait until our little Kiy could come home and share it with us. The morning's trip to the doctor and our wonderful news of the successful ultrasound for our seventh child seemed a lifetime away.

Christmas morning dawned beautifully, even for us in the PICU. Other parents were there, sharing Christmas morning with their sick and dying little ones. Santa Claus came and brought some gifts and candy, and I couldn't help wondering if Kiy would ever be able to play with the little stuffed animals or eat the gingerbread.

Toward noon, our doctor came in to check on Kiy. We were all exhausted and hoping for good news. She was still under anesthesia and full of tubes and wires. Her tiny face was swollen from the IV, a respirator covered her mouth and nose, and heart monitors dotted her little chest. The doctor picked her up and stood her right up on her feet. She moaned and opened her eyes. The doctor paused for only a moment, then he said with conviction,

"She's going to be fine, but plan on her being here at least a week."

We were thrilled! No one knew how long she was underwater, and with the risk of infection, she could have stayed at the hospital for weeks with respiratory problems or pneumonia. Friends and family were completely supportive with prayers, hugs and food. Their collective faith and a priesthood blessing brought her home far earlier than the doctor thought was possible. Forty-eight hours later, Kiy was ready to go home. It was nothing short of a miracle.

Christmas morning dawned bright and early for us on December 27, 1997. The sounds of paper tearing and happy voices were never more appreciated. Kiy sat weakly on my lap and carefully opened her packages. I gave her a little squeeze and blinked back the tears. I could think of no better gift than to see the gift of life . . . our little Kiylee, wrapped in a warm quilt from the hospital, snuggled in my lap on Christmas day.

Sandy Christensen

Heaven Was So Close

I will both lay me down in peace, and sleep: for thou, LORD, only makest me dwell in safety.

Ps. 4:8

Life had always been a little different for me, but it was about to be turned upside down—and I didn't even know it. I was busily involved in preparing for my wedding, which was due to take place in December 2002. My fiancé had flown in from Utah, and we were enjoying the time that we were spending together—even if it was filled with wedding-dress fittings, flower selection and all the other frills that go along with a wedding.

It was a normal October evening, and I had gone to bed, but found myself unable to sleep because of a pain in my neck; eventually, I did manage to get to sleep. I awoke the next morning still not feeling well. I mentioned my difficulty sleeping to my mother and fiancé; it was then that they noticed that my neck was very swollen on one side. We called the doctor but were unable to arrange an appointment, so we decided I should probably go to the emergency department at my local hospital. When I arrived, they gave me some medication, as my temperature was dangerously high. The doctor was unable to determine what was wrong with me, and sent me home.

Later the following week, I could feel pressure on the front of my throat, and noticed that the swelling had spread to the front of my neck. We made an emergency appointment with our family doctor. I was admitted to the hospital right away, as there was danger of my windpipe collapsing. In the hospital, numerous unpleasant tests were run to try to discover what the problem was. Fluid was drawn from my neck and sent for biopsy; it was a painful procedure, but my mother and fiancé were with me through it all.

Months passed, and repeated biopsies were taken to try to determine if the mass in my neck was cancerous. Each time, the results came back as being inconclusive.

As my wedding day drew nearer, we decided to postpone the wedding; I was sick, and we thought it was probably better to wait. Christmas came and went; it was a wonderful time with my family and fiancé there with me, and we were almost able to forget what the future might have in store. January arrived all too quickly, and it was almost time for him to leave and fly back home. We decided I would fly to Utah with him so that I could have a break before the surgery I was scheduled to undergo.

A couple of days before we were due to leave, I had to have one final test—a scan, during which more fluid would be drawn from the front of my throat. The next day I received a telephone call from the doctor who was to perform my surgery; he told me not to go to Utah, as there was a danger that the tumor in my neck would collapse my windpipe. He also told me I needed to prepare myself for the fact that the tumor might well be cancerous. My fiancé had to leave without me—and I had no idea that it would be the last time I would ever see him.

Over the next few weeks I spent most of my time thinking about how I was supposed to come to terms with the fact that, at the age of twenty-seven, I might have cancer. Throughout it all, I tried desperately to hide the fear I felt from my family and friends.

My surgery was scheduled for a Monday. A stake fast had been organized on my behalf and was due to start the Sunday evening before the surgery. It was such a humbling experience to think that there were people who were willing to fast for me. I had never been so scared in my life; the prospect of having the surgery was the most terrifying thing I had ever faced, and I found myself unable to cope with the prospects that awaited me. I spent most of the day crying; I couldn't hide it any longer. Then my miracle happened: The stake fast began.

I don't know how many people fasted for me, but regardless of whether it was five or five hundred, the Lord truly heard their prayers. I have never experienced anything like it in my life. Every bit of fear that I had felt left me; I was totally at peace. I slept better than I had in months. The next morning I awoke and drove to the hospital with my parents. I don't remember much about that morning, but what I will always remember are the feelings that I had inside. It is difficult to find words to describe it! There is no doubt that when I needed Him most, the Savior carried me! I could literally feel myself being carried. I knew that no matter what the outcome of the surgery, everything would be okay, that I wasn't alone and that I never had been. Heaven was so close that day that I felt I could easily reach out and feel the Savior's hand.

The surgery was a little more complicated than was expected, because the tumor was larger than the doctors had initially thought, but they were able to remove it successfully. Although I was in pain and had a lot of bruising, I had never felt more peaceful at any point in my life. I didn't want the feeling to ever end.

After two weeks of waiting, I learned that the tumor was benign.

Not long after that, my fiancé ended our engagement. A month later, my grandmother, to whom I was extremely close, passed away unexpectedly.

I have learned that life doesn't always turn out the way that we plan, or even the way we want it to. I am still single at the age of twenty-nine, but I am single with an even stronger testimony of a loving Heavenly Father who will never leave me alone. When there are things that are difficult to come to terms with, I know I can turn them over to the Lord. We are His, and He will always remind us of that at the times we need it the most.

My life has changed so much from that happy holiday spent with my family, but it is okay. I am His, and He will carry me when I need Him to. There is nothing I wouldn't give to experience once more the feelings I had that day as a result of faithful members who fasted on my behalf.

I learned that each of us has an inner power that we can hold on to, and that power is the knowledge that the gospel of Jesus Christ brings. We are part of a great and perfect plan, and each of us has a unique role within it. I have felt the peace that can be ours when we come to that knowledge, and I will be eternally grateful for it. There is nothing we cannot overcome with the help of the Lord.

Kirsty Hale

There Were People Praying

Wherefore it came to pass that my father, Lehi,
as he went forth prayed unto the Lord, yea, even
with all his heart, in behalf of his people.

1 Ne. 1:5

We were your typical LDS couple, married for less than a year and already expecting our first baby. We were ecstatic and joyful as we waited for our little boy to make his arrival. Based on how big I had gotten, we knew he'd be a handful, but little did we know what the Lord had in store for us. . . .

Andrew James Abbott arrived on June 5, 2001, after a long, difficult labor. After three hours of pushing, my doctor decided Andrew was not going to come out nature's way, so we proceeded with a cesarean section. As the medical team lifted him out, I had five seconds of pure joy seeing his beautiful face for the first time. That was followed by 119 days of unbelievable pain, grief and shock as we struggled to keep him alive.

He was floppy and gray at birth, nearly unresponsive. He was rushed to the neonatal intensive-care unit, where they began a battery of tests to determine what was wrong with our baby. He had a few stable hours before things grew very serious. He was then taken to the operating room, where the surgeon discovered that all of his large bowel and 75 percent of his small intestine had been attacked by aggressive bacteria—and had to be removed. He was near death as the bacteria shut down his liver, kidneys, lungs and heart. We were horrified at this turn of events. I was now facing the prospect of selecting a funeral home instead of birth announcements. I've never felt such pain or sadness.

Several doctors told us we'd need to decide if or when we wanted to withdraw the life support that was keeping him alive. Was he suffering? If we kept at it, what quality of life would he have? Our bishop gave us permission to give him a name and blessing right there in the NICU. As my husband laid his hands on our precious baby's head, the Holy Spirit confirmed to him that Andrew was a very special child of our Heavenly Father and his mission here on Earth may indeed be very short. We opted to keep the life support going and leave it in God's hands. It was the best decision we've ever made. He survived his ordeal and has taught us more about gratitude and compassion than any book or lesson ever could.

Andrew was in the NICU for 119 days. He was on and off life support, and endured nine surgeries, unending pain and thousands of blood draws. He also required twenty-three blood transfusions, because his own blood was so toxic from the bacteria and its by-products.

I won't lie and say that I never lost faith. I did. At times I questioned why God would allow this to happen to my sweet, innocent baby. At times, I prayed for God to let him die, let his suffering end. What kind of God would let this drag on for four months?

I'll tell you what kind of God would do it: our Heavenly Father. He has unending wisdom, and His plan for each of us is not haphazard or random. He knows our needs. He knew that our baby needed to come to Earth to teach our family, our ward and the world about the strength of prayer and faith. You see, even when I was weak, curled up in a fetal position and so sad I didn't want to be alive anymore, there were people praying for our miracle baby. There were people in holy temples who had faith in our Lord and who knew of our son. Word spread all across the country—people in our home ward called everyone they knew and asked them to fast and pray, and they did.

My visiting teachers never failed. They visited me at least once every week as I sat by Andrew's isolette. They brought me healthy snacks because they knew I wasn't eating. They prayed with me and for me. They cried with me. I felt the love of our Savior through these sisters. I will never forget all the kind acts that were bestowed upon us.

Ultimately, Andrew defied all the odds. He is now three years old—and unless you lift up his shirt, you'd never guess there was ever anything wrong. He was on IV nutrition and tube feedings for two years, but now eats a regular diet by mouth. He is tall and stocky and smarter than his old mom! He runs and talks and sings and smiles and lights up the world with his energy. Every medical professional that knows his story is amazed. His odds of survival were next to zero. His odds of being a "normal" kid WERE zero. But here he is, as normal as he can be. He goes to preschool, he colors outside of the lines and he loves to kiss his new healthy baby brother.

People ask me all the time, "What did you do? How did he turn out so great?" As if I had something to do with it. . . . It was purely God's grace. He is the result of sincere prayer and faith. He is a walking miracle, and I have the unbelievable joy of spending each day with him. Through him, Heavenly Father has given our family gratitude that defies description.

Heather Abbott

To the Very Core of My Soul

But Jesus turned him about, and when he saw her, he said, Daughter, be of good comfort; thy faith hath made thee whole. And the woman was made whole from that hour.

Matt. 9:22

Sophomore year of high school, fifteen years old, a time for fun and youthful memories.

I was optimistic and excited about life!

Things soon changed for me when during a fall volley-ball practice, while simply bending to pick up a volleyball, a sharp pain in my back brought me to my knees. This event was followed by regular acute backaches and pains that would leave me in tears, and laid up, unable to move for the remainder of that year. Each time I had an acute back spasm I would wonder what was happening to my back. Why was I experiencing so much pain?

The acute back pain was frequent and severe; it consumed that entire year. Despite a first doctor's opinion of "muscle tightness" and prescribed muscle relaxants, the only relief I ever experienced was laying in bed with my knees up. Instead of doing fun teenage things, sometimes I would spend hours, days, attempting to relieve my back pain.

I was convinced there was something I could do to help myself or to fix my back. I remember one Saturday walking to a friend's house for a girls' fun afternoon. Carrying a bag full of stuff, I counted every ten steps I took and switched hands so my back wouldn't lean to one side too much. Relieved, I arrived at her home without incident, only to sit on her bed and to be gripped with another attack of acute pain. I was so depressed! It seemed no matter what I did, nothing was making my back better; the pain seemed endless.

That summer, instead of spending fun days doing things I loved—jogging, hanging out, going out on the weekends, playing outdoor sports—I spent a lot of time at home, laying on my back, watching TV, but also spending time with my younger sister Elizabeth.

It was also during this summer I had time to consider a more spiritual aspect to my pain.

My father had given me a blessing earlier that spring with a promise that I would heal and the pain would subside and I would be made whole. I believed that I would; if I had enough faith and was worthy of the blessings, my back would heal and I wouldn't have the excruciating pain—I would be whole again.

However, no matter what I did, or didn't do, I continued to have aches and overwhelmingly painful back spasms. Even at girls' camp that summer I had another of these acute attacks of pain, and another priesthood blessing— that the pain would subside, my back would heal and I would be made whole. I began to become so confused: Was I not worthy to be healed? Was my faith not strong enough? What more could I do to help myself?

My junior year of high school began a new struggle: a struggle to find the Lord and discover why my faith was not strong enough to make me whole.

While I was wrestling with my thoughts, we continued to pursue medical relief. A second opinion found a condition called spondylolisthesis. An X-ray discovered two fractures of the lower vertebrae, a condition the doctor proclaimed he usually only saw in geriatric patients. He gave me a list of exercises and stretches that I could do to strengthen my back, combined with physical therapy. However, he laid an emotional bomb: He also told me that I should not jog, play volleyball, or any other sport that involved bending or twisting of my back. He said too that I would not be able to carry a child to full term because my back would not be able to handle the weight. If I were ever to get pregnant, I would have to remain in bedrest for the majority of the pregnancy. I was sixteen years old, and I had just been told that my life as I had known it and loved it would never, and could never, be the same. The things that I enjoyed, and looked forward to—even pregnancy—were no longer an option.

However, I had the optimism of youth. The doctor knew what was wrong and how to fix it. I followed his program meticulously for months, but was continually plagued with the acute attacks of pain. After all my diligent efforts brought no relief from pain, I found myself more emotionally lost than ever. The only difference these months had produced was not physical, but spiritual; I had begun a change of heart.

We were studying the Book of Mormon in seminary that year and I loved it! I looked forward to the emotional relief that the Spirit of the Book of Mormon provided in a time of physical and emotional agony. I found solace in the words of Christ as He appeared to the Nephites; as he blessed them, taught them and healed them. However, I still felt personal inadequacies; I felt that I lacked the faith, because if I had faith, then my back would heal.

Several blessings later, and after many days of pain and tears, we found another doctor, who offered a third opinion. An MRI revealed two herniated discs surrounding my fractured vertebrae, and these herniations were pinching the nerves, which caused the acute attacks of pain. The doctor scheduled surgery and that March, I began the healing process. I wore a back brace, which I affectionately referred to as my plastic milk jug, for several months after surgery, even to my junior prom and through the beginning of my senior year.

The summer before I left for college at BYU I received the final clearance from my doctor that I was completely healed. I could jog, play volleyball, do anything I wanted—and even have babies! Three years of suffering had finally come to an end.

As a young college student, in retrospect I saw so much good that came from this experience. Being a high-school invalid kept me home to grow closer to my family. It also brought me closer to my Savior through the need I felt for spiritual relief from my physical and emotional anguish.

But still, I had a lot of confusion in my heart. Why had it taken almost three years for a blessing to be fulfilled? During a discussion with a college friend, relating this intense test of faith, I shared with him that when my physical pain and heartache was so intense that I couldn't handle it one day longer, I had finally found a doctor who could save me from my pain and suffering. My friend offered that this was no coincidence.

The Savior knows our breaking point. He knows when we can't take it any longer; He will take us to that point— but no further. And He will bring us back. And He did. But it wasn't until I looked back on those three years of my life that I realized it. I had faith that the first blessing my father gave me would come to pass; what I didn't realize was that it was in the Lord's own time and according to His will. It wasn't that I was not worthy or that my faith was not strong enough—on the contrary! It was simply that the test was not over. The Lord was aware of my pain, and he was aware of the blessing I was promised through the priesthood. But it was in His own time and in His own way that the blessing and my prayers would be answered. I wanted the pain to be taken away the first day I experienced it, and I wanted to do it myself—by myself with my own work.

But the Lord knew me better than I knew myself, and neither was it time for that healing to occur, nor could I do it alone. I needed to exercise my faith, increase my testimony and humble myself to the very core of my soul so I could learn to depend on Him, place all faith in Him and place my life in His hands. I could no more save myself from my pain physically than I can save myself spiritually. The Lord intervened in my life specifically, like He has done for all of us through the atonement. He did for me what I could not do for myself. And if I have faith in him, all blessings promised to me by the Holy Priesthood will come to pass, in His own time.

Shelley Ball Andrus

Reprinted by permission of Patrick Bagley ©2004.

8

PRAYER

Praying always that they faint not; and inasmuch as they do this, I will be with them even unto the end.

D&C 75:11

Better than Bedtime Checklists

And they shall also teach their children to pray, and to walk uprightly before the Lord.

D&C 68:28

Getting the kids to bed every night, and getting them to stay in bed, was a very difficult chore for me. We would begin early, but it would take hours for them to settle down. By that time I was too tired to enjoy the company of my loving husband.

I decided to get organized, and I came up with a Bedtime Checklist. I even got the kids to help me with it. We had everything on this checklist from putting toys away to getting a good-night kiss. We had it all.

Each night, we started at the top of the list, checking things off as we went and making sure everything was done so there would be no excuses for getting up after getting into bed.

It worked in theory, but *not* in practice. There was always one more drink, one more trip to the bathroom because of the drink, and so on.

Then one night Marty and I were reading one of the Church magazines, and we saw an article on prayer. The article said that we should have family prayer every morning and *evening*! Wow! I knew that, but we were not doing it.

We tried it the next night. After family prayer, we went from room to room, tucking in the kids and listening to their individual prayers. As soon as we were done, there was silence. I couldn't believe my ears. The kids were all asleep.

The Bedtime Checklist went into the trash can. Prayer works!

Barbara Hausen

Wrestling with the Lord in Lake Simcoe

*But verily God hath heard me; he hath attended
to the voice of my prayer.*

Ps. 66:19

It was amidst the waves of Lake Simcoe that I first
learned how to pray for a result and obtain it.

Before becoming an independent branch, the Korean
group from our stake in Toronto held an annual family and
friends campout on the second-to-last long weekend of
the summer. My wife is native South Korean and one of
the first Korean members of the Church to live in Toronto,
so, naturally, we attended whenever we could.

Let there be no mistake: This is not an adventure story.
This wasn't wilderness camp by any means. In the public
campground at Lake Simcoe, well-paved roads lead to carefully cropped fields surrounded by controlled tree growth,
providing several spaces for individual and group camp-
sites. There is running water and electricity at the camp.
Brother Park always strung up so many wires for lights, rice
cookers and radios that the area around his tents looked

more like a Christmas display than a campsite.

Camp activities were well planned. Sunday included church services and gospel-centered fun. The last day of camp included group competitions and sports. Among the more spontaneous events over the weekend were hiking, crawfish hunting and swimming.

One year a group of us were swimming on Saturday afternoon. The campground had a large beach with demarcated swimming areas of various depths. On that day the beach was crowded; the sun was warm and the water refreshing. Waves lapped steadily. Children and adults who were laughing, leaping and splashing seemed to cover every inch of sand and water.

I was out in the water some distance with my children, David and Hannah, and our friends, Alma (an Iranian-born member who always tagged along with the Korean group) and his son David, when we heard that one of the boys had lost his glasses in the water. Apparently the glasses had been in the pocket of his trunks until just a few minutes earlier.

Had it not also been pathetic, it would have been humorous to see us all carefully charting every inch of the swimming area to see if we could find the glasses. But with the number of people swimming and the constant flow of the current, the glasses would have been quickly carried off or sifted deep under the churning sand. Our efforts seemed unpromising.

I had lost a pair of glasses in a lake once, and I sympathized with the boy. It would be expensive for his family to replace them, and the loss would limit his enjoyment of the weekend. So we kept searching.

As we searched, most of us were uttering simple, silent prayers that we might find his glasses; still, our efforts seemed to be to no avail.

It occurred to me then that I ought to pray harder and

really mean it. I closed my eyes and said, "Heavenly Father, surely you can help us find these glasses. Please show me where they are." Images of the areas we had already searched passed through my mind, but I felt certain about none of them. I continued, "Father, you have parted the Red Sea and guided people safely through. Surely, this is a small thing to ask."

I began to feel in my imagination somewhat like the Old Testament patriarchs who would, as the scriptures say, "wrestle" with the Lord to obtain His blessing. At the very least, I was reasoning with Him, trying to give Him all the reasons I could think of that it should be a simple thing for Him to grant this request.

I continued to pray in that manner for several minutes, recommencing my prayer at least five times—and, each time after I finished a prayer, waiting for some kind of answer. Strangely, while I was actively searching for the glasses I felt more and more feeble and uncertain—but while I prayed I felt only bolder, more confident and more faithful.

Finally, at the conclusion of what I think was the fifth prayer, I saw a clear image in my mind of the large podium in the swimming area that marks where the "deep end" begins. I felt that it was possible the glasses were there. I turned immediately and walked toward it. One, two, three steps, and suddenly something hard and thin was under my feet. I grappled at it gently with my toes, then bent down and picked it up. There were the boy's glasses. They had been barely covered by the sand, but ready to slip away forever. I lifted them first gingerly and then triumphantly, and thankfully held them overhead.

This was a minor miracle on any scale, but the experience illustrated to me how the exertions of our faith can qualify us for the miracles we desire. I have since had other occasions to seek the Lord's help in more serious matters. I now have a better understanding of how willingly He answers, how ready He is to give us the good things that we desire, and how fervently He wants us to try our faith and exert our wills to approach and obtain His grace.

Michael Clifton

To Bless a Patriarch

I have seen his ways, and will heal him: I will lead him also, and restore comforts unto him and to his mourners.

Isa. 57:18

Since September 1999, our stake patriarch, Harvey Lee Smith, and I have served each Thursday in the Oakland California Temple—Brother Smith as a temple sealer, and I as the shift coordinator. The weekly commute from our homes in Oroville, California, takes six hours of driving time—which, combined with our eight hours at the temple, gets us back home at about nine o'clock in the evening.

After several years of serving in this capacity, the trip started becoming rather taxing for the patriarch, who was more than eighty years old. As I got Brother Smith home at the conclusion of one such trip to the temple, he suffered a stroke. He was unaware of the seriousness of the injury that now rendered his right arm and leg powerless. Throughout the night, unable to sleep, he tried to regain use of his right side.

In the morning, his wife quickly realized that something was amiss, since Brother Smith was using his left hand to eat his breakfast and his speech was slurred. She insisted that he see a doctor immediately, and so drove him to the emergency room at our local hospital.

Upon completing a battery of tests, the ER physicians explained to the couple what had happened to Brother Smith—and that because of the amount of time since the stroke had occurred, they were unable to treat him with the clot-dissolving drugs that might have prevented the paralysis which he was now experiencing. Instead, doctors told the couple to return to the hospital if his symptoms worsened, and he was released from the hospital.

Sister Smith called me at 11:30 A.M. as they arrived back home. She described the ordeal they had just endured, and relayed the patriarch's wishes that I might stop by in the evening to give him a blessing. I assured her that I would get another brother to assist me in performing the ordinance, and we would meet them at six o'clock that evening.

As I hung up the telephone, I was completely overwhelmed by the task now before me. Here was the temple sealer and stake patriarch who had pronounced a patriarchal blessing upon me and upon my family members—and who had also used the sealing power of the priesthood to bind my family together throughout the eternities—asking me to give him a blessing.

I called another member of our high priest group, receiving a commitment from him to meet me at the patriarch's home that evening and then retired to my bedroom. Dropping to my knees, I opened my heart to our Father in Heaven. I pleaded with Him that I might be receptive to the will of the Father and to the promptings of the Spirit, and that His will might be manifest in the blessing that I was to deliver.

As soon as I finished my prayer, I was overcome with a

prompting that I needed to call the hospital where the patriarch had been treated. Before asking for help in being sensitive to the Spirit's promptings, I had had no such feelings—but now I was consumed with the need to contact the hospital.

The clerk at the hospital's information desk transferred my call to the emergency room, since that's where Brother Smith had been treated earlier that morning. I inquired about the patriarch and was put on hold as the clerk checked the records for him. In a few moments the clerk returned to the phone, excitedly reporting that Harvey Smith had just come through the door of the ER seeking help.

I raced to the hospital, arriving in fewer than five minutes, and met Sister Smith in the emergency waiting room. She told me that the patriarch had suffered another stroke and that he was much worse than before. While I sat visiting with her, the thought came to me that Sister Smith didn't seem surprised at my sudden appearance in the ER. (I later learned that she had left a note for me on her front door in anticipation of my 6 P.M. arrival, and she had assumed that I had gone to her home early and had seen her note.)

Telephoning another ward member, I asked that he meet us in the ER as soon as he could. About twenty minutes later, the doctors allowed Sister Smith, the other ward member and me into the exam room as they were completing the neurological tests to determine the extent of Brother Smith's injuries.

We watched as the doctors cataloged the many deficits their patient now exhibited: extremely slurred speech and a complete loss of strength throughout his right side. As they completed their tests, they stepped from the room for a few moments. While they were gone, the brother with me anointed the patriarch, after which I sealed the anointing and pronounced a blessing upon him.

One of the doctors returned to Brother Smith's bedside within about four minutes to find him speaking coherently. The doctor then began retesting the patriarch and found that he had regained most of the strength and use of both his right arm and leg.

Patriarch Smith continued to improve during the following weeks, regaining all that had been lost in the two strokes that he had suffered.

I, in turn, spent those weeks in prayerful gratitude to my Heavenly Father for answering my prayer. For although I had pled for help in being sensitive to the promptings of the Holy Spirit in hopes of ascertaining the Father's will during the impending blessing, He had answered my prayer far sooner than I had imagined. He knew that the patriarch needed His help sooner than I had arranged to provide it.

The Lord has promised us that He will take an active, day-to-day involvement in our daily lives if we will give regular temple service. It has been four years since we were blessed to experience the fulfilling of that wonderful promise. Patriarch Smith continues to travel with me weekly, though each trip still entails him leaving home before sun-up and returning long after dark.

Douglas Scofield

The Lord Will Provide

Then shall ye call upon me, and ye shall go and pray unto me, and I will hearken unto you.

Jer. 29:12

I was too proud to ask for a handout. Our cupboards contained only some miscellaneous grains and our fridge had little more than condiments, so naturally our three small children were getting bored with the meals I fixed. But our paucity was wearing on me, causing my temper to be short—and their complaints only frustrated me all the more.

We weren't entirely destitute; we had a home and my husband had a decent job. But we had more expenses than we had income, and in an attempt to keep our promises to our creditors and to keep me home as the primary caregiver to our children, our grocery bill repeatedly ended up last on the priority list.

Finally, I realized that I needed to take the opportunity to teach my children something about faith. I asked them to join me for a prayer, telling them that we should ask

Heavenly Father to provide. If they wanted better food, they needed to stop asking me for it and put up their petition to the Lord Himself.

We knelt down in the entryway of our home next to the kitchen. My oldest was probably about five years old, and each of the children seemed eager to give it a try. I tried not to doubt; in fact, I found myself relying on their purely innocent faith, hoping the Lord would answer their prayers in spite of my own negativity. How would He answer them? I had no idea.

We took turns, each of us expressing the desire of our hearts. I spoke first, demonstrating the proper pattern of prayer. "Heavenly Father, thank thee for all that thou hast blessed us with. We come before thee now to ask thee to please bless us to have better food . . ." I explained why we needed it, and that we were simply trying to do the right thing in keeping our bills paid and keeping me home. Then I closed my petition, "in the name of the Lord, Jesus Christ, Amen."

After we were done, I reminded them to believe and to trust God. Inside I pleaded with Him that He would answer their prayers—not so much for the food we needed, but for the testimony that He lives and that He is there for us, something that would serve them throughout their lives.

How grateful—and amazed—we were when a few hours later our good bishop showed up at our doorstep with bags of groceries that he had personally brought from the Bishop's Storehouse. He had asked me days earlier if we needed it, and I had told him no. Nevertheless, there he stood. And, tearfully, we accepted. My children will always remember that experience, and how timely his arrival was.

We no longer want for groceries. I have since discovered how dependable the blessings of the Lord can be when we live in harmony with His laws. Heavenly Father has since helped us find the way to keep our bills paid and keep me home with the six children we now have. For as we know, "the Lord giveth no commandments unto the children of men, save he shall prepare a way for them that they may accomplish the thing which he commandeth them" (1 Nephi 3:7).

Through that experience I learned that pride can sometimes get in the way of our needs being met. The good news is that even when it does, the Lord knows just how to turn the situation into something that can bless the lives and strengthen the faith of everyone involved. It strengthened not only me, but my children and the bishop himself, as he realized how perfectly he had been an instrument in God's hands. It was his privilege and our blessing that he was the messenger sent to answer our prayers that day.

Leslie Householder

We Forgot to Pray

And again, O God, when I did turn to my house thou didst hear me in my prayer.

Alma 33:6

My grandparents always gave me and each of my brothers and sisters twenty dollars for our birthdays. My brother and sister share a birthday, and my mother was going to take them toy shopping when she realized she was missing her wallet, which had the money in it.

Mom put my little brother in his stroller, and we started looking for the wallet. We looked all over the neighborhood. Suddenly I stopped.

"Mommy," I said, "we forgot to pray."

Mom took us back to the house, where we asked Heavenly Father for help. We went to look again, but we still couldn't find the wallet. When we returned to the house, Mom got a phone call. A lady down the street had found Mom's wallet in the middle of the road; she had looked through the wallet to find out whom it belonged to.

I know that Heavenly Father answers our prayers, because He answered the prayers of little children who were looking for a wallet.

Laura Denhalter

Pick Up the Phone

Learn of me, and listen to my words; walk in the meekness of my Spirit, and you shall have peace in me.

D&C 19:23

I've been taught that in order for the Lord to answer my prayers, I need to think the problem out in my mind and go to the Lord with a solution. If what I have decided is right, then I will receive a confirmation of the Spirit. That confirmation may come through a burning in my bosom or a feeling of peace. If I don't get my "answer," then I need to rethink the situation and go back to Him again. I've learned that sometimes it really doesn't matter whether I move to Boise or Virginia Beach, because the Lord can use me wherever I am—but that other times there are definite right or wrong choices.

At one point in my life I was seeking the answers to a serious problem. I had prayed about it and felt like I knew what direction I should take. On one particular Sunday, I went to the Lord again to confirm my decision.

"Heavenly Father, please help me to hear something today that will help me know that my decision is right," I pleaded.

I was Young Women's president at the time, and we had a problem that seemed to affect more than one of our girls. We had a leader who had overcome this problem, and I had asked her to speak to the girls about it. As I sat in the audience and heard her talk about how important it is to love ourselves and to expect respect from others, I received the answer I needed. Her topic had nothing to do with my problem, and I don't remember exactly what she said, but her words seemed to be spoken directly to me. I felt a burning in my bosom and clarity of thought. I knew that the Lord had given me the confirmation I needed, and I could hardly contain my excitement. The Lord was speaking directly to me!

The information presented to you may not have anything to do with what you need to hear. The important thing is that the Lord will speak to you, and if you are prepared to hear, you will receive the answers you need. However, I know that the whisperings of the Spirit often come so quietly that if we're not paying attention, we'll miss them entirely.

The voice of the Spirit is referred to as that "still, small voice." We refer to our prayers as "cries for help," and that's truly what they are. We cry out to the Lord, hoping He will answer us before we get off our knees. Unlike the parent who may brush a child away because he or she doesn't want to be interrupted right then, our Heavenly Father always has time for us. We speak to Him in our prayers; He speaks to us through the scriptures and through the Holy Ghost. But why do we think our work is done once we've uttered the prayer? Why bother to ask the question if we're not going to listen for the answer?

The Lord is there to lead and guide us. Too many times

He can't get through because of our cluttered lives. Like the cell phone commercial, I'm sure He tires of saying, "Can you hear me now?" After awhile, the connection is lost, and it's not because He hung up on us, but because we never answered the phone.

Joyce Moseley Pierce

Hymns During the Hurricane

And by day have I waxed bold in mighty prayer before him; yea, my voice have I sent up on high; and angels came down and ministered unto me.

2 Ne. 4:24

The Lord truly knows our individual needs and answers our prayers. We joined the Church of Jesus Christ of Latter-day Saints years ago, and were blessed with a beautiful daughter and two handsome sons. All three of our children love the Lord, and our two sons both served missions for our Savior. Our youngest son left the comforts of home in 2003 to serve in Virginia—and shortly after he arrived there, his experience with hurricanes began.

We will never forget September of 2003, when Mark was serving in an area near the Atlantic coast. The hurricanes were threatening the area where he was serving, and we watched every development on The Weather Channel. I was getting more frantic by the hour. I had faith that he was in a safe place; there was no doubt that the mission president was busy evacuating missionaries away from areas of danger. Still, my heart was troubling me. "Where is my child?" I asked in prayer.

As the storms approached Virginia, I expressed my concern to my husband. He assured me our son was fine. I knew that—but WHERE was he fine? Praying for everyone in the hurricane's path, I contemplated calling the mission home, but knew they were undoubtedly preoccupied with their tasks. I also thought about calling our stake president. My husband chuckled at the suggestion. "We are probably more informed than he is. Watching The Weather Channel 24/7 gives you an edge."

Finally, I called the sister missionaries who were serving our ward. They were supportive. "Oh yes, call the mission home," one of them told me. "People call for silly reasons, but this is a good reason." Still, I felt my call would be a burden. The sisters called back a little while later; they still felt it was absolutely acceptable and valid to call the mission home. Again we hung up. The phone rang again immediately. I thought the missionaries were calling back to add still more comforting words to my dilemma. Instead, a sweet voice on the phone asked, "Is this Sister Hartje?"

"Yes," I replied.

"My name is Sister McWiggins. You don't know me, but ..."

A wonderful sister in Virginia was calling to tell me she had just seen my son! The missionaries in the area had been evacuated to her stake building in Suffolk, and she had gone to check on them.

Did they have enough food? What about other supplies, like flashlights?

The elders were assigned shifts at the stake center and were taking turns filling sandbags in other areas. It had been my son's shift as one of two young men at the stake center and Sister McWiggins had thoughtfully asked if she could take phone numbers and call their parents. As I talked with her that day, I sighed with relief and offered a quick prayer from my grateful heart during our conversation.

The Lord not only knew my needs that day, but He answered my prayer while the missionaries served their community and the mission president worked to keep his mission family safe. He may have been praying for parents not to call, since his work was a pressing and immediate need! I believe that Sister McWiggins was the Lord's angel that day. She may live in Provo now, but I will always consider her my "angel" from Virginia.

About five weeks later we received a cassette tape and photographs. The missionaries were singing hymns during the hurricane; we could hear them laughing, making up silly songs and taking pictures as shingles were being torn off the roof of the stake center. One of the missionaries from Tonga climbed barefoot up a flagpole, comparing these winds to a "real" storm—one of his island typhoons!

Through this experience, my testimony of prayer grew deeper, and my prayer of gratitude became more sincere. The Lord promptly answered a mother's prayer. He DOES hear every prayer. He knows each one of us. My prayers are more meditative and reverent. I am now at ease with hurricanes (and everything else), and I take nothing for granted. This experience has also left me eternally grateful for angels on Earth and for the profound love from our Father in Heaven.

Loralee Hartje

Never Really Alone

And ye cannot bear all things now; neverthe-
less, be of good cheer, for I will lead you along.
The kingdom is yours and the blessings thereof
are yours, and the riches of eternity are yours.

D&C 78:18

Feeling particularly discouraged and downhearted, I headed for the temple, knowing I could find peace and comfort in the house of the Lord. My spirits lifted somewhat as I put on my white clothing and sat in the chapel, the muted strains of familiar hymns drifting through my mind. As our group filed down the hall and entered the endowment room, I silently prayed for the peace I needed to stay positive and in tune while dealing with very difficult circumstances.

I sat on the end of the row and concentrated on what was happening around me. As the endowment ceremony progressed, however, I began feeling more and more discouraged: Glancing around the room, I saw glittering diamonds and thick gold bands everywhere. Everyone in our small company was married—all except me. I began aching anew from the loneliness of losing a companion to divorce after twenty-six years of marriage, and a wave of sadness washed over me. I felt alone, betrayed and rejected.

Wanting desperately to feel peace instead of sorrow, I offered another silent prayer. Tears stung my eyes, and I know that Heavenly Father must have felt my intensity as I silently cried out, "Please, Heavenly Father, let me know that you are aware of me and that you love me."

At that very moment, the temple worker who was sitting at the rear of the endowment room got to her feet, walked to where I was sitting, smiled at me with a radiant glow and gently stroked my arm several times. Then she squeezed my hand, gazed deeply into my eyes, smiled again and returned to her seat, without speaking a word.

I was humbled and grateful to know that my Heavenly Father loved me enough that He inspired that sister to come directly to me and provide a handful of loving gestures. I know they were from Him, and my heart soared. I may not have had a companion in mortality, but I know with a sweet assurance that I am never really alone.

Kathy Frandsen

Reprinted by permission of Patrick Bagley ©2004.

9

SERVING OTHERS

When ye are in the service of your fellow beings, ye are only in the service of your God.

Mosiah 2:17

Anywhere

During my years as a graduate student at Columbia University, I served as the New York Stake Young Women's president. One summer, I was working on girls' camp. I had a funny little car, bought on a shoestring and dedicated to the Lord's service. It was called a Gremlin. Most are probably too young to even remember that model, but it did have four wheels and was put together with spit and glue. One of my assignments for camp was apples. We needed lots of apples.

Very early one morning, I headed out to Hunt's Point Market, the local wholesale market, to pick up the apples. Upon arriving, I simply opened up the hatchback and said, "Fill 'er up."

With the back of the car full of apples and a few miscellaneous camp items, I headed upstate. I had to negotiate a number of cloverleaf turns in order to make a switch in direction. On the side of the highway just to the right as I entered the interstate on-ramp, I caught a glimpse of a young hitchhiker standing with a sign and a paper shopping bag. The sign said ANYWHERE. I quickly passed by.

While my father had set a family standard for picking up almost any stray, whether animal or person, and bringing it home, I had never stopped for a hitchhiker before in my life, especially not in New York. At that moment, however, something prompted me to reenter the cloverleaf and come back around. I thought to myself, *If she is still there, I will pick her up.* Honestly, I was hoping that she would be gone, but as I came around, there she was. So I stopped.

She opened the car door and got in. She was unkempt and did not smell like she had bathed that morning or any morning recently. I could not be certain how old she was, although she was clearly old beyond her years. Thinking to break the ensuing silence, I asked, "Are you hungry?"

"Yes," she responded.

I motioned and, reaching to the back of the car, she grabbed an apple. That is all I had to eat: a car full of apples. She ate quickly and put the core on the dashboard by wedging it tightly against the windshield. Usually I'm pretty good at conversation, but not this time. All I could get out of her to my queries were short "Yes" and "No" answers, a shrug of a shoulder or no answer at all. I finally asked, "Where are you going?"

"Anywhere," she answered.

Somewhat concerned, I searched for a way to connect. "Are you still hungry?"

She reached for another apple until there were five cores lined up on my dashboard.

Two can play this game, I thought. In silence I paid the tolls as we made our way upstate. As I was about to turn off the thruway onto a little road where our camp was located, I said, "I'm about to leave the thruway. Would you like to get out now?"

"No."

"Well, I'm going to a camp with some young women, and I'll just have to drop you off there."

Without looking up, she responded, "Okay."

I turned off and we traveled on.

As my car pulled into camp, a literal throng of young women surrounded the car. They were so happy to see us and I, needless to say, was thrilled to see them. As my passenger got out, there were some surprised young women. You could hear the whispers.

"Who is she?"

"What is she doing here?"

"Where did she come from?"

I suggested to my passenger that she might want to wait by the mailbox near the road for another ride. Perhaps somebody would pick her up there and she could be on her way to ANYWHERE.

The day passed. We had lunch and went about all the things you do on the first day of girls' camp. Just before dinner one of our young women came to me and said, "Sister Mouritsen, what are we going to do with *it*?"

"What do you mean, *it*?"

Pointing in the direction of the road, she rephrased her question, "What are we going to do with *her*?"

"I don't know," I said. "What do you think we should do with *her*?"

"I think we should invite her to dinner."

Wow, I wish I had thought of that, but I was so consumed with taking care of the trivial details of getting girls' camp going that I had neglected to notice this "lost lamb." It took a sweet "under" shepherd in the form of a Mia Maid to do that.

"Let's go together," I said, "and we'll invite her to dinner."

We walked together to the mailbox by the roadside. "It" accepted the sweet invitation of the Mia Maid to join us for dinner, and she ended up staying with us the entire week.

I must admit that I was somewhat anxious thinking that

"she" was a risk. I didn't know who she was or where she had come from or what she might have experienced. But those young women embraced her in a most marvelous way. I saw her at the waterfront (someone had apparently loaned her a swimming suit), I saw her at the craft tent, I saw her around the fireside, and I saw her at flag ceremony and at morning and evening devotionals. I watched as she bowed her head at meals as we prayed and as we began and closed our days with prayer. I watched her and the young women all week long. When camp was over, she was sitting by my car. I asked, "Can I take you somewhere?"

She replied, "Anywhere."

I don't know why I was surprised by her answer. I guess I thought that maybe the spirit of our girls and our camp experience had given her a bit more direction.

"Well, I'm headed back to New York City."

"I don't want to go there," she snapped. "Just let me off on the thruway."

We got in my car—minus the apples—and made our way to the thruway and then, a bit reluctantly, I let her and her tattered shopping bag out. Driving off, I watched her disappear in my rearview mirror as she stood on the roadside posting her clumsily written sign, ANYWHERE.

Over the years, that image has come to mind many, many times. In fact, it is one image that came to haunt me.

Some years later I had completed my degree work, moved to Utah and was working as Dean of Students at Brigham Young University.

"There is a young woman with a baby here to see you. She said it won't do any good to give you her name—you won't recall her by name."

I invited her into my office and she sat at my table holding a beautiful baby girl.

"Do you recognize me?" she asked.

"No, I'm sorry, but I don't." This would happen quite often when students I had counseled or taught would return and drop by to share their stories.

"I have known that you were here, but I haven't quite known what to say or do. I'm the young woman you picked up on the thruway in New York some years ago. Do you remember? Although I was very angry and hard, I was touched by what I heard and saw and felt at girls' camp."

She continued to explain that it had been a horrible life for her, including a long history of abuse and neglect at a very young age. *Finally,* she thought, *there has got to be something better than this out there.*

So she ran. As you might expect, a young women of her age with no resources ended up in desperate, dark places. That is when we found each other on the New York State Thruway.

"When I left girls' camp, I stole some money. Now I know that all I had to do was ask and you or anyone would have given me money. But I stole the money from the suitcases of some of the girls who had befriended me."

By this time, we were both in tears.

"When you drove off and left me on the side of the road, I had time to think. It was several hours before somebody picked me up. I went to the very next city and found a telephone booth. I thumbed through the Yellow Pages until I found 'The Church of Jesus Christ of Latter-day Saints.' I dialed the number. I wanted to see if the things I had heard and seen and felt at girls' camp were true. A pleasant woman answered the phone and I asked for the bishop. I'd heard the girls use that term at camp and I had met some of those men when they came up to camp for the last evening."

"He isn't home right now," was the response, "but I would be happy to have him call you back."

"I don't have a telephone. I'll call him back."

A few hours later she did. The bishop was home.

What happened after that is a true miracle, the kind we learn about in the Church when individuals take their role as their "brother's keeper" seriously.

This good family took in this waif and over time made her a member of their family. They cared for her and taught her and helped her to find the resources to heal her broken life. Eventually she joined the Church, met a returned missionary, and they were married. He was now a student at BYU. She came that day with her sweet baby, newly adopted, to extend an invitation.

"I would like to invite you to the sealing and blessing of our baby. Can you come?"

"ANYWHERE, anytime," I replied, my tears acknowledging the miracle of the Spirit and love evidenced in this incredible moment.

There, of course, is a continuation of this story, and more details of the intervening years between our good-bye on the thruway and our hello in my office. The important detail is the power of love, of service and of the Spirit, in teaching and touching the hearts of even those who seem untouchable and even unlovable. Our opportunities to touch lives can be endless when we allow the Spirit to be in charge. He truly does love each of us and sends His "missionaries" in the humble form of Mia Maids and Young Women's presidents and bishops and their families.

Maren Mouritsen

A Positive Mormon

For I have given you an example, that ye should do as I have done to you.

John 13:15

At the age of eighteen, I received the Melchizedek priesthood and was ordained to the office of elder by the bishop of my ward. During that ordination, the bishop also pronounced a blessing upon me and issued a call from the Lord for me to serve in the armed forces of our country.

As I was preparing to depart for active duty, the bishop gave me a pocket-sized book titled *Principles of the Gospel.* This book instructs servicemen in the performance of priesthood ordinances, outlines the conduct that is expected of a Latter-day Saint soldier while in combat and when facing moral adversities, and offers other items of counsel. It also instructs that we should not allow "Protestant" to be stamped on our army dog tags, but rather that we should insist that "Mormon" or "LDS" was indicated so that if we were wounded on the battlefield, we might receive a blessing from another priesthood bearer.

During the first few days of basic training, we underwent a battery of medical tests, received vaccinations, and completed administrative in-processing involving wills, finances and similar things. At each point in the process, yet another document was generated and inserted into our personnel file. At the very last station, a clerk reviewed the file to insure that each step had been properly completed. Then, using the information that had been documented, she would begin stamping out dog tags for each of us.

The only information that didn't appear in our file was our religious affiliation. So as the clerk was completing each man's dog tags, she would ask him for his religion and then stamp that on his tag in addition to the other information.

As my turn for the religion question came, I remembered the counsel I had received, leaned fully halfway across her desk and, pointing right at her, I yelled "Mormon!" The clerk finished stamping my tags, then handed them to me and asked that I verify that everything on the tags was correct. She had listed my full name, my service number, and then had stamped: "A Positive Mormon." I have to admit that I felt pretty smug as I thought to myself, *Wow, I guess I got that across to her!*

Our four months of training sped by, and I was shipped to Southeast Asia. My barracks there housed 360 GIs and two soft-drink machines. Of the twelve selections those machines offered, one was a caffeinated drink and the other eleven were different brands of beer at fifteen cents each. I think it's pretty safe to say that the conditions we faced overseas probably led to the nightly drunken stupor and immorality that many of those servicemen unfortunately chose. And yet, for a few, it made us stronger and made us appreciate even more having been introduced to the gospel and receiving the subsequent blessings. I was humbled and brought to tears many times as I thought of that proclamation, permanently stamped in stainless steel and lying against my chest, which testified of my resolve and stance—that I was indeed "A Positive Mormon." Those dog tags became an ever-present reminder for me, throughout my career, of just who and what I was.

As you might well imagine, though, I was indeed humbled even further several months into my overseas duty when I finally realized that the young clerk back in basic training hadn't been trying to describe my attitude and my commitment towards the gospel when she stamped those tags. Instead, she had indicated my blood type—A positive—and my religion!

Douglas Scofield

Doing What Simon Says

My great-great-grandfather, Simon Baker, was the third child in a family of five, born October 18, 1811, at West Winfield, Herkimer County, New York. Not much is known about Simon's childhood; he went to school at West Winfield and lived with his parents until he was seventeen, when he secured a position to work by the month. His father drew his wages.

At the age of eighteen, Simon married Mercy Young. They started their married life with only one dollar, which they gave to the minister who married them. Simon was hired at first by a Mr. Sheppard and later by Elijah Risley, a merchant of Fredonia, to manage the operation of a sawmill. Simon received twelve dollars a month for his work. On December 1, 1833, Simon started working for E. H. W. Risley & Co., one of the most important merchants in the region. His account book states: "Dec. 1, 1833, Commence work for E.H.W. Risley for one hundred ninety five dollars." He continued working for Risley for six years, managing the lumber mill and hiring and paying help as the occasion required.

Near Fredonia was the village of Laona; in 1835, five years after the organization of the Church, there were already thirty-five members of the Mormon faith in Laona. One evening on his way home from work, curiosity led Simon Baker to stop and listen to a street meeting. The doctrine that the missionaries preached captured his attention so much that he was late for supper—something that rarely happened. When he told Mercy of his interest in the new religion, she began to weep, thinking her husband was being led astray by false doctrine. Simon calmed her fears by telling her that he would take her to hear the missionaries so she could decide for herself.

Upon hearing the missionaries, Mercy also believed their message; later, through the teaching of Benjamin Brown, both Simon and Mercy accepted the gospel and were baptized by him. Mercy was baptized on March 4 and Simon on April 16, 1839.

It must have been a considerable sacrifice for Simon Baker to leave the place where he had worked those six years, pick up his little family, and move west with nothing more than a team of horses and a light wagon. But in the spring of 1839, soon after embracing the gospel, he moved to what was then called the Half Breeds Land in Lee County, Iowa, across the river from Nauvoo. There he located a small farm, lived on it for a year and then sold it for a larger farm that consisted of eighty acres of tillable land and eighty acres of timber. He built a cabin on the farm and moved into his new home in the spring of 1841.

Four of their children were born in that cabin. One of the twins born there died two and a half months later. Mercy seemed unable to recover from this experience, and she died March 4, 1845—leaving eight small children, the oldest only fourteen years old.

On April 5, Simon decided he needed to get someone to help care for his children. He was going to Nauvoo to attend conference, and he promised his children he would bring them a new mother. While on his way to Nauvoo, he asked a friend if he knew of a woman who would make a good mother for his children. This friend referred him to Charlotte Leavitt, the daughter of a widow who lived in Nauvoo. After the morning services of the conference were over, he went to the widow's cottage and made his intentions known, leaving the matter up to Charlotte. She consented to go home with him and take care of his children; if she liked him she would marry him, and if not, he would pay her for her services.

On April 8, Simon and Charlotte started for his home with this understanding. While crossing the Mississippi River on the ferryboat, they decided that they would marry at once—so, securing the services of Elder William Snow, the ceremony was performed between the two states, Illinois and Iowa. That saved them a trip to the county seat for a license, since the state had no jurisdiction over marriages performed on the water.

Simon Baker was an ingenious man who could make all kinds of mechanical devices, and he always had full command of his senses when any emergency arose. Those qualities made him an essential man in the community and on the westward trek.

He was a devoted follower of the Prophet Joseph Smith, and often guarded the Prophet while he slept. He was a courageous man whose life was dedicated to his family and to the Church. In a brief autobiography, he wrote, "I feel thankful that I am permitted to live in this age of the world. My desire is that I may keep the commandments of God and be saved in His Celestial Kingdom."

Simon Baker and Charlotte were sealed in the Nauvoo Temple on January 6, 1846. Charlotte was then proxy in the sealing of Mercy to Simon. Their daughter, Abigail, was born the next day, January 7, 1846.

During the spring of 1856, Simon Baker was called to assist in the colonization of Carson City and the surrounding valley. He had just finished building a house on his lot at the corner of First North and West Temple streets. One of the Church leaders told him, "Brother Baker, before you go on this mission, we want you to do something to help pay off the church debt."

"Whatever is expected of me, I am willing to do," Simon replied.

"We want fifty head of your best cattle, and we also want you to turn your house and lot over to the Perpetual Emigration Fund," the leader instructed. Simon did so, without questioning.

I have often contemplated the love that my great-great-grandfather must have had for the Prophet Joseph Smith, demonstrated by his willingness to guard the Prophet as he slept and to give his own life if necessary. That thought has caused me considerable soul-searching: Would I be willing to give my own life to protect the Prophet as he slept? After much pondering and prayer, I have concluded that I, too, would be willing to guard this great man who communed with Jehovah.

I have also had to ask myself, *Am I willing to do whatever is expected of me?* Sometimes, I believe that we make excuses instead of doing the small things we are asked to do in building the kingdom. We are rarely asked to give up all that we have—instead, we are only asked to fulfill the callings that our bishops and stake presidents extend to us. Each calling we are given is in some way related to the three-fold mission of the Church: to preach the gospel, perfect the saints and redeem the dead. Each of us should strive to be able to reply, as did Simon Baker, "Whatever is expected of me, I am willing to do."

Tom Baker

The Power of One

But charity is the pure love of Christ, and it endureth forever and who so is found possessing it at the last day, it shall be well with him.

Moroni 7:17

I was almost always in my office on Tuesday and Thursday mornings by 6 A.M. Those were my Book of Mormon teaching days. I was, however, a little later on this particular Thursday because it was an exam day.

As was my custom, I had stopped by Winchell's to get some doughnuts, hoping to sweeten the experience just a little. It was a gray day, dark and dim.

As I went in, there were two lines. In the line to my right was a young man whom I recognized as a participant in one of our leadership programs. We chatted. "How are you? How is school going?" The usual conversation.

There was an older man standing just in front of this student. I had not paid much attention, but did notice the man fumbling through his pocket and counting his change. Looking up at the order board, he changed from a drink and a doughnut to a hot drink.

I went about my business, ordered my doughnuts and said good-bye to this young man as he went on his way.

Shortly, I saw the clerk come from behind the counter and walk over to the man with his drink. She laid a doughnut on the table and said, "That young man has bought you a doughnut."

I watched the student as he walked down the street toward school. He never looked back. Not for credit. Not for admiration. He simply walked on, his backpack flung across his shoulder and his physics book under his arm.

I think of the everyday embodiment of the "small acts of kindness" that this young man represented.

Small acts of service are done so willingly and so lovingly every day by so many. "Compassionate service" goes on in the quietest places and the most anonymous corners.

The "power of one" is real.

Maren Mouritsen

Living the Golden Rule

For all the law is fulfilled in one word, even in this; Thou shalt love thy neighbour as thyself.

Gal. 5:14

When I first started my college education, we had one child. We lived in a very humble but affordable house. We painted, cleaned, and did repairs and yard work as part of the rent. I did early-morning janitorial work, then rushed to classes and studied late at night. It was a struggle, both financially and emotionally.

During the week of mid-semester exams, the plumbing went out in our house, and a contractor attached a condemnation order on the house. The college squeeze was so stressful, we decided I needed to remain another week in that house and continue doing my part-time job. Because of sanitation issues, my wife and son went to stay a week with her parents.

It was four days until payday. I came home from work Saturday morning and opened the refrigerator. There was nothing but a half cube of slightly wrapped butter and one stalk of celery. The celery was rubbery, and one end had turned black with reeking rot.

It was at that moment I felt guilt. I was hungry, with nothing at home to eat, and no cash in hand to purchase food. I started contemplating dropping out of school.

I forced myself to study that day and late into the night. I decided to get at least four hours of sleep before leaving to do my early-morning job. I was glad the morning was a Sunday. When I got in our Volkswagen Bug, I saw a ten dollar bill fastened to the steering wheel. Who could have given that to us? With tears filling my eyes, I realized I could now buy some bread to go with the butter, and I could continue until payday.

While I was sitting in our church meetings, I wondered if the Good Samaritan was the bishop or the Sunday school teacher. As I sat in the various meetings and participated in the activities, I smiled at everyone. I monitored people's faces. I maintained eye contact to see if anyone recognized my inquisitive smile.

I was in awe all day and into the next week. I was so appreciative; I treated everyone as if they were an icon and my salvation.

It was this experience and others like it that motivated me to practice the Golden Rule. I have found delight in doing something that causes people to say, "Thank you—that made my day."

Think how fulfilling it would be to secretly do something nice for neighbors—or for a less active member of your ward. He or she would try to find out who did the act, and would start to smile at everyone. He or she would maintain eye contact and see if anyone recognized such an inquisitive smile. Someone might even decide to return to full activity as a result!

John Nield

He Changed My Life

By this shall all men know that ye are my disciples, if ye have love one to another.

John 13:35

As a senior at James Marshall High School in West Sacramento, California, I did not have much ambition for college. I was baptized a member of the Church of Jesus Christ of Latter-day Saints when I was twelve; I was active in the Church for four years, then went inactive from my sixteenth to my eighteenth year. In April 1966, just before graduation, my biology teacher, Harold Jeters (the only African-American at my high school)—who taught like a college professor—pulled me aside and asked, "Kenn, what are you going to do after high school?"

I told him I was probably going to go to American River Junior College in Carmichael, California, but I wasn't certain what I wanted to do. He quipped, "Wait a minute, aren't you a Mormon kid?"

"Yes."

"Then why aren't you going to BYU?"

"I don't know."

"You get your application papers from BYU and see me here next week. We will sit down and fill out your papers and submit them right away. You are going to Brigham Young University."

Wow! I knew he was trying to mentor me, as he taught a very demanding course of biology and expected the most from his students, but this one really threw me off. His stare went deep into my soul, and I knew how he felt about what he was telling me to do.

I did get my application from BYU and met with Mr. Jeters the following week. We sat down at his desk after school and filled out the papers, page by page. It was a late submission for admission, but I was accepted to BYU. I met my wife, Barbara, during my first year there. With her zeal for education, I continued and graduated with a degree in biology. I was then accepted into the Aviation Reserve Officers' Candidate Program, and served as a naval flight officer for eight and a half years. Following my time in the navy, I attended the University of Washington, where I received my DDS degree.

I owe my current quality of life to Mr. Harold Jeters, a special agent of the Lord who helped me find my way back into activity in the Church and helped me carve out a career that has allowed me to serve actively for many years since. I am now fifty-six years old and take every opportunity I can to encourage youth to continue their education. I was far off the LDS track when Mr. Jeters grabbed me one day in that biology classroom, but his insistence changed my life. I am ever grateful to him for his devotion to his students—especially to me.

Kenneth Stinchfield

The Shoes She Left at the Chapel Door

Too often, charity is extended to another when his actions or conduct are acceptable to us. The exhibition of charity to another must not be dependent on his performance. It should be given because of who we are—not because of how we behave.

H. Burke Peterson
Ensign, May 1981

Bishop Peterson's thought reminds me of Darla, a woman I knew some years ago who conducted the music in sacrament meeting. The Lord had blessed Darla with a beautiful voice and a real talent for conducting music, but she had endured a difficult and turbulent life. She often came to church wearing the same dress—sometimes it was clean, sometimes not. But every Sunday, she was there.

Darla had two small children who often ran around in the chapel while Darla conducted the music. Her husband had stopped coming to church a few years earlier, and it was difficult for Darla to take care of her children while she conducted the music.

What offended people so much, however, was not the fact that Darla's children were unattended in the chapel. That was understandable—her husband was inactive, and children's behavior can be excused. What was upsetting so many people was the fact that Darla conducted the music in front of the congregation, in sacrament meeting . . . barefoot.

Darla's bare feet became a topic of conversation both in and out of various meetings at church. I remember asking our bishop why he didn't just ask Darla to put her shoes on. There was concern that her feelings could be hurt. So as a member of the Relief Society presidency, I was asked to visit Darla.

Darla was different. Her boisterous, loud character was often viewed as crass and "uncouth." She was overweight, and sometimes she smelled offensive. In her hectic rush to get herself and her children to church, she periodically wore her dress inside out.

But Darla had a wonderful testimony of the gospel of Jesus Christ, and she loved her Father in Heaven. In fact, here is what I learned: Darla so loved her Heavenly Father that she could not offend Him in His chapel by wearing her dirty, worn-out shoes while she conducted music on Sundays. In her difficult life situation, Darla felt more reverent toward her Heavenly Father when she removed her shoes and left them outside the chapel door.

Melinda Gardner

More Chicken Soup?

Many of the stories and poems you have read in this book were submitted by readers like you who had read earlier *Chicken Soup for the Soul* books. We publish at least five or six *Chicken Soup for the Soul* books every year. We invite you to contribute a story to one of these future volumes.

Stories may be up to twelve hundred words, and must uplift or inspire. You may submit an original piece, something you have read or your favorite quotation on your refrigerator door.

To obtain a copy of our submission guidelines and a listing of upcoming *Chicken Soup* books, please write, fax or check our Web site.

Please send your submissions to:

Chicken Soup for the Soul
P.O. Box 30880, Santa Barbara, CA 93130
Fax: 805-563-2945
Web site: *www.chickensoup.com*

We will be sure that both you and the author are credited for your submission.

For information about speaking engagements, other books, audiotapes, workshops and training programs, please contact any of our authors directly.

Supporting Others

In the spirit of supporting others, a portion of the proceeds from *Chicken Soup for the Latter-day Saint Soul* will be donated to the General Missionary Fund of the Church of Jesus Christ of Latter-day Saints.

The General Missionary Fund is used to support Third World LDS missionaries who are called to serve in other parts of the world and who would otherwise be unable to serve missions.

Sherm and Peg Fugal plan to match the *Chicken Soup for the Soul* donation. They encourage fans of *Chicken Soup for the Soul* to do the same.

General Missionary Fund
Missionary Department/3WW
LDS Church Office Building
50 East South Temple
Salt Lake City, UT 84150
Web site: *www.LDS.org*
Phone: 801-240-2221

Who Is Jack Canfield?

Jack Canfield is one of America's leading experts in the development of human potential and personal effectiveness. He is both a dynamic, entertaining speaker and a highly sought-after trainer. Jack has a wonderful ability to inform and inspire audiences toward increased levels of self-esteem and peak performance. Jack most recently released a book for success titled *The Success Principles: How to Get from Where You Are to Where You Want to Be.*

He is the author and narrator of several bestselling audio- and videocassette programs, including *Self-Esteem and Peak Performance, How to Build High Self-Esteem, Self-Esteem in the Classroom* and *Chicken Soup for the Soul—Live.* He is regularly seen on television shows such as *Good Morning America, 20/20* and *NBC Nightly News.* Jack has co-authored numerous books, including the *Chicken Soup for the Soul* series, *Dare to Win* and *The Aladdin Factor* (all with Mark Victor Hansen), *100 Ways to Build Self-Concept in the Classroom* (with Harold C. Wells), *Heart at Work* (with Jacqueline Miller) and *The Power of Focus* (with Les Hewitt and Mark Victor Hansen).

Jack is a regularly featured speaker for professional associations, school districts, government agencies, churches, hospitals, sales organizations and corporations. His clients have included the American Dental Association, the American Management Association, AT&T, Campbell's Soup, Clairol, Domino's Pizza, GE, Hartford Insurance, ITT, Johnson & Johnson, the Million Dollar Roundtable, NCR, New England Telephone, Re/Max, Scott Paper, TRW and Virgin Records. Jack has taught on the faculty of Income Builders International, a school for entrepreneurs.

Jack conducts an annual seven-day training called Breakthrough to Success. It attracts entrepreneurs, educators, counselors, parenting trainers, corporate trainers, professional speakers, ministers and others interested in improving their lives and the lives of others.

For free gifts from Jack and information on all his material and availability go to:

www.jackcanfield.com
Self-Esteem Seminars
P.O. Box 30880
Santa Barbara, CA 93130
Phone: 805-563-2935 • Fax: 805-563-2945

Who Is Mark Victor Hansen?

In the area of human potential, no one is more respected than Mark Victor Hansen. For more than thirty years, Mark has focused solely on helping people from all walks of life reshape their personal vision of what's possible. His powerful messages of possibility, opportunity and action have created powerful change in thousands of organizations and millions of individuals worldwide.

He is a sought-after keynote speaker, bestselling author and marketing maven. Mark's credentials include a lifetime of entrepreneurial success and an extensive academic background. He is a prolific writer with many bestselling books, such as *The One Minute Millionaire, The Power of Focus, The Aladdin Factor* and *Dare to Win,* in addition to the *Chicken Soup for the Soul* series. Mark has had a profound influence through his library of audios, videos and articles in the areas of big thinking, sales achievement, wealth building, publishing success, and personal and professional development.

Mark is the founder of the MEGA Seminar Series. MEGA Book Marketing University and Building Your MEGA Speaking Empire are annual conferences where Mark coaches and teaches new and aspiring authors, speakers and experts on building lucrative publishing and speaking careers. Other MEGA events include MEGA Marketing Magic and My MEGA Life.

He has appeared on television (*Oprah,* CNN and *The Today Show*), in print (*Time, U.S. News & World Report, USA Today, New York Times* and *Entrepreneur*) and on countless radio interviews, assuring our planet's people that "You can easily create the life you deserve."

As a philanthropist and humanitarian, Mark works tirelessly for organizations such as Habitat for Humanity, American Red Cross, March of Dimes, Childhelp USA and many others. He is the recipient of numerous awards that honor his entrepreneurial spirit, philanthropic heart and business acumen. He is a lifetime member of the Horatio Alger Association of Distinguished Americans, an organization that honored Mark with the prestigious Horatio Alger Award for his extraordinary life achievements.

Mark Victor Hansen is an enthusiastic crusader for what's possible and is driven to make the world a better place.

Mark Victor Hansen & Associates, Inc.
P.O. Box 7665
Newport Beach, CA 92658-7665
Phone: 949-764-2640, ext. 101
Fax: 949-722-6912
Web site: *www.markvictorhansen.com*

Who Are Sherm and Peg Fugal?

Sherm and Peg Fugal are college sweethearts who met while they were students at Brigham Young University. They have been married for thirty-four years and are the parents of four grown sons and grandparents of three grandchildren (to whom this book is dedicated).

Sherm was born and raised in Pleasant Grove, Utah, where his Mormon ancestors from Denmark settled in the 1860s. Peg was born in Vermont, where her paternal ancestors were original colonists. She was raised on a dairy farm in western New York. While Sherm was serving a mission in Guatemala-El Salvador in the late 1960s, Peg was investigating the Church in western New York, which she joined just shy of her eighteenth birthday during her senior year of high school.

Sherm is a real estate investor. Peg owns the oldest, continuous advertising agency in Utah (the only one founded, owned and operated by a woman). Together, they invented the only no-bend, no-lift snow shovel in the world, on which they have a patent, and which they sell all over the country via their Web site: *ezplow.com*.

Stan and Sharon Miller compiled the first three volumes of *Especially for Mormons;* Sherm and Peg helped compile the fourth and fifth volumes. Five years ago, the Millers turned *Especially for Mormons* over to the Fugals, who compiled three new volumes.

Sherm and Peg are both prolific readers and have more books than they can possibly shelve. Peg is also a prolific writer. She began writing at the age of ten, got a job as a stringer for the local newspaper when she was only sixteen, sold her first magazine article when she was a college freshman and worked for the campus daily newspaper at BYU. Before graduating from BYU, she worked as a freelance writer, a radio and television personality, and started her advertising agency. She has authored, coauthored and/or edited eleven best-selling books.

Sherm and Peg spend their free time enjoying their sons and grandchildren. Their oldest son Jayson was one of the first missionaries to serve in Romania; he worked for his mother's advertising agency for ten years before moving to Manhattan where he is an advertising executive with *National Geographic Adventure* magazine; he is married to his college sweetheart Cori, who served a mission in Portugal; they are the parents of Ayden. Their second son Josh served a mission in Brazil; he works for Diebold, the banking products company; his college sweetheart Stephanie teaches at BYU; they are the parents of Halle and Maddie. Like their parents, both Jayson and Josh graduated from BYU. Their third son Jake served a mission in southern California and put himself through college on basketball scholarships (Utah Valley State College and East Carolina University); like his father, he is a real estate investor. Their youngest son Jer served a mission in Korea; he is still in college and works for his father and brother.

Contact Sherm and Peg at: *peg@pegfugal.com*

Contributors

The majority of stories in this book were submitted by our readers' response to our call-out for stories. If you would like to contact any of the contributors for information about their writing or would like to invite them to speak in your community, look for their contact information included in their biographies.

Heather Abbott received her bachelor of science degree in nursing from the University of Nebraska in 1997, and worked as a pediatric intensive-care unit nurse for four years. She is currently serving as a Primary teacher in her northern Virginia ward; she and her husband, James, have two young sons.

Robert Allen is the author of some of the most popular financial books of all time. His *New York Times* bestsellers include *Nothing Down, Creating Wealth, Multiple Streams of Income, The One Minute Millionaire* and the forthcoming *Cracking the Millionaire Code.* He and wife Daryl have been married for twenty-eight years and have three children.

A lifelong member of the Church, **Lori Amavisca** was born and raised in California; she spent twelve years in Prescott, Arizona. She has worked in many fields, including the aerospace industry, and is now a stay-at-home mom in Hilo, Hawaii. She is active in the Honomu Branch, where she teaches the young single adult gospel doctrine class; she and her husband, Mark, have one son, five daughters and three grandchildren.

Charlotte Andersen is an associate professor of computer information systems and writes novels in her spare time (between one and two in the morning). Currently she serves with her husband as activities chair in the Edmonds Ward, Shoreline Washington Stake. They are the parents of two boys under the age of three.

Originally a western New Yorker, **Shelley Ball Andrus** now lives in east Idaho, where she works from home as an educator for Idaho Virtual Academy. She is active in the Church, and serves her community as a city councilwoman. Shelley and her husband, Jason, are the parents of three children.

Julio Arciniega is a convert from Mexico City; he served a mission in Mexico and graduated from BYU. He has been a translator for the Church for more than thirty years; he also teaches (and loves to) dance. Active in the Edgemont 8th Ward of the Provo Utah Edgemont Stake, he has one daughter and three sons; he recently added four more daughters through marriage.

A lifelong member of the Church, **Sue Ayres** was born in Utah—but as a military dependent, she has lived all over the world, including Japan. She attended BYU and currently works as a secretary/receptionist. She enjoys creating woodcrafts and spending time at the family cabin. She serves on the Relief

Society enrichment committee of the Kaysville 10th Ward, Kaysville Utah Crestwood Stake and is the mother of two sons.

Pat Bagley is a graduate of Brigham Young University, and for twenty-seven years has been the editorial cartoonist at *The Salt Lake Tribune*. He is famous for his cartoons that skillfully deflate the pompous and poke gentle fun at his own Mormon culture, nine of which appear in this book. His previous books include *I Spy a Nephite* and *Mormons: History, Culture, Beliefs.*

A native of Salt Lake City, **Tom Baker** graduated from Stevens-Henager Business College in Ogden, Utah, with degrees in accounting and business management. He moved to Seattle in 1986. He is married to Kathryn, with whom he shares a yours-mine-and-ours family of eight children and six grandchildren. Tom is the ward mission leader in his Des Moines Ward, Seattle Washington Stake.

Valerie Baker grew up in Boulder, Colorado, and attended Utah State University. She has been married for twenty-seven years and is the mother of three grown children. She has served in the Primary, Sunday school, Relief Society and Young Women's organizations. For the past fifteen years, she has facilitated a pediatric brain-tumor support group.

Betty Bayne was born and raised in Chicago and joined the Church at age twenty-five. She attended ECC and is currently the cafeteria manager of two middle schools. She and her husband, Rick, have five children and seventeen grandchildren. Betty produces the ward bulletin in the Schaumburg 2nd Ward, Schaumburg Illinois Stake.

SummerDale Beckstrand was born and raised in Long Beach, California. She just returned to the Long Beach 10th Ward, Long Beach East Stake, from a Spanish-speaking mission in Houston, Texas. She is single and is majoring in physics and astronomy at Brigham Young University, where she is a teacher's assistant.

Ann Best's writing has appeared in numerous publications and she has won numerous awards. She recently wrote a young-adult novel. She lives in Salt Lake City, is the caretaker of a brain-injured daughter, and is a visiting teaching supervisor in the Cottonwood 1st Ward, Salt Lake Cottonwood Stake.

Valaree Brough serves as Relief Society education counselor in the Grants Pass Oregon Stake and as advancement chairman for the Grants Pass 3rd Ward Scout Committee.

Douglas Brown has been writing since sixth grade and has been published in the *New Era* and *Friend* magazines. Doug currently serves as ward clerk for the River 2nd Ward, West Jordan River Stake. He and wife JuVene live in West Jordan, Utah, and have seven children.

Heidi Butters has been making up and writing stories and plays since she was a little girl. Some of her poetry has been published by *poetry.com* and some of her stories have been published by *Short Stuff Magazine* and *The Storyteller*. She also self-publishes on her Web site. Heidi is a visiting teaching supervisor in the Wallsburg 2nd Ward, Midway Utah Stake.

Meli Cardullo was born and raised in Pennsylvania and joined the Church at the age of forty-four. She graduated from MCC with four AAS degrees, and now works for the college assisting disabled students. Most recently, she was editor of the Relief Society newsletter in her ward in Mesa, Arizona. She has four children and three grandchildren.

Esmeralda Carter has been a retired United States Navy veteran of the Persian Gulf War since 1996. She serves as a Sunday school teacher for youth in the Mount Pleasant Ward, Chesapeake Virginia Stake. She lives in Chesapeake with her hero and husband, Bry—a naval officer—and their daughter.

Sandy Christensen was born and raised in Ephraim, Utah, and married her husband, Carl, right after high school. She earned an associate degree from Snow College, a bachelor's degree from University of Utah and a master's degree from Utah State University. She worked for ten years as a technical writer while teaching English at Columbia College. She is now a full-time mom with nine children ranging in age from eighteen months to twenty years.

Michael Clifton, a lawyer for condominium developers, boards and managers, has a master's degree in philosophy and is a freelance writer. He is currently the high priest group leader in the Waterloo Ward, Kitchener Ontario Stake. Michael's wife, Marhee, is Young Women's president; they are the parents of two children.

Susan Watts Coon was raised in Provo, Utah, where she met husband Richard while they were still in high school. Susan received a degree in nursing from Brigham Young University (where her father, Stan Watts, was the basketball coach). She enjoys sewing, cooking and reading. She volunteers for LDS Family Services and serves with her husband in a singles ward.

Pamela Coyle is a twenty-eight-year-old wife and mother of two. She currently serves as a ward adult Sunday school teacher and as a Relief Society teacher in the Irvine Ward, Paisley Scotland Stake.

Laura Craner was born and raised in Utah and now lives in Colorado with her husband and daughter. She enjoys being a full-time mother and uses her spare time to write. Laura is currently serving in the Primary presidency of the Longmont 4th Ward, Longmont Colorado Stake.

A lifelong member of the Church, **Laura Denhalter** was born in Orange, California, but was raised primarily in Utah. Currently in the tenth grade, she is trying to get a job as a recording artist. She has one sister and two brothers.

Alexandra Domingues immigrated to the United States and studied at Utah Valley State College in Orem, Utah. She teaches English classes and does translation work. She currently serves as a visiting teacher, adult Sunday school teacher, seminary teacher and Relief Society music leader in the Set`bal Ward 1, Portugal Set`bal Stake (near Lisbon). She and her husband, who joined the Church in 1983, are the parents of three boys.

Susan Durgin was born in historical Charlestown, Massachusetts, where she lived until she married at the age of twenty-four. She joined the Church at age thirty-one. She works as an accountant and teaches Relief Society in the Revere 2nd Ward, Cambridge Massachusetts Stake. Widowed at age forty-one, she has one son and one daughter.

Susan Eliason was born in Utah and raised throughout the world. Baptized at age eight, she holds bachelor's and master's degrees from Brigham Young University, is an instructional design consultant and teaches part-time at the Marriott School of Management. Susan serves as ward music chair in the Orem 5th Ward, Orem Utah Stake.

Annaliese Enderle was born and raised in the Church in Fairbanks, Alaska. She is currently serving as the Relief Society second counselor in her Vista, California, ward. She and husband Vance were married in 1996. She is a stay-at-home mom of three children.

Kirsten Fitzgerald was born in Ohio, and raised in many different states. Her parents joined the Church while expecting her. Shortly after high school she married her husband, Kurt, in Utah; they have four children. Kirsten volunteers for her community, and serves as the enrichment leader in the Tallmadge Ward, Akron Ohio Stake.

Heather Ford grew up in Cody, Wyoming, and graduated Cum Laude from Brigham Young University with a degree in business management. While at BYU, she was a Hinckley Scholar and studied abroad in Southeast Asia. After graduation, she worked in human resources and corporate training. Heather currently serves as the Young Women's music director in the Lehi 26th Ward, Lehi Utah North Stake, stays at home with her two daughters and aspires to write as much as possible.

Kathy Frandsen, a writer and editor by profession (she helped edit this book), also loves genealogy and family history work. She and her ex-husband adopted five children, and she has one granddaughter. She is currently the Relief Society pianist and ward choir pianist in the Lakeridge 13th Ward, Orem Utah Lakeridge North Stake; the assistant webmaster and newsletter editor in the Genesis Branch; and is a worker at the Mt. Timpanogos Temple.

Lisa Freeman was born and raised in Idaho. She earned both her bachelor's and master's degrees at Brigham Young University, and is currently a Ph.D. candidate at the University of Virginia. She lives in Illinois with her husband, Robert, and her five stepchildren. She is the Primary Activity Days leader in her ward.

Melinda Gardner has served as the gospel doctrine teacher for the past four years in the Banbury Ward, Northampton Stake in England. She and her husband, Ian, have three children and two grandchildren. Her oldest son is currently serving in the Salt Lake City Utah Mission.

Kimberlee Garrett served a mission in the Brazil São Paulo Interlagos Mission and attended Brigham Young University and Utah State University, where she majored in English. She currently serves as the marriage and family relations teacher in the American Fork 21st Ward, American Fork Utah East Stake. Kimberlee and her husband, Layne, have three children.

Britnee Gilbert was born and raised in Brigham City, Utah. She has been an active member of the LDS Church her whole life. After graduation she had the opportunity to be a nanny in New York. She has since moved home to Utah to pursue an education in computer science.

Jennifer Gowans was born in Bountiful, Utah, and was raised in the Salt Lake Valley, where she joined the Church at the age of nine. She has an EMT Certification through Utah State University, works for UBMC and is a volunteer firefighter. She and her husband, Andrew, have three young children and serve as a home teaching couple.

Nancy Reynard Gunn was born in Orlando, Florida, was raised as an Air Force "brat" and attended Brigham Young University. She later returned to BYU to earn her master's degree in English; she currently teaches part-time at BYU. Nancy teaches Primary in the Lakeview 7th Ward, Orem Utah Lakeview Stake. She and husband DeVerl have six children and eleven grandchildren.

Kirsty Hale is a seventh-generation member of the Church; she lives in the South Shields Ward, Sunderland England Stake, where she currently serves as the first counselor in the Young Women's presidency and as the gospel principles teacher.

Loralee Hartje and her husband were already married when two LDS missionaries came to their door; they joined the Church in January 1979. They have a daughter and two returned missionary sons at Brigham Young University. Lori has served in all auxiliaries in the Church and belongs to the Crystal Lake 2nd Ward, Buffalo Grove Illinois Stake.

Jody Hastey was born and raised in California and joined the Church at age forty-three. She worked in office management and childcare until she moved to Utah after the death of her husband, Michael. She has two daughters and seven grandchildren. Jody is the visiting teacher coordinator in her Utah ward.

Barbara Hausen was born in Fitchburg, Massachusetts. She earned a master's degree from Louisiana Tech University. Barbara enjoys being a full-time mother. She is currently the ward employment specialist in the San Antonio 6th Ward, San Antonio Stake. Barbara married in December 1976 and joined the Church three months later; she and Marty have eight children and seven grandchildren.

April Homer is a young mother of three children, who loves teaching preschool, decorating her home, scrapbooking on the computer and playing the piano. She currently serves as a Relief Society instructor in the Kennewick East 1st Ward, Kennewick Washington East Stake.

Leslie Householder, a wife and mother of six young children, is the author of *The Jackrabbit Factor* and *Hidden Treasures: Heaven's Astonishing Help with Your Money Matters*. She currently serves as the family preparedness specialist in the Lindsay Ward, Mesa Arizona Citrus Heights Stake.

A fifth-generation member of the Church, **Lester Ann Jensen** was born, raised and educated in southern Alberta. She and her husband have visited many nations through their work in the travel/hotel business. Lester Ann also loves to sew, craft and write. The mother of three and grandmother of five, she serves as second counselor in the Relief Society presidency in the Lethbridge Fairmont Ward.

Rochelle Johnson was born and raised in Ohio, and joined the Church at the age of twenty-two. She earned a master's degree in special education at George Washington University, and currently teaches special needs children in an urban Washington, D.C., elementary school. Rochelle is single and serves on the compassionate service committee in her Virginia ward.

A convert to the LDS Church, **Sammie Justesen** lives on Rooster Ranch with her husband, Dee, in the Sunnyside Ward, Sandpoint Idaho Stake. She is a registered nurse, a writer and a professional editor. Sammie has served in three Relief Society presidencies and is currently a literacy and genealogy specialist.

Barbara Keller was born and reared in New Jersey. She joined the Church at age thirteen, graduated from BYU, and earned a doctorate at Bowling Green State University. She spent her career in higher education and retired as dean of students at Weber State College. Barbara is a family history consultant in her Utah ward.

Marie Kirkeiner was born and raised in Indiana. She and her husband joined the Church in 1989 while her husband was stationed with the U.S. Army in Germany. She graduated from Indiana State University with a degree in music education. She currently serves as the Beehive adviser in the Fisher's Ward, Muncie Indiana Stake. Marie and her husband are the parents of three children.

Vickie Mattson is a lifelong member of the Church, born in Logan, Utah and reared in Washington state. She and her husband, Gary, of forty-one years have four children and eight grandchildren. She continues her chosen career as mother and homemaker while serving as the stake Young Women's president.

Lisa May enjoys writing short stories and poetry; she has been published in local and city papers and ward publications. She also enjoys photography and is currently teaching piano. Lisa is the Primary and choir pianist in the

Meadowview Ward. She lives in the southern California countryside of Temecula with her husband, son, daughter and yellow Lab.

Deborah McIff works as a grants administrator for nine charter schools in Arizona. She was previously Young Women's president and is now serving as the Cubmaster in the Vineyard Ward of the Mesa Arizona Maricopa Stake. She and her husband have three children.

Patricia McKenna-Leu was born and raised in Liverpool, England, where she joined the Church at the age of twenty-two. Married to her childhood sweetheart, Patricia went back to school when Martin was disabled in a traffic accident; she is now a graduate midwife working in Melbourne, Australia. She currently serves in the Blackburn Ward, Maroondah Australia Stake as a Primary teacher, temple preparation instructor, ward missionary, family history worker and visiting teacher. She and her husband, Martin, have four daughters.

Stan Miller was born in Arizona, attended Brigham Young University and spent his career in Utah as a business consultant. He is the originator of the bestselling *Especially for Mormons* books. He and his wife, Sharon, have five children, many grandchildren, and live in Lindon, Utah.

Ruth Moore was born in Massachusetts, raised in Maine and joined the Church in 2004. She has a master's degree in social sciences and is both a teacher and an athlete. She and her husband, Alfred, have one daughter. They are members of the Ellsworth Branch, where she is an enrichment co-leader.

Diane Moss is currently finishing her master's degree in nursing science and teaches part-time in the nursing program at Salt Lake Community College. In order of importance, she is a mother of three children and six stepchildren, a grandmother of six, a wife, a sister and a daughter. Her mother is still alive, enjoying her forty grandchildren and thirty-seven great-grandchildren. Diane is currently a Webelos den leader and a visiting teacher in the Pleasant Grove 4th Ward, Pleasant Grove Utah Stake.

Professor emeritus of religious education/ancient scripture, past administrative assistant to President Jeffrey R. Holland, and former Assistant Vice-President and Dean of Student Life at Brigham Young University, **Maren Mouritsen** earned her degrees at Northwestern and Columbia Universities, with additional studies at The Chicago Art Institute. A popular speaker and writer, Maren is a contributor to *The Mormon Encyclopedia* and *The Book of Mormon Reference Companion*. She served in the Northern Far East Mission and on the Young Women's General Board, helped produce the opening and closing ceremonies of the 2002 Salt Lake Winter Olympics, and currently teaches gospel doctrine at Utah State Prison.

A lifelong member of the Church, **John Nield** was born in Montpelier, Idaho. He earned a doctorate from Idaho State University, retired from college teaching and currently serves as the ward mission leader in the Spanish Fork 12th

Ward, Spanish Fork Utah South Stake. John and wife Sally have five children and sixteen grandchildren.

Silvana Norat was born in Argentina in 1970, raised in Buenos Aires and joined the Church in the United States at the age of twenty-five. She graduated from University of Córdoba and is currently the Primary president in her San Antonio, Texas, ward. Silvana and her husband, Sergio, have two children.

Cheryl Panisiak was born and raised in Manitoba and joined the Church at age twenty-four. She has taken early childhood education courses. She is single but has many special "children of the heart" from all her years of working with little ones. She is a nursery teacher in her Edmonton ward.

A lifelong member of the Church, **Nadja Pettitt** was born and raised in Switzerland. She graduated from Brigham Young University and is currently a SAHM and a freelance translator. Nadja serves in the Primary presidency in the Cergy Paris France Stake. She and her husband, Hugh, are the parents of five daughters and two sons.

Joyce Moseley Pierce was born and raised in Missouri and joined the Church in Oklahoma in 1978. She owns a publishing company and does freelance work. Joyce is the information specialist in her Houston, Texas, ward. She and her husband, Ed, have three children and six grandchildren.

Bridget Rees is an editor and writer with *LDS Living* magazine. She currently serves on her ward's Relief Society enrichment committee. She and her husband, Ryan, live in Draper, Utah, with their pug dog, Slim.

A native of Utah, **Chrystine Reynolds** has a bachelor's degree in English and history from Utah State University, and loves writing, singing, historical reenacting and doing family history. She participated in three LDS wagon trains and in Seatrek 2001. Chrystine is the Relief Society compassionate service leader in the Ames Ward, Ames Iowa Stake. She and her husband, James, are the parents of six children.

Rich Rogers is a Utah-based freelance writer specializing in arts and entertainment. He is also a literary and theater critic. Rich is the Service Committee cochairman in the Union Fort 9th Singles Branch, Midvale Utah Union Fort Stake. He is permanently single and enjoys being a bachelor uncle.

A lifelong member of the Church, **Larisa Schumann** was born in Utah and spent her childhood in California. She has degrees from Brigham Young University and BYU-Hawaii, and she currently teaches at Utah Valley State College. She teaches family history and is a visiting teacher in her Utah ward; she is also a temple worker and extraction coordinator.

Douglas Scofield, a retired military police officer, was raised in northern California and joined the Church at the age of fifteen. He is an Oakland Temple coordinator and member of a bishopric in the Gridley California Stake. Doug and his wife, Cindy, have two daughters, a son and a grandson.

Born in Sacramento, California, **Kenneth Stinchfield** is a retired navy commander who gave twenty-seven years of active duty and six years of reserve duty. He is an oral and maxillofacial surgeon who was a naval flight officer early in his military career. Kenneth is a high priest who currently serves as the Young Men's president in the Salmon Creek Ward, Vancouver Washington West Stake. He and his wife, Barbara, have been married for thirty-five years and are the parents of seven children.

Terry Tippets lived in Utah during most of his school years, served in the U.S. Air Force after graduation from high school, and then served a two-year Church mission in Scotland. Married for thirty-two years and a father of five, he is currently the financial clerk, chorister and assistant organist for his Omaha, Nebraska, ward.

Lehi Yanez was born in Muzquiz, Coahuila, Mexico, and is currently serving as a full-time missionary in the Mexico Oaxaca Mission.

Permissions *(continued from page iv)*

Three Wheels of Hope. Reprinted by permission of Susan Elaine Durgin.©1998 Susan Elaine Durgin.

The Greatest Glory. Reprinted by permission of Marie Annette Kirkeiner. ©2005 Marie Annette Kirkeiner.

The Fast I Have Chosen. Reprinted by permission of Douglas M. Brown. ©2004 Douglas M. Brown.

An Incredible Calm. Reprinted by permission of Cheryl Ann Panisiak. ©2004 Cheryl Ann Panisiak.

He Will Provide. Reprinted by permission of Joyce Ann Pierce. ©2005 Joyce Ann Pierce.

The Mommy Store. Reprinted by permission of Lisa Marie May. ©2005 Lisa Marie May.

She Has Always Been There. Reprinted by permission of Robert Grant Allen. ©2005 Robert Grant Allen.

Stopped at the Gate. Reprinted by permission of Betty Bayne. ©2004 Betty Bayne.

Pizza, Soggy Cereal and the Atonement. Reprinted by permission of Deborah L. McIff. ©2005 Deborah L. McIff.

A Family for Me. Reprinted by permission of Ruth Amy Moore. ©2004 Ruth Amy Moore.

Jesus in the Sky. Reprinted by permission of Jennifer Lyn Gowans. ©2005 Jennifer Lyn Gowans.

Brothers by Chance, Best Friends by Choice. Reprinted by permission of April JaNae Homer. ©2005 April JaNae Homer.

In Memory of Our God and Our Children. Reprinted by permission of John B. Nield. ©2005 John B. Nield.

The Greatest Sacrifice. Reprinted by permission of Leigh Baugh. ©2005 Leigh Baugh.

Years of Pent-Up Emotion. Reprinted by permission of Joyce Ann Pierce. ©2004 Joyce Ann Pierce.

Confessions of a Scrapbooking Skeptic. Reprinted by permission of Bridget Bosworth Rees. ©2004 Bridget Bosworth Rees.

A Simple Sheet of Paper. Reprinted by permission of Kathy Frandsen. ©2005 Kathy Frandsen.

My Search for Roots. Reprinted by permission of Rolando Julio Arciniega. ©1980 Rolando Julio Arciniega.

He Healed Me. Reprinted by permission of Kathy Frandsen. ©2005 Kathy Frandsen.

Two and a Half Miracles. Reprinted by permission of Charlotte Hilton Andersen. ©2005 Charlotte Hilton Andersen.

Good Fruit. Reprinted by permission of Pamela Coyle. ©2005 Pamela Coyle.

I Will Pray Every Birthday. Reprinted by permission of Maria Alexandra dos Santos Mendanha Degues da Cunha Mendes Domingues. ©2004 Maria Alexandra dos Santos Mendanha Degues da Cunha Mendes Domingues.

Collective Faith and a Priesthood Blessing. Reprinted by permission of Sandy Christensen. ©2004 Sandy Christensen.

Heaven Was So Close. Reprinted by permission of Kirsty Hale. ©2004 Kirsty Hale.

There Were People Praying. Reprinted by permission of Heather Ann Abbott. ©2005 Heather Ann Abbott.

To the Very Core of My Soul. Reprinted by permission of Shelley Ball Andrus. ©2005 Shelley Ball Andrus.

Better than Bedtime Checklists. Reprinted by permission of Barbara A. Hausen. ©1987 Barbara A. Hausen.

Wrestling with the Lord in Lake Simcoe. Reprinted by permission of Michael Howard Clifton. ©2005 Michael Howard Clifton.

To Bless a Patriarch. Reprinted by permission of G. Douglas Scofield. ©2004 G. Douglas Scofield.

The Lord Will Provide. Reprinted by permission of Leslie Kaye Householder. ©2005 Leslie Kaye Householder.

We Forgot to Pray. Reprinted by permission of Laura Denhalter. ©2004 Laura Denhalter.

Pick Up the Phone. Reprinted by permission of Joyce Ann Pierce. ©2004 Joyce Ann Pierce.

Hymns During the Hurricane. Reprinted by permission of Loralee H. Hartje. ©2004 Loralee H. Hartje.

Never Really Alone. Reprinted by permission of Kathy Frandsen. ©2000 Kathy Frandsen.

Anywhere. Reprinted by permission of Maren M. Mouritsen. ©1996 Maren M. Mouritsen.

A Positive Mormon. Reprinted by permission of G. Douglas Scofield. ©2003 G. Douglas Scofield.